Fleur de Lys and Calumet

Fleur de Lys and Calumet

Being the
Pénicaut Narrative
of French Adventure
in Louisiana

TRANSLATED AND EDITED BY

Richebourg Gaillard McWilliams

WITH A FOREWORD BY

Robert R. Rea

THE UNIVERSITY OF ALABAMA PRESS
Tuscaloosa and London

LIBRARY OF CONGRESS
Library of Congress Cataloging-in-Publication Data

Pénicaut, André.
    Fleur de lys and calumet : being the Pénicaut narrative of French
adventure in Louisiana / translated, edited by Richebourg Gaillard
McWilliams ; with a foreword by Robert R. Rea.
        p. cm.
    Bibliography: p.
    Includes index.
    ISBN 0-8173-0414-2 (pbk.)
    1. Louisiana—Discovery and   exploration. 2. Louisiana—History—
To 1803.   3. French—Louisiana—History—18th century.
4. Pénicaut, André—Diaries.   I. McWilliams, Richebourg Gaillard.
II. Title.
F372.P4 1988
976.3'01—dc19   88-14203
                                                                                  CIP

British Library Cataloguing-in-Publication Data available

Contents

List of Illustrations

Foreword

ROBERT R. REA

THE TRANSLATOR AND EDITOR of this book, Richebourg Gaillard McWilliams, belonged to a generation of Alabama scholars that linked the past and the present in personal as well as professional terms. Born to the traditions of a landed rural society, aristocratic by virtue of ancestry and education, passionately dedicated to their chosen professions, and imbued with a deep love of their state and all that its past represented to them, they lived to see social and economic transformations of the most fundamental sort—and in their various ways they contributed to those changes without losing the best distinguishing qualities of the receding past of their youth. As a scholar, Richebourg G. McWilliams reached back to the very origins of that past and brought them to life for generations to come.

Born on June 24, 1901, in tiny Oak Hill, Wilcox County, Alabama, McWilliams was the son of a long-established and well-placed Black Belt family. His father, though trained in dentistry, became involved in the timber business and in a lumber mill at the neighboring town of McWilliams. Young Richebourg was educated in the little three-room school at Oak Hill; there he was exposed to the rigorous discipline of mathematics and the intellectual virtues of classical Latin. The linguistic exactitude demanded of the student helped to shape the future scholar, and to it he credited much of his mature achievement. He enjoyed close association with two physicians who lived in the family home, his uncle Dr. Edward C. McWilliams, and an aunt's husband, Dr. Samuel Swift Boykin. Richebourg often accompanied these men as they drove around the county in their buggies making house calls. Perhaps these relationships encouraged McWilliams to consider entering the medical profession, for with that in mind he enrolled at the University of Alabama in Tuscaloosa in 1918.

Four years later, McWilliams received a Bachelor of Science degree in Biology, but his interests had turned toward the humanities, particularly the study of literature and languages. Following graduation in 1922, he went to Puerto Rico where he taught English and mathematics in the Continuation School at Cabo Rojo. When the school year ended, he seized the opportunity to study Spanish at the University of Puerto Rico during the summer of 1923.

His undergraduate study of French and his unique experience and study of Spanish enabled Richebourg McWilliams to return to the University of Alabama in 1924 in the dual roles of instructor in Romance Languages and graduate student in the English Department. His fascination with literature and creative writing was spurred by Hudson Strode, who was just then beginning a distinguished professorial career at the Capstone. In 1925, McWilliams received a Master's degree in English and a Phi Beta Kappa key. He continued to teach Spanish and French, winning promotion to assistant professor in 1926, and he secured appointment to the English Department in 1927.

Languages and literature were intimately associated in McWilliams's professional development. In 1927 he spent the summer studying German at the University of Wisconsin, and that fall he began graduate study in English at Harvard University. There he found inspiration under the tutelage of George Lyman Kittredge and the Pulitzer prize-winning poet Robert Hillyer; he was drawn toward creative writing, but he had also to earn a living. In 1928 he joined the English Department faculty at Birmingham-Southern College and began an association that would last until 1970. His intellectual curiosity and academic ambitions were far from satisfied, however. During the summer of 1933, McWilliams traveled to Germany to study that language at the University of Munich and complete requirements for his Harvard Master of Arts degree. The following academic year, 1934–1935, he was back at Cambridge as a doctoral student, and later there would be summers in New York at Columbia University. But with aspirations of becoming a novelist, McWilliams accepted his mentors' suggestions that the Ph.D. was not requisite for success in the writing of fiction.

Richebourg McWilliams returned to Birmingham-Southern's hilltop in 1935, a published author by virtue of the short story,

"They Were Seven," which appeared in *Story* magazine that spring.[1] Inspired by his sojourn in Munich, and perhaps sobered by the echo of triumphant storm-troopers' boots, "They Were Seven" caught and contrasted the joy of a German couple's silver wedding anniversary party—interrupted by the startling news of the assassinations at Sarajevo—and their subsequent grief as they decorated the graves of their five sons after the ensuing war had ended. The brooding prescience of the vignette had yet to be disclosed; the thrill of first publication was immediately encouraging to the novice author.

Through the next several years, McWilliams pursued the writing of major fiction. Two novels with familiar and contemporary south Alabama settings were well advanced during summer vacations when Richebourg secluded himself in a rented office in Camden, a few miles from the family home at Oak Hill. Two prestigious publishing houses expressed interest in his work, but McWilliams never released the manuscripts to the press. These years did, however, mark a significant and happy change in his life. His had been the common existence of many a bachelor-scholar. In 1937 he married Miss Dorothy Schultz, and a whole range of new felicities opened to him. They became delightfully visible in his next short story, "Spare the Lark's Nest," a very personal episode drawn from the McWilliams's domestic life.[2] Set in a small cottage on Miami Beach, the scene included Dorothy and an infant son nearby in a playpen. Derived in part from Robert Frost's poem, "The Exposed Nest," the story recounted Richebourg's concern for the fate of a mother lark and her hatchlings whose nest lay in the path of destruction by a giant mower. The theme reflected McWilliams's love of nature and his sensitivity to its fragile dependence upon human consideration—for the operator of the mower passed around the lark's nest and the story came to a happy ending.

Richebourg McWilliams loved nature in all its forms. With his growing family of three boys, he spent many summers on the Gulf Coast at Orange Beach, Alabama. As his son Tennant remembered it,

Our entire family of five (plus mutt dog) would go floundering at night along the edge of the bay; he would position his sons fore and aft in the skiff in order to shine the lights and use the gigs; and he and Mother would sit in canvas camp chairs in the bottom of the boat while he provided a running narrative of inquiry on stars, changing coastlines, sleeping seabirds, the differences between sting rays and flounders as they appeared on the bottom of the bay, and what seventeenth-century Frenchmen would have thought upon first seeing what we saw. In short, he was intensely interested in everything around him and loved to discuss it.[3]

Summer holidays were also devoted to scholarly work, for the increasing demands upon an English professor at Birmingham-Southern left little time for creative activity. The task at hand in the late 1940s was the preparation of André Pénicaut's journal, the collation of manuscripts (of necessity working from microfilm and transcripts of the sources), the pursuit of supplemental materials with which to give clarity and background to the Frenchman's exotic experiences and far-ranging travels, and the painstaking translation of his narrative into effective modern English. As scholars love their work, so did Richebourg McWilliams revel in his labors, and in his wife Dorothy he enjoyed an eager audience for his ideas.

In the spring of 1951, McWilliams published a third short story, "The Marster and the Minder," a tale told by a young black boy, recounting the impact of war's end in 1865 upon a south Alabama plantation.[4] The sense of time and place and the intimacy of the local color reflected McWilliams's origins; the kindly wit that enlivened the story said even more about the author.

That same spring McWilliams introduced his work on Pénicaut to the public in a paper presented before the Alabama Historical Association meeting in Auburn.[5] He dealt with Pénicaut as a literary figure, as Alabama's first historian, and he pointed out the dependence of previous generations of scholars upon badly flawed versions of Pénicaut's journal. "As historian he [Pénicaut] should be used with caution," McWilliams warned;

"as literary man he can be used with pleasure." The occasion heralded the completion of McWilliams's translation of the journal, and his paper sent a thrill of anticipation through his audience. The study of the state's colonial history had been dormant since Peter J. Hamilton's work at the beginning of the century; it was exciting to hear that the field was about to be reopened.

In addition to his last short story and his first essay into French colonial history, the year 1951 saw also the publication of *The Memoirs of a Circuit Rider: Being excerpts from 'The Life and Times of A. C. Ramsey and Others.'*[6] The selections printed in this monograph represented only a small part of Ramsey's lengthy manuscript, but they sharply illuminated pioneer life and backwoods Methodism in south Alabama and southeastern Mississippi in the period 1807–1837. This remarkable document required little editorial attention, and the names of those responsible for its publication did not appear in print, but Richebourg G. McWilliams was prominent among them. He doubtless found its preparation a delightful change from the French documents he had long been studying, for the *Memoirs* provided an exceptionally early and intimate glimpse of that part of Alabama he had known as a boy.

A grant from the American Council of Learned Societies enabled McWilliams to devote the academic year 1951–1952 to reading and research on "French Colonial Culture in the Old Province of Louisiana, 1698–1763" and rapidly advanced his work on Pénicaut. The Louisiana State University Press having accepted McWilliams's manuscript for publication, on August 15, 1952 he put the finishing touches to the front matter and dedicated the book to Dorothy Schultz McWilliams "who enjoyed this work with me." Published in 1953, *Fleur de Lys and Calumet* attracted considerable attention, and the jubilant author celebrated its appearance by writing a delightful *jeu d'esprit*, "Armadillo—Alabama's Armored Pig," which was first printed in the *Birmingham News Magazine*, then reprinted in *Alabama Conservation.*[7] Like "Spare the Lark's Nest," this brief essay was taken, literally, out of the family's Orange Beach front yard.

Perhaps Richebourg's undergraduate studies surfaced momentarily as he watched the "long-faced little pig wearing two turtle shells," for he settled by experiment the question of whether the armadillo could swim. It could.

At the same time, another short piece emerged, but this one reflected considerable professional application. Published by the Mobile Chamber of Commerce and the Dauphin Island Land Sales Corporation, McWilliams's *History of Beautiful Dauphin Island*, subtitled "Dramatic History of Dauphin Island," was a thirty-two page pamphlet designed to serve the purposes of local real estate developers, but its author's scholarship could not be hidden.[8] McWilliams went to the original sources and even made reference to Marcel Giraud's very recent *Histoire de Louisiane Française.* Not surprisingly, the text of the pamphlet focused attention upon the early French colonial and American Civil War periods of Dauphin Island's history. A catalogue of street names for the new development was included, and no one could have so readily provided brief identifying sketches of the persons and places whose names were proposed to adorn the next stage of the island's history—including Pénicaut Street—as Richebourg G. McWilliams.

Following the publication of *Fleur de Lys and Calumet*, McWilliams turned his attention to the records left by the greatest of French Gulf Coast explorers, Pierre LeMoyne d'Iberville. The translation and annotation of Iberville's journals would occupy him the rest of his active life, but after a decade of study the fruits of his labors began to appear. In 1964 McWilliams attended the gathering of "a lot of curious people" drawn by John Francis McDermott to St. Louis to celebrate the bicentennial of the founding of the city and to form the First Conference on the French in the Mississippi Valley. There McWilliams read the paper, "A Kingdom Beyond the Rockies: The El Dorado of Mathieu Sagean." Centered upon the fanciful story concocted by Sagean in 1700 and demonstrating the state of geographic knowledge (or innocence) at that date, McWilliams's essay again remarked upon the relationship between literature and history, for Sagean's El Dorado was largely inspired fiction.[9] The work on

Sagean was refined and its biographical elements incorporated in a brief, factual contribution to the *Dictionary of Canadian Biography* a few years later.[10]

The St. Louis conference expanded McWilliams's acquaintance in the small circle of French colonial scholars, and he happily returned to the Second Conference, held at Southern Illinois University, Edwardsville, in 1967. The paper he read, "Iberville at the Birdfoot Subdelta: Final Discovery of the Mississippi River," dealt with a subject that long fascinated him—the "black rocks" or "petrified trees" that had blocked Spanish entry at the mouth of the river and had posed no less a challenge to Iberville.[11] The French explorer also provided source and subject for the address McWilliams delivered at the annual dinner meeting of the Alabama Historical Association in Mobile, May 5, 1967. "Iberville and the Southern Indians" was drawn from observations of the natives' manners and mores as set forth in the Frenchman's journals.[12]

Although he had achieved recognition as a leading authority on early French Louisiana, the burdens of academic duty—teaching English literature, American literature, and advanced writing—lay heavily upon him as a research scholar. By the late 1960s, Richebourg McWilliams had served as Professor of English at Birmingham-Southern College, Head of the English Department, Chairman of the Humanities Division, and Acting Director of the M. Paul Phillips Library. He held the Mary Collett Munger Chair of English, but he was approaching the age of retirement, and the horizons and demands of research in his field were widening. Reviewing the third volume of Marcel Giraud's epochal history of French Louisiana in 1968, a sigh of regret seemed to escape him when he wrote, "No one antedating Giraud had the proper skills or access to proper guides to manuscripts in France to write a general history."[13]

A scholar deeply absorbed by his study of Iberville might bemoan the passage of time and opportunity; the students who passed through his Birmingham-Southern classroom during some forty years could celebrate their good fortune and his many contributions. In 1970, colleagues and former students presented him with a *festschrift* entitled *Essays in Honor of Richebourg Gaillard McWilliams*.[14] Eight studies of both English and American literary figures ranging from the medieval to the modern period demonstrated the emphasis upon style, tone, and linguistic discipline inculcated by the master. As a teacher, Richebourg McWilliams will long be remembered for insisting upon precision, restraint, and clarity: qualities that were invariably evident in his own writing.

The outer figure of the man was impressive and all but changeless: lean, straight, with what the eighteenth century would have termed a noble head though spare of hair, a crisp moustache, sharp features that hardly softened with the years. His green Harvard book-bag was a trademark. He was no lecture platform thespian or orator, yet he exuded style—formality, intellectual integrity, and a wide-ranging interest in all that touched the world of literature. If he intentionally sought to present this professional persona, he succeeded magnificently, and students who once thought him a bit old-fashioned came to realize that it was they who were yet unformed. To those students he was *Mr.* McWilliams, and even though he might have had long acquaintance with any one of them, in the classroom they were always *Mr.* or *Miss.* The teaching of fine writing requires great fortitude when it comes to the reading of student papers. McWilliams was generous with comments and corrections—to the point that it was said his observations were sometimes longer than his students' essays.

The personal and professional aura of distinction that surrounded Richebourg McWilliams led to a welcome invitation to teach for three years at the University of South Alabama, Mobile, after his retirement from Birmingham-Southern College in 1970.

Although full of years, McWilliams had not completed his work; Iberville had yet to be finished. In 1978, at Mobile, he again addressed the annual dinner meeting of the Alabama Historical Association. "Glances into Iberville's Gulf Journals" drew upon two decades of research and contemplation, but the excitement of discovery was quite as evident on this occasion as it had been a quarter of a century earlier when he introduced Pénicaut to this same audience. The completed book appeared in print in 1981 as *Iberville's Gulf Journals*.[15] Younger scholars in the field described McWilliams's last work as "most informative and very readable," a "lucid translation"; that they also noted weaknesses in an etymological approach, in ethnographic and cartographic details, demonstrated that McWilliams's lifework had indeed pushed forward the boundaries of scholarship.[16] That work completed, Richebourg G. McWilliams died in Mobile on February 13, 1986, at the age of eighty-five.

Fleur de Lys and Calumet stands as McWilliams's major contribution to the study of the vast region that was once known as French Louisiana and extended from Alabama's Gulf Coast to the upper Midwest. The journal of André Pénicaut may still be described as "the best sustained piece of literature portraying early French dominion in old Louisiana" (xv). The carpenter-craftsman of old Mobile was unique, and his narrative remains basic to the "new evaluation of the whole period of France's colonial culture in Louisiana" (xvii) for which McWilliams called in 1952. By bringing together the faulty and partial states of Pénicaut's journal as published by B. F. French and Pierre Margry in the nineteenth century, and by collating and completing the text from other sources, McWilliams raised Pénicaut's work to a higher level of scholarly utility. Though frequently forced by time and circumstance to depend upon older works in print, such as Peter J. Hamilton's *Colonial Mobile*, he was also in communication with the recognized modern leader in the field, Marcel Giraud. McWilliams's scholarship was cautious, which militated against overly facile translation and led to the retention of the changing, uncertain seventeenth-century forms of proper names in the original manuscripts. The nature and extent of the problems he faced may be suggested by noting the continuing argument among scholars as to the most desirable spelling of the Frenchman's name—Pénicaut or Pénigault.[17] At the same time, as an editor he took infinite pains in tracing the names and locations of places and persons, both French and Indian, and he made full use of the extant forms of Pénicaut's journal, carefully indicating significant variations when they appeared. The caliber of his work fully warranted the Louisiana Library Association's Certificate of Merit for the most distinguished book on Louisiana published in 1953, and the French Ministry of Education award to the author of the *ruban violét* of the *Palmes Academiques* in 1954.

The book was widely reviewed upon its initial publication; as is often the case, its reception clearly reflected the reviewers' interests, not always the translator's intent. A. P. Nasitir remarked of McWilliams in *Americas*, "Had he been an historian, he might have been tempted with the Herculaean task of fully editing the history and . . . correct[ing] the errors of Pénicaut." That was not McWilliams's purpose; he approached the journal as a man of letters dealing with a priceless piece of literature. But the historians' complaint was echoed by Joseph B. Tregle in the *Journal of Southern History*, Charles S. Davis in the *Florida Historical Quarterly*, and John H. Kennedy in the *American Quarterly*. Edwin A. Miles, writing in the *North Carolina Historical Review*, struck a more balanced note: "The book's main virtues and faults are those of Pénicaut and not the editor." Recognizing the historiographic importance of the journal, John Francis McDermott, in the *Mississippi Valley Historical Review*, found the translation "pleasantly rendered and ably edited"; it made Pénicaut "charmingly available." The anonymous *Georgia Historical Quarterly* reviewer, who thought it a "superb work," hit the mark dead center: "Pénicaut could never have hoped . . . to be translated into English in a better flowing engagingly interesting style." Richebourg McWilliams might well have smiled upon reading Rhoda Coleman Ellison's assertion in *The Alabama Review* that he had indeed succeeded in catching "the gusto and imagination of his seventeenth-century Frenchmen."[18] What more should literature do for history?

Fleur de Lys and Calumet stands on it own merits. What it did not do—and in many instances could not do—is being done today by a new generation of scholars. They are fortunate and may be proud to stand upon the shoulders of Richebourg G. McWilliams.

NOTES

In addition to the sources cited, biographical information may be found in *Birmingham News* obituaries of February 14, 1986, p. 13C and February 15, 1986, p. 3A; E. L. Holland, "A Green Bookbag Some Years Ago," *Birmingham News*, February 2, 1964, p. 14; Ben Windham, "Influence of 'Mr. McWilliams' continues each day," *Tuscaloosa News*, May 18, 1986; Howell Raines, "A Mentor's Presence," *New York Times Sunday Magazine*, July 20, 1986, p. 46; Robert W. Houston, "A Tribute to Richebourg Gaillard McWilliams," manuscript. Former students, colleagues, and members of the McWilliams family have generously shared materials and remembrances for which this writer is most grateful.

1. Vol. 6, No. 34 (May 1935), 92–96.

2. *Yale Review*, 31 (1942), 764–69. McWilliams's original title for this story, "Not Everyman But the Poet Shall be Thy Guide," was set aside at editorial insistence.

3. Tennant S. McWilliams to Robert R. Rea, November 5, 1987.

4. *Georgia Review*, 5 (1951), 94–107. McWilliams was particularly fond of the story's title.

5. Read April 7, 1951. "Pénicaut as Alabama's First Literary Figure," *Alabama Review*, 5 (1952), 40–60.

6. Birmingham-Southern College *Bulletin*, 44 (No. 4, 1951).

7. *Alabama Conservation*, 26 (No. 4, January–February 1955), 8–9, 21–23.

8. The pamphlet is not dated; first published in 1954, it has been erroneously attributed to 1956 and 1960.

9. John Francis McDermott, ed., *Frenchmen and French Ways in the Mississippi Valley* (Urbana, Ill.: University of Illinois Press, 1969), v; McDermott, ed., *The French in the Mississippi Valley* (Urbana, Ill.: University of Illinois Press, 1965), 175–95.

10. "Mathieu Sagean," *Dictionary of Canadian Biography* (Toronto, 1969), 2: 589–90.

11. McDermott, ed., *Frenchmen and French Ways in the Mississippi Valley*, 127–40.

12. *Alabama Review*, 20 (1967), 243–62.

13. Ibid., 21 (1968), 156.

14. Howard Creed, ed., Birmingham-Southern College *Bulletin*, 63 (No. 2, 1970).

15. Tuscaloosa, Ala., University of Alabama Press.

16. Reviews by Carl A. Brasseaux, *Louisiana History*, 23 (1982), 215; Jack D. L. Holmes, *Florida Historical Quarterly*, 61 (1982), 78–80.

17. E. g. Jay Higginbotham, *Old Mobile: Fort Louis de la Louisiane, 1702–1711* (Mobile, Ala.: Museum of the City of Mobile, 1977).

18. *Americas*, 10 (1954), 497; *Journal of Southern History*, 19 (1953), 376; *Florida Historical Quarterly*, 32 (1954), 304; *American Quarterly*, 7 (1955), 90–92; *North Carolina Historical Review*, 31 (1954), 591; *Mississippi Valley Historical Review*, 40 (1953–54), 724–25; *Georgia Historical Quarterly*, 38 (1954), 97; *Alabama Review*, 6 (1953), 235–36.

Acknowledgments

I AM GLAD that I now have the opportunity to publish an expression of gratitude to those persons, libraries, and institutions that have generously and enthusiastically assisted me in the preparation of this book: The Bibliothèque Nationale, the Library of Congress, the Massachusetts Historical Society, and the Ayer Collection of the Newberry Library, Chicago, for permitting me to use microfilm of the Pénicaut manuscripts in their custody; the Most Reverend T. J. Toolen, Bishop of Mobile, for opening the Mobile Baptismal Records to me; Mrs. Emily Danton, Director of the Birmingham Public Library, and Miss Jessie Ham, Custodian of the Southern Collection; Mrs. Marie Bankhead Owen, Director, and Miss Frances M. Hails, Archivist, of the State Department of Archives and History, Montgomery, Alabama; Dr. William Stanley Hoole, Director of Libraries, University of Alabama, for use of the T. P. Thompson Collection; Miss Marguerite D. Renshaw, Reference Librarian of the Howard-Tilton Memorial Library, Tulane University; William R. Sieben, Reference Librarian of the E. M. Cudahy Memorial Library, Loyola University, Chicago; Stephen T. Riley, Librarian of the Massachusetts Historical Society, Boston; Mrs. Ruth Lapham Butler, Custodian of the Ayer Collection of the Newberry Library, Chicago; Miss Irene B. Pope, Reference Librarian of the Russell Library, Northwestern State College, Natchitoches, Louisiana.

I am grateful to the Oxford University Press for permission to reprint a satirical quatrain from Harry Kurz' edition of L'Abbé Prévost's *Histoire du Chevalier Des Grieux et de Manon Lescaut,* and to the Smithsonian Institution of Washington for permission to reprint plates of DeBatz's drawings of early Indian life. The translation, the research, and the background reading were made possible by a grant from the Carnegie Foundation for the Advancement of Teaching and by a fellowship of the American Council of Learned Societies. To the founder and the trustees and officers of both of them I am deeply indebted.

Mrs. William R. Lathrop, Jr., and Rucker Agee, both of Birmingham, kindly lent me eighteenth century maps essential to an understanding of the French exploration in Louisiana.

I have received the enthusiastic help of Margaret H. Hughes, head of the Birmingham-Southern College Library, and extraordinary assistance from Monsieur M. Chabrier, Chef du Service Photographique of the Bibliothèque Nationale, Paris.

And finally, from my colleague Dr. Anthony Constans, philologist and phonetician, I had expert advice on many a difficulty I met in translating eighteenth-century French script to English. No one could have been kindlier than he.

R. G. M.

Birmingham-Southern College
August 15, 1952

Editor's Introduction

IN LATE SUMMER, 1952, I am writing the preface to a book, the Pénicaut Narrative, that was completed in manuscript by late summer, 1723. It is the earliest full-length account written by a Frenchman participating in the first exploration and first settlement of France's province of Louisiana. And judged solely by the use that historians and other writers have made of it, it is valuable as history and entertaining as reading. Yet it has never appeared before as a book unto itself or appeared in a complete English translation.[1]

During the last hundred years this one book, in manuscript or in Margry's French edition, has made a greater contribution to published books about French dominion in the Lower Mississippi, I dare say, than has any other single source. Accordingly, I think it is high time for someone, in all fairness, to proclaim the debt—sometimes acknowledged, often suppressed—that so many writers owe to this one source: the Pénicaut Narrative. They have used it as a primary source of historical facts, for which, being memoirs with the faults of memoirs,

---

[1] Benjamin Franklin French made a fragmentary translation of the Pénicaut Narrative and published it in *Historical Collections of Louisiana and Florida*, n.s. (New York, 1869), pp. 33–162, with the title "Annals of Louisiana . . . By M. Penicaut." Pierre Margry edited and published the whole text in the original French in *Découvertes et Établissements des Français dans l'Ouest et dans le Sud de l'Amérique Septentrionale*, V (Paris, 1883), pp. 375–586, with the title "Relation de Pénicaut" as a part of the great six-volume collection of original documents concerning the French in America. *Découvertes* was published by means of a $10,000 subsidy from the Congress of the United States. Francis Parkman was the most active lobbyist for this subsidy. See the interesting letters edited by John Spencer Bassett and Sidney Bradshaw Fay, which show both Parkman's and Margry's activities in this cause: "Letters of Francis Parkman to Pierre Margry," in *Smith College Studies in History*, VIII (April–July, 1923), 123–208.

it is not altogether suited. They have used it as a grab bag from which to snatch many a revealing interpretation, or illustrative anecdote, or colorful scene to garnish their own dishes of Louisiana life. Ironically, then, the Pénicaut Narrative, which has helped write so many books [2] and which is better reading than the majority of them, has remained unpublished as a book for 229 years. I do not know why an English edition of the full manuscript has been so late in appearing. The neglect may have been accidental. French-reading scholars who used the manuscript in the Bibliothèque Nationale or Margry's French edition may have assumed that there

[2] Writers who have made considerable use of the "Relation de Pénicaut" or of the manuscript in the Bibliothèque Nationale include Father Pierre François Xavier Charlevoix, Charles Gayarré, Peter J. Hamilton, Henri Gravier, the American ethnologists Frederick W. Hodge and John R. Swanton, Grace King, and Émile Lauvrière. Their books are given in the bibliography.

Hamilton, aware of his debt, wrote: "He [Pénicaut] will be our chief authority for many years." (*Colonial Mobile* [Boston and New York, 1897], p. 33.) And Pénicaut was; for in Part II, "The French Capital, 1670, 1699–1722," pp. 25–101, Hamilton drew on Pénicaut fifty-five times in the seventy-six pages, according to my tally. The "Relation de Pénicaut" was one of Doctor Swanton's three favorite primary sources even though he was critical of some inaccuracies in Pénicaut's chronology. (*Indian Tribes of the Lower Mississippi Valley* [Washington, 1911], p. 4.) Grace King, in an enthusiastic expression of indebtedness, reveals the cause of Pénicaut's popularity as a primary source: "It [available material about the French] was not all, however, nor even the best of it, in Bienville's reports, nor in the reports sent to the government by the facile, if unorthographic pens of his companions, . . ; for there is Pennicaut! The literary pilgrim comes to many an unexpected oasis in the arid deserts of colonial research. . . ." (*New Orleans, the Place and the People* [New York, 1928], pp. 16–17.) See also Henry E. Chambers, *History of Louisiana* (Chicago and New York, 1925), I, Chapter IX, "France's First Foothold upon the Gulf Coast," in which Pénicaut's name is mentioned once, though Pénicaut supplied three fourths of the material in that chapter. See Charles Gayarré, *History of Louisiana* (3d ed., New Orleans, 1885), I, 165–82, and compare the account of St. Denis in Mexico with Pénicaut's description of the same drama. Pénicaut's name is not mentioned. Perhaps it is futile to try to examine Gayarré's sources, since his expressed purpose was to write "historical truth set in a gilded frame" (*ibid.*, I, 189), which is not a bad definition of epic fiction.

was a complete English translation by Benjamin Franklin French; and those scholars who read only B. F. French's "Annals of Louisiana . . . By M. Penicaut" could only assume that it was the complete translation, since the author offered it as a translation without qualifying it as a fragment.[3] Not many scholars went to the trouble to collate the two. The few who did, having their own particular interests, did not choose to prepare an edition in English.

I am offering this first complete edition in English in the belief that it is perhaps the best sustained piece of literature portraying early French dominion in old Louisiana—that is, along the Gulf Coast from Florida to Texas and in the Mississippi Valley from the Balize to the Illinois Country. So far, no books written by Frenchmen who lived in this area have been accepted by the general public as literature. Being written in French, the early books about Louisiana may be excluded from the canon of American literature on the grounds that a nice strictness may not admit translations. But I believe other causes have determined this neglect.[4]

[3] This edition has sixteen chapters; the manuscript has twenty-three. But only about half of B. F. French's chapters are directly translated from the manuscript without alterations, including the insertion of new material. Some chapters are abstracts; others are chiefly of B. F. French's own composing, drawing much of their material from other sources or from French's own knowledge of Louisiana history. There are no suspension points or footnotes or any other form of editorial discrimination which tells where Pénicaut ends and B. F. French begins. Including space given to footnotes, this edition is 38,000 words, and the manuscript is 69,500, by my tally.

[4] George Washington Cable is the earliest Louisiana writer included in the new anthology *The Literature of the South* (Chicago, 1952). The experienced anthologist Dr. Richmond Croom Beatty and his fellow critics, who undertook in that anthology "to represent Southern literature from its colonial beginnings to the present," totally ignore French dominion in the South. They saw Louisiana—the Louisiana after the Purchase—only as an area that created one social and one

Students of American civilization begin their studies with Virginia and Massachusetts and proceed through the colonial period to the formation of the republic. During these formative years the people of the province of Louisiana, being subjects of a foreign power, were not a part of the society that laid the cornerstones of the nation. As Frenchmen or, after 1763, as subjects of England or of Spain they made no intellectual contribution to our national culture comparable to that of, say, the New England Puritans or even to that of the *métropole*, France, whose philosophers—directly, and not by way of Louisiana—influenced American democracy.

By the time the whole of Louisiana became a part of the United States, the founders of Louisiana and whatever books they produced had been long forgotten. The first, and perhaps the only, popular books about the old area—*Manon Lescaut* and *Atala* with its companion volume *Les Natchez*—were written, not in Louisiana, but in Europe. The authors of these novels knew very little about life in the area, and nothing firsthand. In the United States no book about the Louisiana area won a place for itself in American literature until William Bartram's *Travels* appeared in 1791—nearly a generation after France had lost her colonial empire in the heart of America. After Bartram's *Travels* at least a half century passed before Longfellow's *Evangeline* and George Washington Cable's Creole stories brought Acadians and Creoles to the attention of the general reading public, to the chagrin of Creoles if not of the Louisiana Acadians.

political problem: it drew population from Carolina and other parts of the East; and, as a slaveholding area, it helped promote the Civil War.

Meanwhile, France's colonial life at her early posts and settlements—Biloxi, Fort Louis de la Mobile, Natchez, Natchitoches, the Illinois Country—was all but lost from the national consciousness. For a public interested chiefly in superficial vestiges, state historians and state societies did what they could to withhold France's colonial culture and her colonial leaders and explorers from oblivion.[5] Iberville and Bienville have been commemorated in the nomenclature of the Gulf Coast and the Lower Mississippi Valley. But the explorers Le Sueur, La Harpe, St. Denis, Du Tisné and others have suffered an oblivion hardly merited by their exploits. Except for minor local interest they are forgotten men. Occasionally, professional writers lug into light histories of New Orleans some of the choice episodes from the great journeys these explorers made into the far wilderness.

A new evaluation of the whole period of France's colonial culture in Louisiana, 1699–1763, is needed, particularly of the literature, which is written in French. The Pénicaut Narrative, with its emphasis on exploration and relations with Indians, represents only the first third of the period. As Indian literature it is an authoritative source upon which leading ethnologists have freely drawn for material about Southern tribes. As exploration literature it may be compared with Captain John Smith's histories or even with William Bradford's *Of Plymouth Plantation*. As first observer and interpreter of events,

---

[5] The reputations of these men have suffered from the want of good biography. Not even Iberville was adequately portrayed in a biography until 1944, when Guy Frégault's brilliant book was published.

Pénicaut represents the French on the Gulf Coast the way Smith and Bradford represent the English on the Atlantic Coast. The two Englishmen were, of course, Renaissance writers, and one would hardly expect a book by this Frenchman of the eighteenth century to be of the same temperament and same material. Such an assumption would be partly incorrect, however, for the Pénicaut Narrative is essentially Renaissance literature even though the Renaissance had been ended for half a century by the time the Iberville expedition entered the Gulf of Mexico in the winter of 1698–99 to found a French establishment at the mouth of the Mississippi River. Pénicaut came with Iberville. But, late as the French were, the conditions affecting French exploration differed only slightly from the conditions affecting Spanish and English exploration in South and North America between 1500 and 1630.

When those first men of the Renaissance—Spaniards, Englishmen, Frenchmen—won their beachheads on the shores of the two Americas, established settlements, and explored deeper into the land, the people back home in Europe expected to be given oral or written reports of the wonders of the New World—exciting tales that would catch the fancy of rulers and ministers and would serve the Crowns of Europe as intelligence reports when they sent out other expeditions to the Americas. Chronologically and spiritually, the first written accounts to go out of the Americas were Renaissance literature. As one follows the relations of the explorers and first settlers, he finds the same themes repeated, repeated again: "the dangers I had passed"; the wonders of the New World—

strange animals, strange birds, plants of astonishing prop-
erties; savages—even Othello's anthropophagi—living
according to their individual barbarism; and almost invariably the expectation of discovering mines—copper,
silver, gold.[6]
Such Renaissance themes reappear with fresh material
and a new geography in the narratives of eighteenth-
century Frenchmen in Louisiana. Even before Pénicaut
arrived in America, he was temperamentally prepared to
follow such themes. For three years—ever since he was
fifteen, he tells us—the urge had been on him, the longing to see foreign lands. Beginning with January 31,
1699, when Iberville's ships dropped anchor off Mobile
Point,[7] he was to lead a life that should have satisfied his
youthful curiosity. He was far from home, and the shore
that he could see that day from the decks of *Le Marin*
was the margin of a vast Louisiana, many times larger
than France. In this Louisiana, savage tribes lived along
the river courses only a few miles inland; strange creatures, such as the buffalo, the raccoon, the opossum, and
new plants and trees awaited an observer; and great
rivers would give access to still remoter regions—all in
a world still unexplored or seen only by a few white
priests or forest rangers, if seen at all. Pénicaut was young
and, as he himself said, fond of rambling; and, standing

[6] This paragraph and the next one have been adapted from parts of my essay
"Pénicaut as Alabama's First Literary Figure," which appeared in the *Alabama Review*, V (January, 1952), 40–60, and is used with permission of the editor. That
essay examines Pénicaut as a belated Renaissance writer.

[7] Pierre Margry, "Navigation de la *Badine*," [Iberville's Log], in *Découvertes*,
IV, 145. These observations are based on textual statements that Pénicaut came
to Louisiana on Iberville's first voyage, and not on the second, as some confusion
in his account of the events of 1698–99 might indicate.

offshore that afternoon in the winter of 1699, was he not on the eve of a Renaissance experience comparable to that of a Spaniard in South America or an Englishman on the Atlantic Coast? The book he began in the colony [8] and finished in France is, according to his own statement, an eyewitness account of the events he reports. It is written in the form of annals. He says he kept a yearly account. Although some of the author's dates of events during the early exploration have been successfully challenged,[9] there is no doubt that the book remains a valuable and entertaining narrative of the first years of the French colony.

No other Frenchman with an ability to write appears to have had so good an opportunity as Pénicaut had to witness the important events of those years. Pénicaut's trade of ship carpentry caused him to be picked as a member of historic expeditions. He was needed, he states, to repair boats used by exploring parties. He was needed, too, to serve as interpreter of Indian languages, for which he had an aptitude.

Accordingly, he accompanied Le Sueur on his ascent of the Mississippi River in 1700 to work a copper mine on the Blue Earth River, in present-day Minnesota. He went with Juchereau de St. Denis on the great journey, the first one, from Mobile to the Red River and overland to the Rio Grande, to open trade with the Spaniards in Mexico. He helped build the first post in Louisiana, at Old Biloxi, and the second post, on the Mobile River. He

[8] He may have left at Natchez a copy of the finished chapters when he sailed for France in October, 1721. Such inference will be supported in Chapter VI.

[9] By Elizabeth McCann. See her scholarly article Pénicaut and His Chronicle of Early Louisiana," *Mid-America*, XXIII, n.s. (October, 1941), 288–304.

witnessed the moving of the capital from upriver to the present site of Mobile, and from Mobile to New Biloxi. He saw the building of New Orleans, in the very beginning. He was acquainted with Iberville, Bienville, Dartaguette–Diron, Cadillac, and other prominent men. With a shipbuilder's eye and an explorer's knack for measuring distances, he participated in the transportation of hundreds, perhaps thousands, of the colonists shipped by John Law's Company to Dauphin Island and New Biloxi, whence they had to be removed to their concessions along the Mississippi, from New Orleans as high as the Arkansas River.

In October, 1721, suffering from inflammation of the eyes and losing his eyesight, Pénicaut returned to France for treatment, taking with him a yet-unfinished manuscript that drew its material from his twenty-two years in the colony.

All that I have so far told about the author has been gleaned from his own book. There are some other facts, a few, which are not without interest, since they represent a problem of identity. Who was Pénicaut?

Up until 1919 he was commonly called Jean Pénicaut by the older historians.[10] His last name is often written Pénicault and occasionally Pénicaud. The older historians who gave his name as Jean cited no authority for the name. Not Jean but André appears as his Christian name on the title page of two of the manuscripts of his book.[11] But this name was unknown for a long time be-

---

[10] Hamilton, *Colonial Mobile*, p. 87, and Alcée Fortier (ed.), *Louisiana* (n.p., 1914), II, 299.

[11] See the description of the Parkman and the Rouen manuscripts in the Bibliography.

cause it is missing from the Bibliothèque Nationale manuscript, on which both B. F. French and Pierre Margry based their editions of his book. André Pénicaut also appears on a map, made by f[rançois] B[oüet], which accompanies the Rouen manuscript. In 1919 the official catalog listing of the Library of Congress was changed from Jean Pénicaut to André Pénicaut.[12]

Among the hundreds of names I have examined in Louisiana documents I have not run across the name Pénicaut, either Jean or André. But I have found the name André Pénigault several times, twice as clear autographs. Once I found the printed form André Pemgant,[13] which is a likely misreading of André Pénigaut as written in an eighteenth-century document.

Three entries in the Mobile Baptismal Records, now in the residence of the Bishop of Mobile, show André Pénigault's signature. On April 7, 1708, he became godfather of a slave at Fort Louis de la Mobile. When his child René André was baptized, October 27, 1708, Pénigault signed the entry made by the priest.[14] A second child of his, Jacque, was baptized on March 28(?), 1710, and again André Pénigault signed the entry.[15]

[12] Miss Jane C. Hall, assistant chief of the Descriptive Cataloging Division, the Library of Congress, reports that she cannot locate an authority card showing the cause for the change.

[13] N. M. Miller Surrey, *Calendar of Manuscripts in Paris Archives and Libraries Relating to the History of the Mississippi Valley to 1803* (Washington, 1926–28), I, 204.

[14] "Ce jourd'huy 27 d'octobre de l'annee 1708 a este baptisé René André né le jour de devant, fils d'André Penigault Me Charpentier et de Marguerite Catherine Prevot [or Prevost] son epouse. Le Parrein a este René Boyer Me Arquebusier, et Marie Linand la Marreine.
[Signatures:] boye marie Linant andrepenigault ca[t]hrine christophe
F. Le Maire, Miss. Aplique"

[15] "Le 28 [20 or 29?] de mars de lan 1710 a été baptisé iacque——[middle

His wife was named Marguerite Catherine Prévot, according to the priest's entry, when René André was born. About a year and a half later, when Jacque was baptized, a different priest gave Marie Prévôt as the name of the wife. Meanwhile Marguerite Catherine Prévôt may have died, and André Pénigault may have married her sister Marie; or a different priest may have entered a different part of the multiple Christian name of the same wife.

The André Pénicaut who wrote the narrative was a master carpenter, had lived at Fort Louis de la Mobile, and was a married man when he left the colony in 1721, according to his own statements.

The André Pénigault who signed the Baptismal Records was a master carpenter, had lived at Fort Louis de la Mobile, where he owned a lot in 1706 (?),[16] and was a married man, the father of children in 1708 and 1710, according to historical records.

Since there were few people in Mobile, and indeed few carpenters,[17] I cannot believe there were two master

---

name not yet chosen?] né en et de legitime mariage d'andré penigaud maitre charpentier et de marie prevot sa femme. le parrein a été iacque le compte maitre charpentier [et la marraine] marie anne nadoüe.

[Signatures:]   Alexandre Huvé pretre missionnaire
                                  Jacque Le Conte
    marque de marie anne nadoüe
    andrepenigault"

[16] In the revised and enlarged edition of *Colonial Mobile* (Boston and New York, 1910), p. 84, Hamilton published a map, "Fort Louis de la Mobille, 1706?" which shows the house lots and the names of the owners. André penigau is marked on a lot fronting on Ruë St. Denis.

[17] The population—garrison and *habitans*—was 337 in 1708. (Hamilton, *Colonial Mobile*, pp. 58–59). In his financial report for October 12, 1713, Duclos listed one master carpenter, with wages of fifty livres a month, and two carpenters serving with the navy. Dunbar Rowland and Albert Godfrey Sanders (ed. and tr.), *Mississippi Provincial Archives* (Jackson, Miss., 1927–32), II, 145. (Hereinafter cited as *MPA.*)

carpenters at Mobile at the same time named André Pénigault and André Pénicault or Pénicaut. There could just
as well have been a Tweedledum Me Charpentier and a
Tweedledee Me Charpentier, and both at Fort Louis de
la Mobile at the same time.

Furthermore, as this goes to press, I have received from
Professor Marcel Giraud, of the College de France, a
description of a document [18] that definitely establishes
André Pénigault as the author of this book because it
identifies him as one of the *engagés* brought to Louisiana on Iberville's second voyage by Le Sueur, with
whom André Pénicaut, of the manuscripts, says he
ascended the Mississippi River in 1700.

According to Professor Giraud, in the seventeenth
and eighteenth centuries there were several Pénigault
families in La Rochelle, writing their name Pénigault or
Pénigaut. Pénicaut, pronounced the same, was a later
spelling of the same family name. In the document, a deed
of indenture, André Pénigault—his middle name was
Joseph—is identified as a "garçon charpentier de navire,"
born in La Rochelle, and "demeurant en cette ville [La
Rochelle]."

Here is proof that Pénigault came on Iberville's second voyage along with the other *engagés* brought to
Louisiana by Le Sueur. But in his book Pénigault as
writer says he came to Louisiana on the *Marin* in 1698.
Can he still be believed? Professor Giraud thinks not; he
suggests that Pénigault's putting himself on the first

[18] Identified in n. 1, p. 2, Chapter V of Professor Marcel Giraud's history
of French colonial Louisiana, 1698–1715, which will be published this year.
With scholarly courtesy, Professor Giraud mailed me the page proof of two
pages of his book, with permission to draw upon them.

voyage is due either to a faulty memory or to a desire to boast.

But there is still, by inference, the possibility that he did come on the first voyage, as he says he did. If he returned to France with the expedition, he was back in La Rochelle by the first week in July, 1699, some three months before he signed the "contrat d'engagement." The *Marin* was back at La Rochelle on July 2. Since the contract of indenture lists Pénigault as "garçon charpentier de navire," one may infer that he had been to sea already. Accordingly, lacking a photostat of the deed of indenture, I cannot exclude the possibility that on September 24, 1699, Le Sueur bound under a three-year contract the young man André Joseph Pénigault, who had just been to Louisiana on Iberville's first voyage and, with an urge to travel, was easily induced to go on a second.

Whether André the literary man was successful in petitioning the French government for a gratuity or recovered his eyesight and returned to Louisiana and his Houssaye property at Natchez, I do not know. Alcée Fortier believed he did: he identified Pénicaut with a man named Perricault,[19] a carpenter who escaped the Natchez Massacre in 1729 and brought to New Orleans the dreadful truth that confirmed the first rumors of the massacre. Fortier says this is the same person as the carpenter named Couillard, given by Dumont de Montigny[20] as the man who escaped and brought the news to New Orleans.

[19] See Fortier (ed.), *Louisiana*, II, 299.
[20] Lieutenant [Louis François Benjamin] Dumont [de Montigny], *Mémoires Historiques sur la Louisiane* (Paris, 1753), II, 170–71.

Professor Fortier did not describe the documents in which Pénicaut shows up in Louisiana after 1729 as Perricault. As for Couillard, I can see no connection between his name and the name of the writer, although the Houssaye concession Pénicaut owned at Natchez could certainly account for his being there in 1729—if he really returned to Louisiana.

I have translated and edited this edition of the Pénicaut Narrative from microfilm reproductions of three contemporary manuscripts and of a transcription of a fourth. For brevity of citation, I have assigned to these manuscripts the names Clermont, Parkman, Spofford, and Rouen, which represent the provenience of the four. A detailed description of each is given in the bibliography. I have not been able to locate the autograph manuscript, which may yet be discovered by some scholar working in libraries in France. Three of the copies I have used are eighteenth-century, contemporary manuscripts. The Clermont manuscript, as I have described it in the bibliography, seems to me to be the most authoritative, since evidence is strong that it was the dedicatory copy, presented to Dartaguiette Diron by the author. To make this edition, I have translated the Clermont manuscript and from the other three manuscripts have supplied those passages dropped from Clermont or confused by the penman.

The title of the Clermont manuscript is "Relation ou annale veritable, de ce qui s'est passé dans Le païs de La Loüisiane pendant vingt deux années consecutifes depuis le commencement de L'etablissem^t des françois dans le païs par Monsieur Dhyberville, et M^r Le Comte De surgere en 1699, continué jusqu'en 1721. . . ." This is, with trivial variations, the title of both Parkman and Rouen. The Spofford manuscript has a new title in a new hand. All except Clermont were prepared by François Boüet. With the Clermont manuscript I have collated Pierre Margry's published text "Relation de Pénicaut" and such chapters as were translated by B. F. French in his "Annals of Louisiana . . . By M. Penicaut." Important variations in the manuscripts and in Margry's text, as well as passages supplied from Parkman, Spofford, and Rouen, have been registered in the footnotes. Minor variations are too numerous to record.

As translator I have withheld every impulse to improve the carpenter's prose style, which is sometimes loose. The shift from French to English syntax forced me to change the construction of some clauses and occasionally to reverse the position of noun and pronoun. One passage—describing the tactics used by both Indians and Frenchmen to force a hibernating bear from a hollow tree—was accidentally improved by translation, since English syntax will not admit of tautology equivalent to the French of this passage.

With the exception of Missicipy River and a few other well-known names, I have left all place names in their French forms, and all names of Frenchmen and of Indian tribes just as I found them in the manuscripts. The reader can readily guess the modern forms even if he does not read French. Difficult names are translated in the footnotes or clarified in some other way. My reason for retaining the French spelling of proper names is that it presents less margin for error. I have tried to avoid the type of error that Margry made when he did not respect the form he found in the manuscript. For example, finding Chaqtos as the name of the Indian tribe the French had to remove from the present site of Mobile before they could start their own town there, Margry changed it to the normal French (*Chactas*) for Choctaw. But Chaqtos are not Choctaws.

Since the name of a given person or given place or tribe may appear with several different spellings in the same manuscript, I had to make some decision that would bring consistency into a confusion of names: I used for each name the spelling of the majority of entries in the Clermont manuscript. This decision forced me to use some spellings that are at variance with accepted usage. D'Iberville appears as D'Hyberville; Boisbriant as Boisbrian; Le Sueur as Le Sueure.

The punctuation, including the sentence stops, is mine, as well as many of the paragraph divisions. Sentences are often run together in the manuscripts, and there are sometimes misplaced indications of paragraphs. The capital letters, too, are mine. Because most readers are used to seeing diacritical marks on French words, I have added such marks to all words I thought should carry them. Passages from manuscripts or books quoted in the footnotes have not been altered, however; there is, therefore, some inconsistency between the spelling in the text and that in the footnotes.

Pénicaut's Narrative

To Monsieur

Monsieur Dartaguiette Diron, King's counsellor, collector-general of the taxes of the district of Auch

Monsieur:—You have always been so kind to me that I can do no less than present to you this first manuscript copy of my narrative as a public mark of my very humble appreciation. To whom else, Monsieur, should I have more naturally addressed it than to you, Monsieur, who have a perfect knowledge of the Province of Louisiana, where you have held command for a number of years, and who have been at the head of war detachments, leading them against the savages that have dared declare war on the French, against those on the frontiers of Carolina or those on the banks of the Mississippi, which you have ascended a number of times? All the troops now in Louisiana and all the habitans in the neighborhood of Mobile who have had the honor of seeing you there, and of obeying you, still long for that happy time when your natural goodness made free to question them kindly and to ask them whether they were content to live in that country. They deeply felt the misfortune they suffered in losing you when the Court, having need of you, Monsieur, wrote you to return to France in order to give you assignments more in keeping with your ability, and merited by your worth; for indeed you were not born, Monsieur, with so much urbanity to remain among savages. So, I count myself fortunate in the affliction that has forced me to come to France, since I have the honor to assure you, in very deep respect, that I am, Monsieur,

> Your very humble,
> very obedient and much
> indebted servant Penicaut

Advertisement to the Reader

This narrative I am giving the public I wrote year by year during the time I lived in Louisiana in the capacity of carpenter for the construction of the King's ships. Since in those faraway lands workmen have to serve in every capacity for the defense of the country, added to the fact that my trade compelled me to be along with the expeditions going out as war parties or exploring units, because I was needed on them to repair longboats and rowboats which transported the troops, plus the fact that my youthfulness and my fiery temperament caused me to take pleasure in being with all the detachments assembled against the savages, I have had, by such means, the opportunity to observe everything that I have described in this narrative.

The opening of this book will not have the attractiveness or the amusement given in novels, which usually begin with whatever is most pathetic and sublime but which, failing to continue in this vein, nearly always end by making the reader languid and bored. So, I am not giving this work to the public as an invented fable but as a sincere and true account of that to which I have been an eyewitness during the twenty-two years I have lived in Louisiana—of everything I have put in it; and proof of its authenticity is in the fact that I report the [events] year by year.

A great number of people who have known me in Louisiana (whose names and deeds are revealed in this narrative), all people of distinction and quality, who are now in Paris, have begged me numerous times to read it to them. For all that, I have not agreed to do so, my purpose being to make a clean draft of it and let the public have it first.

The opening of this book, then, will not give most pleasure to the reader; for naturally when one arrives in a far country where he is obliged to make explorations in order to get acquainted with the land, he can only report the distance from one place to another, together with the incidents and the observations to be made during each day's travel, within the compass of those distances. That is what will be useful to the reader-traveller.

The middle of the book will be for the inquisitive reader: he seeks, in reading, the useful and the pleasant, such as the discovery of mines;

what ore is in them and the places where they are located; trade of the French with the savages; the manners of the savages of each different nation; their religion; their temples; their food; their weddings; their funerals; their festivals; their dances; their pretended nobility; their dress; finally, their warring among themselves and with the French; and the manner in which they make war, and how they are armed.

It contains, too, the galante story of one of the leading French officers of Louisiana and the daughter of a Spanish captain of cavalry of the frontier of Mexico—an event of my time which I learned confidentially from his valet de chambre, who was my friend.

The end of this narrative will be useful to people interested in the country on account of the concessions established, which are owned by a great number of people of quality and private individuals of Paris, who do not know where they are placed or what returns they bring them. Therefore, I am noting the locations of them; the names of these places; at how many leagues they are placed or removed from the town named New Orleans and from the mouth of the Missicipy River; the rivers on whose banks they are placed and the distance from the mouth of each river to the place they are located; the names of the persons to whom they belong; likewise the names of their neighbors, that is, the persons who have concessions next to theirs. This is what the reader will find, for the sake of even greater convenience, marked in like manner on the map that I have made to be appended to this narrative.

Chapter 1

The Years 1698 and 1699

The author takes ship at La Rochelle—His arrival at Louisiana
—Fort Biloxi established—How the savages proclaimed peace—
First discovery of the Missicipy by way of Lake Pontchartrain

EING BORN in La Rochelle,[1] I was no more
than fifteen years old when I had a great urge
to go on a journey. To satisfy my desire, I was
induced, when I was eighteen, to enter the
service of His Majesty on board the Count de Surgère's [2]
ship. It was in the year 1698, in the month of October,
that we sailed from La Rochelle with two ships named
Le Marin,[3] commanded by the Count de Surgère, and
La Renommée,[4] commanded by M. d'Hyberville.[5] Our
voyage was very fortunate because of the constant favor-

[1] A seaport town on the west coast of France.

[2] Usually written Surgères.

[3] Not *Le Cheval Marin,* of forty-eight guns, as several historians have insisted
upon the basis of a single document, but indeed *Le Marin,* a frigate carrying thirty-
two to thirty-six guns, according to all other documents. See the convincing argument made by Guy Frégault, *Iberville le conquérant* (Montréal, 1944), p. 272, n. 27.

[4] An error for *La Badine.* Iberville was in command of *La Renommée* on his second voyage. "Navigation de la *Badine,*" in Margry, *Découvertes,* IV, 131-32; and
"Journal de D'Iberville commandant le vaisseau la *Renommée* dans son second voyage
au Mississipi," *ibid.,* IV, 393-95.

[5] Pierre Le Moyne d'Iberville, the most daring and capable seaman-soldier France
had in American waters at the close of the eighteenth century. Both D'Hyberville
and D'Hiberville are common spellings of his name. His autograph is DIberville.

able winds that brought us as far as Cape St. Domingue,[6] where we remained eleven days to refresh ourselves.[7] We left on St. Thomas' Day [8] to continue our voyage with as favorable weather, thank God, on our way from Cape St. Domingue as we had had on the way over, so that we arrived at the province of Louisiana on Kings' Day [9] of the following year, 1699.

The first lands we discovered on arriving happened to be two islands, to one of which the Count de Surgère gave his own name, as he had been the first to see it. This island is five leagues long and a quarter of a league wide. We anchored in a roadstead that runs between this island and another which took the name Isle-aux-Chats [10] because of the great number of cats we found on it. Similar

[6] Cap François, St. Domingue, now Haiti, is meant. After his arrival in the Indies, Iberville dated his first letter to the minister "Du cap François de Saint-Domingue, ce 19 décembre 1698." Margry, Découvertes, IV, 87.

[7] Translated literally from pour nous rafraischir, which, in language of the sea, meant to get rest, a fresh supply of food, and wood and water. Wood and water are sometimes specified beyond the ordinary rafraîchissements. To this list, my colleague Dr. J. F. Locke tells me, should be added social life for the crew among the women ashore. For example, see School of Naval Administration, Stanford University, Handbook on the Trust Territory of the Pacific Islands (Washington, D.C., 1948), pp. 72–73.

[8] The twenty-first or twenty-ninth of December, which honor respectively St. Thomas the Apostle and St. Thomas à Becket, according to McCann, "Pénicaut and His Chronicle of Early Louisiana," p. 292 and n. 14.

[9] Epiphany, January 6th, called Twelfth Night by the English and jour des rois by the French, whose festivities honored the Magi as kings of Arabia. For jour des rois festivities among the French in the Mississippi Valley, see John Francis McDermott, A Glossary of Mississippi Valley French 1673–1850 (St. Louis, 1941), pp. 18–19.

[10] Cat Island, south of Gulfport, Mississippi, was named for raccoons, which the French called chats sauvages. Dumont de Montigny tells how these chats sauvages, when living on seafood, would open oysters at low tide. When their paws were caught in the shells, they had to wait patiently for a change of tide. Mémoires, I, 82–83. The swine that Bienville put on Cat Island destroyed the raccoons, according to [Antoine Simon] Le Page Du Pratz, Histoire de la Louisiane (Paris, 1758), I, 44. McDermott calls attention to the use of chats alone, rather than chats sauvages, for raccoon skins in the fur trade. McDermott, Glossary, p. 49.

in size, it is seven leagues long and a quarter of a league wide and is one league west of Isle Surgère.[11] We went ashore at Isle Surgère and killed a prodigious quantity of wild geese, locally called bustards,[12] which are once again bigger than the geese we have in France. We took there also such an abundance of fish and of oysters in the shell that the crews of the two ships became upset from over-indulgence. On neither of these two islands did we notice any sign or mark that man had ever been there. We found fresh water good enough to drink, although these two islands are five leagues distant from the mainland.

Sixty of us set out in longboats to follow the mainland in an east-west direction, because all the Florida coast lies that way. We found a bay some two leagues in cir-cumference situated five leagues off Isle Surgère. At the head of this bay there is high ground, where M. d'Hyber-ville planned to have a fort built. We worked on this fort without stopping until it was finished. Before the embouchure of this bay there is an island about one league long and an eighth of a league wide which is a quarter of a league off the mainland. To this day it is called Isle-aux-Chevreuils [13] because of the great quantity of deer to be found on it.

We went a full week working at our fort without see-ing a single savage of the region. When part of our men went into the woods to hunt deer, the reports of their guns, which were heard by some savages staying in the woods, surprised them in the extreme. They resolved

[11] Now Ship Island, south of Biloxi, Mississippi.
[12] The French word is *outarde,* a name the French used for the common wild goose, *Branta canadensis.*
[13] Deer Island, which is the southwest boundary of Biloxi Bay.

among themselves to draw near to see what this could be; and, having descried some of our Frenchmen who were felling trees not far from our fort in order to build themselves some houses, they hid behind trees and watched our men a long time, being quite surprised at our clothes and the color of our faces. Some of our soldiers, observing them, signaled to them to approach and to have no fear. They spoke to them in the Iroquois language, as most of our soldiers were, by nation, Canadians who had often had dealings with the Iroquois. After they had spoken to the savages a long time, they approached our men. When the savages had looked at them, a little reassured, our men led some of them to M. d'Hyberville, who received them very well indeed, having food and drink from our supplies given them; but, either because these things were not to their taste or because they were still afraid, they would not eat these things or even touch them. They only kept gazing at us, astonished at seeing white-skinned people, some heavily bearded, some bald-headed, for such indeed there were among us. Thus we appeared to be quite different from them, who have very tawny skin and heavy black hair which they groom very carefully. These savages belonged to a nation called Biloxi; that is why M. d'Hyberville gave the name Biloxi [14] to the fort we had built in this place. They remained with us two days. M. d'Hyberville gave them several little presents of awls, small mirrors, rings, combs, knives, vermilion and such;

---

[14] Commonly called Fort Biloxi, this fort was officially named Fort Maurepas, for Jerome Phélypeaux, Count de Maurepas. For his assumption of the title Count de Pontchartrain, see N. M. Miller Surrey, *Calendar of Manuscripts in Paris Archives and Libraries Relating to the History of the Mississippi Valley to 1803* (Washington, 1926–28), I, vi and 57.

and he had them told the several uses of these things, which they carried off to their village, to their chief.

A week later—as soon as news of the arrival of the French spread among the savages neighboring to these— they came with the chiefs of several villages and sang their calumet of peace, as all the nations do [15] with people whom they have not seen before, but with whom they wish friendship and peace. The calumet is a stick, or hollow cane, about one ell long, decorated all over with feathers of parrots, birds of prey, and eagles. All these feathers tied together around the stick look just about like several lady's fans from France joined together. At the end of this stick is a pipe which they call *calumet*.

The chiefs of these savages—who were five different nations named the Pascagoulas, the Capinans, the Chicachas, the Passacolas, and the Biloxi [16]—came ceremoniously into our fort, singing the while, to present the calumet to M. d'Hyberville, our commander, who did indeed draw some puffs [17] on that calumet after the manner of the savages. Then, as a mark of honor, they rubbed white dirt over the faces of M. d'Hyberville, his brothers, and several other officers. The feast of the calumet lasted three

[15] The description of the calumet, or peace pipe, ceremony does not appear in the Gentleman of Elvas' account of De Soto's travels in the South, nor do I recall any allusion made to it in Garcilaso de la Vega's *Florida del Ynca*. The ceremonial calumet must have been introduced among Southern tribes within the century and a half preceding the arrival of the French on the Gulf Coast.

[16] The Biloxi Indians, linguistically the most interesting of these tribes, were of Siouan stock. The Capinans, living with the Biloxi and Pascagoula, are called Moctobi by ethnologists. These three tribes had no more than twenty cabins when Iberville arrived on the Coast. The Passacolas, or Pensacola Indians, lived in the neighborhood of Pensacola, Florida. See Frederick Webb Hodge, *Handbook of American Indians North of Mexico* (Washington, 1907–10), I, 147; and Swanton, *Indian Tribes of the Lower Mississippi Valley*, p. 306.

[17] Iberville was not a smoker.

days, during which the savages sang and danced three times a day. On the third day they sank a stake in the clearing in front of our fort and danced around it after they had gone for M. d'Hyberville in the following ceremonious manner: a savage offered his back to M. d'Hyberville, who mounted on the savage's shoulders while another savage held both his feet; thus they carried him to the clearing about the stake, keeping in cadence to the sound of their *chichicois,* which are calabashes as big as one's two fists, filled with small pebbles, and which, when shaken, make a rather mean little noise. They have another instrument, too, made of an earthen pot in the shape of a kettle, containing a little water and covered with a piece of deer skin stretched tight across the pot-mouth like a tambour; this they beat with two drumsticks, making as much noise as our drums.

When they had thus arrived before the stake, they laid M. d'Hyberville on the ground upon a deer skin, and made him sit on it; and one of their chiefs, placed behind him, put his hands on M. d'Hyberville's shoulders and rocked him as if he had been an infant needing sleep. Over the ground they had spread out more than three hundred deer skins, upon which the officers and the soldiers were placed. As soon as everybody was seated on these skins, the savages—with their bows and quivers made of the skins of otter or fox and carried on straps slung across their backs, and with wooden head-breakers [18] held in their right hands—came so accoutered and struck the stake with their head-breakers, telling at each blow whatever

---

[18] The French word for this weapon, *casse-tête,* is often translated tomahawk. But these weapons, being wooden, are more like clubs than hatchets.

PIERRE LE MOYNE, SIEUR D'IBERVILLE. From a portrait in the Louisiana State Museum, New Orleans.

noble deeds they had done in war, and more besides. All of them, women as well as men, are permitted to do the same thing and to accuse one another of telling big lies.

The French then went to the King's warehouse by order of M. d'Hyberville and brought knives, glass beads, vermilion, guns, lead, powder, mirrors, combs, kettles, cloaks, hats, shirts, *braguets*,[19] leggings, rings, and other such trinkets. The *braguets,* made from five quarters of cloth cut in two lengthwise, are worn in front of the body and pass between the thighs, thus covering their nakedness. The leggings are made each one from half an ell of cloth cut in two and sewed like a stocking. Through these they stick their legs. The savages were also given axes and picks. After this M. d'Hyberville went off to his quarters, leaving the savages before the fort dividing the presents and examining them with astonishment, not knowing the uses of the greater part of them. We took keen pleasure in watching their bewilderment. Someone told M. d'Hyberville, who came back to the clearing before the fort with the other officers. He could not keep from laughing. He commanded that the use of each article be demonstrated to them. Thereupon their shirts were put on them, and their *braguets* and their hats; their leggings were stitched together and put upon their legs, as our Canadians, of whom I have already spoken, were familiar with such things. Some powder was put in the powder pans of the guns that had been given them; these were cocked and then fired. But when they saw the powder catch fire, they threw out their arms, dropped the

[19] A loin flap for a man or a kind of apron for a woman. Cf. French *braguette,* the codpiece or fly of a man's breeches.

guns, and shrank back from the fear they had of them. M. d'Hyberville directed the French to fire blanks in front of them, which reassured them.

Now, as there are always certain ones bolder than the rest, one of the savages came over to us, making a sign with his hand that he wished one of their guns to be loaded, signaling that he desired to shoot. The Frenchman who loaded for him—out of mischief or for some other reason—put too heavy a charge of powder in the gun; and the savage, in his eagerness to shoot, leaned backward instead of forward as one ordinarily does. The recoil of the gun knocked him down, the savage in one direction, the gun in another. This accident caused the savages to go more than two weeks without wishing to touch a gun.

Helves were made for their axes and their picks, and they were shown how to use them. They gave evidence by signs that that gave them a great deal of pleasure. As early as that time, though, they did have boats in which they went from one place to another on the river. To make these they kept a fire burning at the foot of a tree called *cypress* until the fire burned through the trunk and the tree fell; next, they put fire on top of the fallen tree at the length they wished to make their boat. When the tree had burned down to the thickness they wanted for the depth of the boat, they put out the fire with thick mud; [20] then they scraped the tree with big cockle shells as thick as a man's finger; afterward, they washed it with water. Thus they cleared it out as smooth as we could have made

[20] In hollowing out a log for a pirogue, the Indian worker used a layer of mud, when necessary, to control the direction of the burning as well as the depth of the trough.

it with our tools. These boats may be twenty-five feet long. The savages make them of various lengths, some much smaller than others. With these they go hunting and fishing with their families and go to war or wherever they want to go. When our fort was finished, M. d'Hyberville returned to France, leaving M. de Sauvol [21] as commandant at Fort Biloxi, with M. de Boisbrian [22] as major, M. de Bienville,[23] his brother, together with several other officers, and the Reverend Father Duru,[24] a Jesuit, as our chaplain. After the departure of M. d'Hyberville we made preparations to go forth in the area, to right and left, to discover the Missicipy. We took some savages with us as guides and went east along the coast, where we found a very shallow bay, which is named Baye des Pascagoulas because in the depths of this bay empties a river on whose banks the Pascagoulas, a savage nation, have a settlement twenty leagues inland; and it is from this nation that this bay and the river have taken their name. This bay is only

[21] M. de Sauvole de la Villantray, often called governor of Louisiana, in the sense meaning commandant of a post or town. It is now customary for historians to identify Sauvole as "not the brother of Iberville." The maudlin scene pictured by Gayarré—Iberville kneeling and weeping at the grave of his brother Sauvole—has made this negative identification necessary. Charles Gayarré, *History of Louisiana* (3d ed.; New Orleans, 1885), I, 79–80.

[22] Pierre Dugué de Boisbriant, who was commandant at Mobile in 1717 and in the Illinois Country in 1718. He became ad interim governor of Louisiana after Bienville's recall in 1724. Pénicaut's memory telescoped events, however, for Boisbriant did not come to Louisiana until Iberville's second voyage.

[23] Jean Baptiste Le Moyne de Bienville, who was several times appointed governor of Louisiana.

[24] Father Paul Du Ru, who came on the *Renommée* on Iberville's second voyage, was chaplain at Biloxi after May, 1700. M. Bordenave should have been listed as the chaplain from May 4, 1699, to April 11, 1700. See Jean Delanglez, *The French Jesuits in Lower Louisiana (1700–1763)* (Washington, 1935), p. 7 and n. and p. 30. Paul Du Ru left an interesting, trustworthy journal translated and edited by Ruth Lapham Butler: *Journal of Paul Du Ru* (Chicago, 1934).

five leagues east of Fort Biloxi; it is one league across and three leagues in circuit. At the mouth of this bay there is an island about one league away called Isle Ronde [25] because of its shape, but it is barren and uninhabited. We continued along the mainland, always to the east, and found one league away a little river that is to this day called Rivière-aux-Poissons [26] because of the great quantity of fish found there. One league farther on is Pointe-aux-Chênes,[27] a fine place for hunting and for the great quantity of pheasants, bustards, ducks, and teal found there, half again larger than those in France. As we continued our route eastward, we came upon a river three leagues farther on, called Aderbane,[28] ten leagues distant from Biloxi; it was named Aderbane for one of our Frenchmen that was lost there, and it is so named to this day. Three leagues farther on, there is a point named Pointe-aux-Huîtres [29] on account of the great abundance of oysters found there. This point is opposite an island [30] one league away. We crossed over to this island and landed.

When we disembarked, we became terrified upon find-

[25] Round Island, in Mississippi Sound, southwest of Pascagoula, Mississippi.

[26] This river, which should be close to South Pascagoula, Mississippi, does not appear on the maps I have examined; nor does a Fish River, the translation.

[27] The southeastern tip of Mississippi is still called Point[e] aux Chenes, which means Oak Point.

[28] Bayou LaBatre, in Mobile County, Alabama. Early maps show it as Rivière-à-Derbane. A certain Sieur d'Herbanne was the keeper of the warehouse on Dauphin Island, nearby, on October 12, 1713, but I do not know that he was drowned or lost at Bayou LaBatre. See Hamilton, *Colonial Mobile*, p. 36, and Rowland and Sanders, *MPA*, II, 144.

[29] Oyster Point, which is now called Cedar Point, is on the southwest shore of Mobile Bay, on Mon Louis Island. Hamilton mentions a nearby pass called Pass Sweet, which was developed by the folk from Passe-aux-Huîtres. (*Colonial Mobile*, p. 325.)

[30] Dauphin Island, at the mouth of Mobile Bay.

ing such a prodigious number of human skeletons that they formed a mountain,[31] there were so many of them. We learned afterwards that this was a numerous nation who, being pursued and having withdrawn to this region, had almost all died here of sickness; and as the manner of savages is to gather together all the bones of the dead, they had carried them into this spot. This nation was called Mobila, and a small number of them survive. This island is covered with two kinds of trees, cedars and pines, which are very fragrant. M. de Bienville, the brother of M. d'Hyberville, who commanded us, named it Isle Massacre on account of all these bones. It is seven leagues long and a quarter of a league wide.

While coasting from there along the island on our way back, we crossed a pass about a half league wide, at the end of which is another island called Isle-à-la-Corne [32] because one of our Frenchmen lost his powder horn there; this island lies three leagues off the mainland and is seven leagues long, like Isle Massacre, and of the same width as it. It is quite barren and has the same trees as the other island. When we reached the point of this island we sailed the three quarters of a league to Isle Surgère, where we had a big hunt, after which we crossed over to our fort to rest for several days.

After resting two weeks at Biloxi, we set out to locate a passage through which we could go to find the Missicipy

[31] Iberville, who saw those skeletons on February 2 or 3, 1699, recorded in his log that there were "more than sixty men or women," and he located the skeletons "au bout du sor-ouest" of the island, which he said he was calling Massacre Island on account of the skeletons. Pénicaut's memory or his pen has enlarged one detail, forgotten other details. Margry, *Découvertes*, IV, 147.

[32] Horn Island, a long, narrow island in the chain that forms Mississippi Sound. It is called Isle Bienville on the chart on p. 236.

River to the west of our fort. All the coastal waters are shallow in that direction as far as five leagues out.

We found a bay one league wide and four leagues in circumference, forming a half circle. We named it Baye de St. Louis [33] because it was on St. Louis' Day that we came there. This bay is eight leagues west of Fort Biloxi. We went ashore there and found such a great quantity of game of all kinds of animals that we killed more than fifty wild animals, [as many buffalo as deer; we made no attempt to kill more].[34] After three days we left that place, and three leagues away we found a creek up which the tide ascends. The savages who were guiding us led us to believe that this creek went into a big lake; but, as we were not sure of their words, we made signs to them that we wanted to go on. Two leagues from there we found, at a quarter of a league from the seashore, a pass or small island called Passe-aux-Hérons [35] on account of the great quantity of herons found there. We quit the sea on our left, and three leagues inland we reached an island that we named Isle-aux-Pois [36] because a sack of peas was left behind there. We departed one hour before daybreak,

[33] St. Louis Bay, Mississippi.

[34] This passage, dropped from the Clermont manuscript copy and from Margry, *Découvertes*, V, 384, is supplied from the Francis Parkman manuscript, p. 23: ". . . tant boeufs sauvages que chevreuils; nous n'en voulumes pas tuer davantage."

[35] This name survives, on the charts I have seen, only in Heron Bay and Heron Bay Point, fifteen miles west of St. Louis Bay. The main pass, between Heron Bay and Grassy Island, is now called Grand Island Pass.

[36] Or Pea Island, neither showing on modern maps. A comparison of the I. aux Pois on H. Moll's "A New Map of the North Parts of America Claimed by France, 1720" and on Guillaume Delisle's "Carte de la Louisiane et du cours du Mississipi," 1718, with Pearl River Island on a detailed modern map shows that Isle-aux-Pois, which was south of the east branch of Pearl River, is Pearl River Island, or the east part of it. The name Isle-aux-Pois survives in Bayou Isle aux Pois, which connects with East Pearl River close to Baldwin Lodge. Doubtless the coast line has changed greatly in 225 years. I can offer no more than a reckoning.

which was contrary to our usual procedure, in order to avoid the stinging of an infinity of little flies or gnats that the savages call *maringouins*,[37] which bite till the blood comes. The creek that we had met with flows by that place; and a quarter of a league farther on, we found a big lake which M. de Bienville named Lake Pontchartrain. This lake is twenty-eight leagues in circumference and seven across. Its embouchure at the entrance is a quarter of a league across from right to left, and both sides of this entrance are covered with shells in such great quantities that they form banks; accordingly it was given the name Pointe-aux-Coquilles.[38] After one enters this watercourse and sails upward for a league and a half from the entrance, he finds on his left a point called Pointe-aux-Herbes; [39] here we sheltered our longboats, because this lake is so shallow that boats are always being lost here in rough weather. Six leagues farther up the lake, a small river flows into it which is called, in savage, Choupitcatcha; [40] the French call it today Rivière d'Orléans be-

[37] A South American Indian word for mosquito. Father Du Poisson, a Jesuit slain in the Natchez massacre, has left a memorable comment on the *maringouins* along the Mississippi: "Since the French have been on the Mississippi, this little beast has caused more cursing than had been done in the rest of the world up to that time." Translated from the French quoted by McDermott, *Glossary*, p. 100.

[38] Contemporary French maps, by D'Anville and Delisle, show that the whole shore of Lake Pontchartrain from Chef Menteur Pass to West Rigolets, and the south shore of the Rigolets, were called Les Coquilles (the Shells). I believe that Pointe-aux-Coquilles was the name given to the spit of land between Lake St. Catherine and Lake Pontchartrain, ending in a point at West Rigolets. Between that point and Chef Menteur Pass there is still a Shell Point Bayou, on this spit. See "Lake Borne and Approaches," U.S. Coast and Geodetic Survey, No. 1268 (1949).

[39] Point aux Herbes, in Orleans Parish, juts prominently out into Lake Pontchartrain from the south shore.

[40] Also spelled Soupicatcha. This bayou has been successively called Rivière d'Orléans and Bayou St. John. Professor William A. Read gives Choupicatcha as derived from Choctaw *shupik*, "grindle or mudfish," and *hacha*, "river." *Louisiana Place-Names of Indian Origin* (Baton Rouge, 1927), pp. 24–25.

cause afterwards (as will be shown at the proper time) there was built near this river, one league away from the lake, the town of New Orleans. Five leagues farther, always turning to the left along the lake shore, one comes to a stagnant body of water that the savages call *bayouque*;[41] it is a drain for waters that flow from high grounds. We made camp near this place because the savages who were guiding us made us understand that we should go by way of it to the Missicipy River.

On the morning of the next day, having left our longboat in that bay, we set out on foot to make our way to the river bank. For three quarters of a league we crossed through a wood filled with cypress; these are trees that grow only in low, marshy regions and that are of a prodigious height, bearing a kind of olive as fruit. Coming out of this wood, we entered some tall reeds, or canes, which bear a grain very much like oats, from which the savages make a quite tasty bread and also a soup which they call *sagamité*.[42] After crossing through these canes for a quarter of a league, we reached the bank of the Missicipy.[43]

This greatly delighted us. We looked with admiration at the beauty of this river, which was at least half a league

[41] This bayou may have been Bayou Piquant or Bayou Labranche. Both flow into Lake Pontchartrain on the west side.

[42] A porridge dish made of ground corn. *Sagamité* almost certainly goes back to Algonquin *kisagamite*, "the water is hot," which Frenchmen thought to be the name of the hominy cooking. With the ground corn Indians sometimes mixed beans, meat, and other food. William A. Read, *Louisiana-French* (Baton Rouge, 1931), pp. 105–106.

[43] Pénicaut is apparently giving an account of Bienville's expedition which reached the Mississippi through Lake Pontchartrain in August, 1699. This part of the narrative has been carefully analyzed by Elizabeth McCann. See "Pénicaut and His Chronicle," pp. 295–97 and notes.

wide at the spot where we saw it, which is forty leagues above its embouchure at the sea. Its water is light-colored, very good to drink, and quite clear. At this place its banks are covered with canes, about which we have just spoken. Everywhere else the area along the river appeared to us to be covered with all kinds of forest trees, as far as we were able to discover, such as oaks, ash, elms, and others whose names we did not know.

That night we slept on the bank of the river under some trees, upon which wild turkeys (of which there are great quantities) came at dusk to perch for the night. By moonlight we killed as many of them as we wanted, without their being frightened away by the discharge of our guns. I can say in all truth that I have never seen such big ones in France, for these weighed as high as thirty pounds when ready for the spit. Next day we returned to our longboats. Those who had remained behind to guard them were very much gladdened when we informed them that we had slept on the bank of the Missicipy River.

We then continued our way on Lake Pontchartrain in order to make the circuit of it, and we slept five leagues farther on, on the bank of a *manchacq* [44]—which in French means a channel—through which runs a creek that comes from the Missicipy River. By way of this stream one reaches another lake which is two leagues from there and which nowadays is called Lake Maurepas. This

---

[44] A Choctaw word meaning "rear entrance," according to Read, *Louisiana-French*, p. 157. This particular *manchac*, between Lake Pontchartrain and Lake Maurepas, is now called Pass Manchac. *N.b.* that Pénicaut was aware of the continuous flow of water from the Mississippi through Bayou Manchac and the Amite River (which he does not name) into Maurepas and then through Pass Manchac into Pontchartrain.

lake is fully ten leagues in circumference and two leagues across. The next day we continued our route, always keeping to the channel of Pontchartrain, and one league from there found another river that the savages guiding us called Tandgepao,[45] which in savage signifies white corn; the water in it is very good to drink. Three leagues farther, on the same channel, one finds a *bayouque*, or stagnant water, called Castein Bayouque,[46] which means the place of fleas.[47] The next day we left there and came five leagues away to a river that flows into the lake, which the savages call Taleatcha,[48] which in French is Rivière-aux-Pierres; in it we found some of those shells, or cockles, about which I have already spoken, with which the savages scrape their boats after they have been burned. In these cockles, pearls are found. We gave two dozen of them to M. de Bienville, who was with us. This river is only three leagues distant from Pointe-aux-Coquilles. Here we left Lake Pontchartrain and took our way on this river, which conducted us, at a half league from there, to another of its branches that flows down to Isle-aux-Pois, only three leagues away. Here we spent the night because of the conveniences of the river, whose water is

[45] The Tangipahoa River flowing into Lake Pontchartrain from Tangipahoa Parish.

[46] Castine Bayou, near Mandeville, on the north shore of Lake Pontchartrain. Margry (*Découvertes*, V, 387) gives Castimbayouque, which is wrong. Castein Bayouque, or Casteinbayouque, is derived from Choctaw *kashti*, "flea," and *bayuk*, "bayou," according to Read, *Louisiana Place-Names*, p. 17.

[47] ". . . lieu des puces," Spofford ms., p. 24. The Clermont ms. has a blur for *puces*, and Margry, having to guess, gave "lieu d'espaces," which makes no sense. *Découvertes*, V, 387.

[48] Pearl River, which is not a translation of the Indian name. Margry (*Découvertes*, V, 387) gives Tulcascha. But all ms. entries have Taleatcha, derived, according to Read, from Choctaw *tali*, "rock," and *hacha*, "river." *Louisiana Place-Names*, p. 25.

very good to drink and is of great help for all Frenchmen who come through these parts, for the water of Lake Pontchartrain is tainted with tidal salt water that comes into it. The next day, leaving Isle-aux-Pois, we passed through some little rigolets,[49] which end up at the sea three leagues away, near Baye de St. Louis. We slept at the entrance of the bay, close by a spring of fresh water that flows down from the mountains and that nowadays is called La Belle Fontaine.[50] We hunted for a few days on the shore of this bay. We loaded our longboats with the buffalo and deer that we killed, and the next day we brought them to our fort.

As soon as we arrived, we gave M. de Sauvol, the commandant, a detailed account of the discovery of the Missicipy, which we had found incomparably beautiful, both for its width and for the charms of its banks. M. de Bienville made him a present of the pearls we had found in the cockles. M. de Sauvol told us that he would give them to M. d'Hyberville. But we never learned afterwards what became of them or whether they were valuable.

Several days afterwards, the savages who had guided

[49] "Des petits rigolets." *Rigolet* is a diminutive of French *rigole,* "channel." These little *rigolets* are not the same channel as the Little Rigolets cutting off Rabbit Island, on modern maps. A detailed inset on Delisle's "Carte de la Louisiane" has Petits Chenaux (Petits Rigolets) marked in the position of East Pearl River; to the south is the main pass marked Gr. Chenaux (present-day Rigolets). Therefore, I believe the French used Petits Rigolets for East Pearl River.

[50] D'Anville's "Carte de la Louisiane" shows a Fontaine (small creek or spring) in the neighborhood of the present-day town of Bay St. Louis, Mississippi. But Belle Fontaine was a common place name throughout the province of Louisiana, and I am not sure about this location. The most southern point between Ocean Springs and Pascagoula is still called Belle Fontaine Point, and there is a Bellefontaine on the west shore of Mobile Bay, both pronounced Belle Fountain by seamen I have interviewed.

us made M. de Sauvol understand that they wished to
return to their villages and wanted us to go with them.
M. de Sauvol made them understand that that pleased
him. Ten of us Frenchmen thereupon set out in one longboat and, coming away from our fort, made camp at the
entrance of their river—named, like them, Pascagoulas
—which flows into the head of the bay of the same name.
We ascended this river for twenty leagues above the
mouth and on the third day reached their village. As it
was near the end of August and very hot, all the savages
—the men and the boys—went as naked as one's hand;
but the women and the girls wore a single hank of moss
which passed between their legs and covered their nakedness, the rest of their bodies being quite nude. This moss
is a very fine plant half an ell [51] long, which the French
in the region derisively name Spanish beard and the Spaniards, to return the favor, call French wig.

We were perfectly well received by their grand chief
and by all the savages of the village: they gave us something to drink and to eat such as buffalo, bear, and deer,
and every kind of fruit in abundance, such as peaches,
plums, watermelons, pumpkins, and all of an exquisite
flavor. The pumpkins are indeed better than those in
France: they are cooked without water, and the juice that
comes from them is like syrup, it is so sweet. As for the
watermelons, they are just about like those in France. The
peaches are better and bigger; but their plums are not so
good; there are two varieties, white ones and red ones.
They served us also some of their sagamité, which is a
kind of pap made from maize and green beans that are

[51] The ell was approximately forty-six inches.

like those in France. Their bread comes from maize and
from a grain that grows on canes. They have some dishes
made of wood and others of clay, which, even though
made by the hands of savages, are nevertheless very well
made indeed. The savages' women also make great earthen
pots, designed almost like big kettles, which hold about
forty pints; in these they cook their sagamité for two or
three families; this is how they contrive among themselves
to avoid the trouble of cooking the same thing every day,
each one in turn doing it. As for their huts, they are made
of mud and are of a round shape almost like windmills.
The roofs of the houses are made mainly from the bark
of trees. There are others that are covered with the leaves
of a bush locally called *latanier*,[52] which is a tree peculiar
to the area. An observation I have made about the savages
is that, however abundant their provisions may be, they
do not overindulge themselves, but eat only what they
need, yet very untidily, most of them eating only with
their fingers, though they possess spoons, which they
make from buffalo horns. Their meat is usually smoked
or in some other way buccaned,[53] as they say in that region. They have, however, a kind of gridiron on which
they put it, but with little fire underneath, doing little
more than drying it, the smoke contributing as much to
the process as the heat from the fire.

The chief orders his savages to dance in the evening,
which they do to the sound of their little drum and their
chichicois. A ring is formed by twenty or thirty, without

---

[52] The *latania*, commonly called palmetto.

[53] Derived from French *boucaner*, "to smoke meat on a frame." According to
Read (*Louisiana-French*, p. 83) *boucan* is a South American Tupi word meaning a
"wooden lattice frame for the smoking of meat." Cf. *buccaneer*.

holding hands; at the head is the leader of the dance, who with one sound of his whistle makes them break their circle; and, as they intermingle among themselves, always keeping to the rhythm, the leader of the dance with another sound of his whistle makes them form their line into a ring again with a surprising precision. They have still other dances about which I shall speak more at length in the course of this narrative.

We spent the night at the house of the Grand Chief, sleeping on flat cane beds stretched and interwoven like camp cots, some tied to others, and all covered with buffalo skins. Next morning we took short walks into their countryside, where they sow their corn. The women were there to work with the men. The savages have flat, hooked sticks with which they pick the ground, as they know nothing about plowing the way we do in France. They scratch the ground with these hooked sticks and uproot the canes and weeds, which they leave on the ground out in the sun for two weeks or a month; and afterwards they set fire to them, and when they are reduced to ashes, they take a stick as big as one's arm and sharpened at one end and make a hole in the ground every three feet, into which they put seven or eight grains of corn per hole and cover it over with dirt. In this way they plant their corn and their beans. When the corn is a foot high, they take great care, as we do in France, to pull up the weeds that grow in it; this they repeat two or three times during the year. They still use their wooden picks nowadays despite the fact that we have given them iron ones, because they find theirs lighter. We stayed a few more days at this village and then returned to our fort.

Chapter 2

The Year 1700

Second discovery of the Missicipy, which M. d'Hyberville ascended from its embouchure at the sea up to the Tinssas—The author's third trip upon the Missicipy, which he ascended as high as the Saut de St. Anthoine—Buffaloes described—Fort Huilier established on the Rivière Verte

E WERE quite impatient for the return of M. d'Hyberville and were constantly out on the point before the fort keeping watch for him. Finally on Kings' Eve, 1700, we heard cannon-firing from Isle Surgère, five leagues from our fort. It was M. d'Hyberville arriving with the Count de Surgère: M. d'Hyberville in command of *La Renommée* and the Count de Surgère of *La Gironde,* a seven-hundred-ton flûte.[1] M. de Sauvol had cannon fired, and all the muskets of the troops, to assemble everybody at the fort for the reception. M. d'Hyberville was received with all possible joy. But he remained at the fort only four days, after which he picked out sixty men to go with him to the Missicipy River. From the officers, he chose to accompany him MM. de Bienville and de Chateaugué,[2] his two brothers, and [MM. Dugué][3] and de Boisbrian, also two

[1] A warship used chiefly to carry supplies.

[2] Antoine Le Moyne de Chateaugué, Iberville's brother who after long and important service in Louisiana became Governor of Île Royale.

[3] Omitted from Clermont and from Margry, *Découvertes,* V, 392; thus Margry's reading "et de Boisbriant, aussy deux frères" is illogical. The prominent one of the Dugué brothers was Pierre Dugué de Boisbriant, the ad interim governor of Louisiana after Bienville's recall in 1724. Grace King has suggested that the Dugué name in the Creole families Dugué de Livaudais and Dugué may have come from the

brothers, and M. de St. Denis.[4] He left M. de Sauvol, who
was commander of the fort, to have the two vessels unloaded and the goods and munitions stored in the King's
warehouse. After M. d'Hyberville had given all his orders,
we left with him to ascend the Missicipy through its embouchure at the sea. First we crossed over to our ships to
take the necessary supplies off them; here M. d'Hyberville conferred with the Count de Surgère about securing
the vessels during the trip. We then left the ships and went
away in three longboats.

We spent the night seventeen leagues west of Fort
Biloxi, near Pointe-à-l'Assiette,[5] so named because M.
d'Hyberville lost a plate there. Twelve leagues farther
from there we camped at a point called Pointe-au-
Trespied.[6] The next day we proceeded and spent the night
on the bank of a small river six leagues farther on. It was
called Rivière-aux-Chiens [7] because a crocodile ate up
one of our dogs there. Ten leagues farther from there we
reached the mouth of the Missicipy. Here we camped on

Canadian Jean Sidrac Dugué, who called himself Boisbriant. Jean Sidrac may be
the name of the other brother. *Creole Families of New Orleans* (New York, 1921),
p. 216.

[4] Louis Juchereau de St. Denis, the romantic explorer and adventurer. After the
events recounted in this book, he was for many years commandant at Natchitoches.

[5] It does not appear on modern maps, nor does Plate Point, the translation. The
map in Charlevoix, *Histoire et Description Generale de La Nouvelle France*, . . .
(Paris, 1744), III, 468, shows Pointe a l'Assiete as the point on the mainland (now
St. Bernard Parish) directly west of the most northern Chandeleur Island and be-
hind the Seven Islands. Delisle's "Carte de la Louisiane" gives the point west of the
Seven Islands as Pointe aux Sept Isles, which may be the same as Pointe-à-l'Assiette.

[6] It does not appear on modern maps, nor does Tripod Point, the translation. By
my reckonings, based on Pénicaut, it was in St. Bernard Parish, between Seven Island Point and Rivière aux Chênes, the west boundary of the parish.

[7] Rivière aux Chênes, emptying into Black Bay and being the west boundary of
St. Bernard Parish, may be a folk development from Rivière-aux-Chiens, Dog River.
It is in the right location.

the right-hand bank going upstream. All the shore line—from Fort Biloxi to the mouth of the Missicipy River and for ten leagues upstream—is low ground. At the river mouth there are three passes made by two small islands. The narrowest of the passes, which is on the right, is the deepest, with only eleven feet of water.

When we had ascended the river for ten leagues, we found the first of the forests that border the river to right and left. At this place, on the right, there is a small channel through which flows water from the river. This little channel is called Mardy Gras.[8] Eight leagues higher up, M. d'Hyberville noted on the right a very good site for a fort, which he resolved to have built when he came back down the river. Eight leagues higher up there is a bend, three leagues long following the shore, which is called Le Détour-à-l'Anglois.[9] (I shall give the reason for that in its place.) Twenty-four leagues higher up, on the left going upstream, one comes to a river called Rivière des Chetimachas.[10] We then found, six leagues higher on the same side, the first savage nation that lives on the bank of the Missicipy River; they are called the Bayagoulas.[11]

As soon as they perceived us, they fled into the depths

---

[8] Perhaps Fort Bayou, east of the Mississippi, in Plaquemines Parish. Jack A. Reynolds was unable to identify Mardy Gras pass with any certainty in "Louisiana Place Names of Romance Origin" (unpublished Ph.D. thesis, Louisiana State University, 1942), p. 332.

[9] Now called English Turn.

[10] Bayou Lafourche. The Chitimacha Indians were of a distinct linguistic stock. Their territory extended from Grand Lake to the Mississippi entrance to Bayou Lafourche. A Chitimacha village was on the site of Donaldsonville, Louisiana. Hodge, *Handbook*, I, 286.

[11] The Bayogoula Indians, a Muskhogean tribe that lived around 1700 in present-day Iberville Parish. The town Bayou Goula carries their name and marks the site, according to Read (*Louisiana Place-Names*, p. 9). Bayogoula means "bayou people," from Choctaw *báyuk-ókla*.

of the woods with their women and children, so that when we entered their village we found no one there, only their little personal effects and other utensils with which they worked. M. d'Hyberville was not surprised at this and remarked that fear had made them abandon their houses. He immediately detailed two Frenchmen and one savage to go to them and reassure them. They ran after them and caught up with them in a short while, as their children hindered them from going fast. Our savage, who was of the Biloxi and knew them all, made them understand that we were good people and encouraged them to return; and, although they had little faith in that, they did not fail to return, their calumet of peace in their hands. When they had come back to their village, they offered the pipe to M. d'Hyberville and all the other officers, and also some flour, which they eat with cold water, some of their bread, some fish, and other foods of their making. A while later they sang their calumet, as is the manner of the savages.

During the evening they asked M. d'Hyberville in their language whether we had had enough to eat and whether we would require as many women as there were men in our party. By showing his hand to them, M. d'Hyberville made them understand that their skin—red and tanned —should not come close to that of the French, which was white. We stayed in their village three days—as long as their calumet lasted.[12] We made them presents of some trinkets, such as mirrors, rings, picks, etc., which they beheld with wonder after they had been instructed in the uses of all these things. M. d'Hyberville told the chief of

---

[12] Notice how life in Louisiana as portrayed in this book falls into three-day periods, so binding was calumet protocol upon the French as well as the nations.

Sauvage en habit d'hiver.

INDIAN IN WINTER DRESS. From David I. Bushnell, Jr., "Drawings by A. DeBatz in Louisiana, 1732–1735," in *Smithsonian Miscellaneous Collections*, LXXX, No. 5.

these savages that he would leave the next morning and needed some poultry to take with him. The village being filled with fowls, they gave us a great number of them. We brought along four savages from their village to serve us as guides. M. d'Hyberville left with their chief a little French boy [13] to be taught the savage language by him. Next morning we departed. Still headed upriver, we found the Manchacq [14] five leagues up on the right side, a little creek of which I have already spoken that empties into Lake Pontchartrain. As the current in it is excessively rapid, it is quite difficult to ascend; added to this, it is very narrow. From there we went five leagues higher and found very high banks called *écorts* [15] in that region, and in savage called *Istrouma*,[16] which means red stick, as at this place there is a post painted red that the savages have sunk there to mark the land line between the two nations, namely: land of the Bayagoulas, which we were leaving, and land of another nation—thirty leagues upstream from the *bâton rouge*—named the Oumas.[17] These two nations were so jealous of the hunting in their territories that they would shoot at any of their neighbors whom they caught hunting beyond the limits marked by the red

[13] One of the six cabin boys that Iberville left in Louisiana to learn Indian languages and serve as interpreters and perhaps as cultural spies. This practice had already been used by the French in Canada.

[14] Bayou Manchac, once called Iberville River. It should not be confused with Pass Manchac, between Lake Pontchartrain and Lake Maurepas.

[15] Usually written *écore* or *écor*, this word, which means "bluff," is common in place names along river courses throughout the province of Louisiana.

[16] Possibly derived from *iti humma*, "red pole," of which Baton Rouge is a translation. A suburb of Baton Rouge is named Istrouma. See Read, *Louisiana Place-Names*, p. 32.

[17] The Huma Indians, whose name is conjecturally derived from *shakchi humma*, "red crawfish," which was their tribal war emblem. Read, *Louisiana Place-Names*, pp. 31–32.

post. But nowadays things are not the same: they hunt everywhere, the ones with the others, and are good friends.

Five leagues upstream from this post, there are bluffs or banks of white dirt on the right side, very high, extending for three quarters of a league. At the end of them one finds a neck of land that juts far out into the Missicipy, making a bend seven leagues around. To avoid the tedious trip around this bend, M. d'Hyberville had the longboats carried across this neck, which is no more than a gunshot wide, and we were presently on the other side upon the Missicipy, where we launched our longboats once more. For some time the river current has been undermining this neck of land, so that the full stream now passes across it. This is why that neck of land now bears the name Pointe Coupée.

Opposite a little island eight leagues upstream on the right there is a portage marked by a cross that M. d'Hyberville had set up there. Here, down on our knees, we sang a *Vexilla Regis,* which greatly astonished the savages. We made them understand that this cross was an object greatly valued in our religion and that they should take care not to knock it down. For this reason this place was named Portage de la Croix.[18] This is the main route to the village of the savages called the Oumas, which is two leagues from there.

M. d'Hyberville and the officers, who had gone ashore at this place, took this route to the village, having ordered

---

[18] By comparing D'Anville's "Carte de la Louisiane," on which this portage is marked, with a modern map, I calculate the position as close to the Mississippi-Louisiana line, in West Feliciana Parish.

us to follow the bend of the shore with our longboats and meet them there. This bend is ten leagues long. Following the shore, we found the mouth of a big river called Rivière Rouge,[19] which empties into the Missicipy on the left. (We shall have more to say about it hereafter.) Two leagues upstream on the right we found the Baye des Oumas,[20] in front of which there is a small island. We landed at the bay, on the bank of which the village stands. Here we found M. d'Hyberville and all the officers, who had got here two days before. We remained here only three days; and after the savages had finished singing their calumet of peace, M. d'Hyberville gave them some presents, as he had given the others. They, too, gave us a great many fowls and some game, which we loaded into our longboats. And we did not fail to get from them four of their savages to serve us as guides, replacing the four Bayagoulas savages, whom we sent back to their village. Thus we exchanged nation for nation so that we would not fatigue them and would at the same time reassure the savages when we came among them: seeing us with other savages, they were not at all alarmed.

From the village of the Oumas, we continued our way, still going upstream; and fifteen leagues higher up, the Missicipy splits into three branches, forming two small islands half a league long; and a league upstream on the right we passed banks of a tremendous height [21] extending for half a league. Beyond these there flows into the river

[19] Red River, Louisiana.

[20] Close to the line between West Feliciana Parish and Wilkinson County, Mississippi.

[21] Identified as Ellis' Cliffs in French's "Annals of Louisiana . . . By M. Pénicaut," p. 57.

a small stream [22] that comes down from a village four leagues up its course and about a league inland from the river. We left our boats and went to this village, where we were received perfectly well. These savages are called the Natchez, and of all the savages they are the most civilized nation. They showed a great many civilities to M. d'Hyberville and to all the officers. They sang their calumet of peace, which lasted three days, after which we departed laden with game and poultry. M. d'Hyberville gave them some presents, too, as he had done to the other nations that had sung their calumet. Hereafter we shall speak of their customs, their religion, their temple, etc.

We left the Natchez, and on our right, still headed upstream, passed along some great rocky banks that extended for twelve leagues; and then we came to a spot that we called Le Petit Gouffre [23] because of the eddies that the river makes for a stretch of a fourth of a league. Eight leagues on upstream is Le Grand Gouffre.[24] We passed this, and two gunshots upstream on the left we landed to go to a village that is four leagues inland from the river bank. These savages are named the Tinssas.[25] We

[22] Marked on D'Anville's "Carte de la Louisiane" as La Petite Rivière, the usual "des Natchez" being omitted. This little stream, south of Natchez, Mississippi, is called St. Catharine's Creek or St. Catherine Creek. Christian Schultz, in *Travels on an Inland Voyage* (New York, 1810), II, 148–49, calls it Catharine's Creek and locates the mouth as nineteen miles below Natchez, and one mile above White Cliffs.

[23] Meaning little eddy or whirlpool. The name survived for years as Petit Gulf. Schultz, who passed it, gives the position as ten miles below Bayou Pierre and twenty-three miles above Coles Creek, both in Mississippi. *Travels,* II, 129–30.

[24] The name survives as Grand Gulf, a place name in Claiborne County, Mississippi, opposite Tensas Parish, Louisiana.

[25] The Taensa Indians were socially and linguistically related to the Natchez tribe. First found on Lake St. Joseph, Tensas Parish, Louisiana, they moved to several other sites in Alabama and Louisiana. As Tensas or Tensaw their name is carried by place names in Alabama and Louisiana. For the history of the tribe, see Hodge, *Handbook,* II, 668–69.

were well received among them. But I have never seen a spectacle more dolorous or more frightful at the same time than what occurred on our second day in this village.

A frightful thunderstorm suddenly arose: lightning struck their temple, burned all their idols, and reduced their temple to ashes. Immediately the savages ran out in front of their temple making horrible shrieks, tearing out their hair, and raising their arms aloft. Facing their temple, they invoked their Great Spirit, like men possessed, to extinguish the fire; then they seized dirt and smeared it on their bodies and their faces. Fathers and mothers brought their children and strangled them and cast them into the fire. M. d'Hyberville was so horrified at such brutality that he commanded us to put a stop to that frightful performance and to take the innocent children away from their parents. In spite of all our efforts they succeeded in throwing seventeen [26] of them into the fire; and had we not hindered them, they would have thrown more than two hundred.

After the three days during which they sang their calumet of peace, M. d'Hyberville gave them a more substantial present than he had given to the others, telling them to abandon that place and come and settle on the bank of the Missicipy. And, seeing that the time was drawing nigh for him to return to France and that the other nations were too far off, he decided to go back down the river.

We departed next morning and on that same day arrived at the Natchez, where we spent the night. Next

[26] Only four or five children were sacrificed, according to soberer accounts of this incident. McCann, "Pénicaut and His Chronicle of Early Louisiana," p. 298.

morning their chiefs came to accompany M. d'Hyberville to the edge of the water. He promised to send them a
small French boy to learn their language among them.
From there we went on and spent the night at the village
of the Oumas, the current being so swift that, going
downstream, we covered much distance in one day. Then
we were at the Portage de la Croix and the next day at
the Bayagoulas, where we found the little French boy that
M. d'Hyberville had left there on the way upriver. He
could already speak their language very well. M. d'Hyberville told him to remain in this village and act as interpreter for the French who should pass this way. From
there we came to the place that M. d'Hyberville on the
way upstream had marked out as a site for a fort, where
we found a *traversier* that M. de Bienville had brought
over from Biloxi; for M. d'Hyberville had sent his
brother, M. de Bienville, from the Natchez in advance so
that he could send the provisions and the tools needed for
building this fort.

On his way down from the Natchez to Biloxi, M. de
Bienville had found a small English ship careened in a
bend three leagues long. M. de Bienville went to him and
asked him what he was seeking on the Missicipy and asked
whether he did not know that the French were established
in the region. The Englishman, quite astonished, replied
that he had known nothing about that and a moment
afterwards departed, headed for the sea, cursing greatly
at the French and at M. de Bienville. This is what caused
that bend to be named Détour-à-l'Anglois,[27] a name that
it bears today.

[27] This account of the English ship on the Mississippi shows that English Turn

To return to M. d'Hyberville. After having the plan and the dimensions drawn for the construction of the fort, which was well advanced in two weeks, he had the munitions and the food supplies unloaded so that they could be carried into the magazines in the fort. He had a battery of six pieces of cannon set up to front the river, and he left M. de Bienville, his brother, there with M. de St. Denis as commander of the fort, with twenty-five men. Then he sailed back to Fort Biloxi in the *traversier,* followed by two of our longboats and five French-Canadians, fur traders who had learned that we were established at Biloxi and had come to barter with us. M. d'Hyberville [28] kept us under way day and night upon leaving Fort Missicipy, and the next day he reached his ships, where he conferred with M. de Surgère about the food supplies remaining in them. It so happened that there was no more than a three months' supply.

He then went to Fort Biloxi [29] to inspect the merchandise and the munitions that were in the warehouses. He increased the garrison of the fort with sixty Canadians, whom he added to the six hundred men [30] that we

means merely the turn, or bend, where the Englishman was found. Yet, people, who have forgotten the old meaning of turn—a bend, in French *détour*—are inclined to associate the word with turning and fleeing. For example, see one explanation of English Turn given by Alcée Fortier, *A History of Louisiana* (New York, 1904), I, 258, n. 12: "They turned back, whence the name 'English Turn.'" But cf. Plaquemine Turn or Bend. The English ship that withdrew so quickly was commanded by Captain Bank, and he had some Huguenots aboard his ship. See Read, *Louisiana Place-Names,* p. 52, and Delanglez, *French Jesuits,* p. 6 and note.

[28] Clermont, p. 42, and Spofford, p. 50, have Bienville, which the context denies. Parkman, p. 53, and the Rouen Manuscript have "nous vogames."

[29] Parkman, p. 53, and Rouen have: ". . . il alla ensuite au fort Louis du Biloxi." The first fort at Biloxi was named Maurepas. I judge that the Parkman and Rouen scribes, or even Pénicaut, fell into this anachronism by recalling the name of the fort at Mobile or New Biloxi: Fort Louis.

[30] This figure is far too high, but all mss. give it. Parkman, p. 54, has: ". . . 600

already had; he had brought them across on his ship with
M. Le Sueure; and having embraced M. de Sauvol and
M. de Boisbrian, he sailed in the month of April in that
year, 1700, on his second return to France.

At his departure he recommended to M. de Sauvol that
he give M. Le Sueure [31] twenty men to go with him to
a copper mine that is in the country of the Cioux, a nation
of nomadic savages more than nine hundred leagues from
the mouth of the Missicipy, as far up as the Saut de St.
Anthoine.[32] M. Le Sueure had had information about this
mine several years earlier when he was on a journey into
the country of the Ataoas,[33] where he engaged in trading.
I was commanded by M. de Sauvol to go on this trip that
M. Le Sueure was undertaking, because, being by trade a
carpenter in the service of His Majesty and being needed
to make longboats and keep them in repair, I have always
been along on all the expeditions that I have reported, and
shall report hereafter, of which I have been an eyewitness.

To return to M. Le Sueure. After he had got all his

hommes que nous etions"; the other mss. write out six hundred. Pénicaut must have
written ". . . 60 hommes," in which a penman's flourish or some blemish suggested
another zero. Margry (*Découvertes*, V, 400) gives "60 hommes."

[31] Pierre Charles Le Sueur, the explorer, was sent to Louisiana so that he could
go up the Mississippi to work or discover mines in the Sioux Country. His wife, a
first cousin of the Le Moyne brothers, resided at Mobile for many years. For events in
the life of his family at Mobile, see Hamilton, *Colonial Mobile*, p. 123. The primary
source is Mobile Baptismal Records, at the residence of the Bishop of Mobile.

[32] The Falls of St. Anthony, the head of navigation on the Mississippi River, in
Minnesota. Towns did not develop there until 140 years later. Minneapolis grew from
two towns, Minneapolis on the west bank and St. Anthony on the east bank. Henne-
pin, captured by Sioux Indians, saw the falls July 1, 1680, and named them. James
Truslow Adams (ed.), *Dictionary of American History* (New York, 1942), III,
26.

[33] The Ottawas. The French also spelled the name Outaouas, which is Margry's
reading. *Découvertes*, V, 400.

supplies and all the tools necessary and had embraced M. de Sauvol, he made his departure at the end of April of that year, with one single longboat in which we were only twenty-five persons. I shall not waste my time by giving a needless repetition of the places we passed on our way up the Missicipy River. I have already given a description of them from its mouth as far up as the nation of the Tinssas, who are the last as far as we went with M. d'Hyberville, who did not wish to go higher than that village. I shall merely say that on arriving at the new fort,[34] where MM. de St. Denis and de Bienville were, we were given a rowboat to lighten our longboat, which, being too heavily loaded, was unable to make more than slight headway each day. The next day we left to go to the Tinssas. It took us twenty-four days to get there, as we were unable to make more than five or six leagues a day going upstream because of the currents, which at the end of April and during the month of May are very swift in the Missicipy on account of the melting of snows which swells the streams flowing into the Missicipy and makes it overflow its banks during that time.

When we had passed the Tinssas, ten leagues upstream on the right we found a river called Rivière des Yasoux. Four leagues up this river we found on the right the villages in which dwell six savage nations, called the Yasoux, the Offogoulas, the Tonicas, the Coroas, the Bitoupas, and the Oussipez.[35] In that village we found a French [mis-

[34] Fort Mississippi.

[35] These small tribes lived in Mississippi, near or along the Yazoo River. The Yasoux, now called Yazoo, were of the Tunican linguistic group. The Offogoulas spoke a Siouan dialect, according to Hodge. The Tonicas, now usually Tunica, were a distinct linguistic family. The Coroas, or Koroa, belonged to the Tunican group. The

sionary named M. Davion],[36] with a French servant, who
showed us many courtesies and was delighted at meeting
us. He had come as a missionary among these savages to
try to convert some. He said Mass for us next morning
before we departed. We told him that M. d'Hyberville
had brought a colony of French people into the region;
but he was already well informed about that. After giving us his blessing, he gave all of us the embrace and accompanied us as far as our longboat, where we bade him
farewell.

From this place we went on up the Missicipy for sixty
leagues, as far as a stream called the Rivière des Arcanssas,
half as wide as the Missicipy, which runs from north to
east. Eight leagues upstream on the same side, the left, is
the nation of the Arcanssas,[37] whose name the river bears.
In their village were two other nations of savages who
lived with them, named the Tourimas [38] and the Capas,[39]
who received us very well and sang the calumet of peace
to us. But they could give us only a little food, because
the Missicipy River had overflowed its banks and beasts
had withdrawn to more than sixty leagues from the river

Bitoupas are correctly Ibitoupa, which Swanton classified as Muskhogean. The
identity of the Oussipez, or Oussepez, is uncertain: they may have been the Taposa
or another band of Ofos. See the entries for these names arranged alphabetically in
Hodge, *Handbook*; also Swanton, *Indian Tribes of the Lower Mississippi*, pp. 9, 33–
34, 308, 332–33, and his linguistic map.

[36] Restored from Parkman, p. 56: ". . . dans ces villages nous trouvames un
missionaire francois nommé Mr. Davion avec un domestique francois."

[37] The Arkansas Indians were the Quapaw, sometimes spelled Kapa. Of Siouan
stock, they had migrated downriver and therefore were called *Quapaw*, "downstream people." Hodge, *Handbook*, II, 333–34.

[38] Identified by Hodge as the name of one of the Quapaw villages. (*Handbook*,
II, 796.) Indians were often given their village name.

[39] The Quapaw. The French designated one particular tribe of Quapaws as the
Arkansas.

bank. This nation is very warlike, and they are great hunters, and when the Missicipy is low they live solely from hunting because then there is plenty of game in their region. That is why they are not industrious and are very little devoted to the cultivation of the soil. It is the women who do the work here rather than the men; they are quite pretty and white-complexioned. Most of the men are heavy and thickset. We found an English trader here who helped us very much out of his own provisions, as ours were beginning to dwindle, which forced us to leave next day.

Twenty leagues away we found the Baye de St. François.[40] We gave it this name, which has remained as its name till this day. It is fully a league in circumference. Twenty leagues upstream are high banks on the right side, and at this spot a small stream flows in, named Rivière-à-Margot.[41] By way of this stream one goes near the village of the Chicachas, which is thirty leagues distant from the bank of the Missicipy River, far inland on the right. As this village was very remote, we did not go to it, but went on up river to a place forty leagues higher up, which is called Écorts-à-Prudhomme [42] because a French-Canadian by that name died there in a fort which he had built and which to this day bears his name. Fifty leagues

[40] The St. Francis River enters the Mississippi today on the west side just north of Helena, Arkansas.

[41] Wolf River, at Memphis.

[42] The Chickasaw Bluffs above Memphis, Tennessee. La Salle built a fort at the mouth of Big Hatchie on his way downstream. The fort and the bluffs, *écores*, were named for Pierre Prudhomme, who, having been lost for ten days, had to be left with several men in the fort while the explorer proceeded downstream to discover the mouth of the Mississippi. Adams (ed.), *Dictionary of American History*, V, 242, and J. H. Schlarman, *From Quebec to New Orleans* (Belleville, Ill., 1929), p. 95.

up stream on the right we came to a place called La Mine de Fer.[43] Five leagues farther, on the right, still going upstream, we found the Rivière Oüabache,[44] which flows from east to west. This river is almost as big as the Missicipy at its mouth. One can go up to Canada by way of this river. Its banks abound in every kind of game. Ten leagues up this river, on the right going upstream, another river flows in called Des Kasquinempos.[45] This river has its source in the direction of Carolina and flows to the village of the Cheraquis, a populous nation that can send more than fifty thousand warriors to war. Fifteen leagues above the mouth of the Rivière Oüabache, on the right side of the Missicipy, we found Cape St. Anthoine.[46] This is the place where the French from the Illinois come for rocks with which to make millstones. Here at this cape our provisions failed us altogether. For twenty-two days we were forced to remain at this place without any provisions, each one going out every morning into the woods to seek his living off the end of his gun. Among us were some who ate wood sap, others the young leaves of vines and shoots of trees, for it was spring time and the waters

[43] My reckonings, based solely on Pénicaut, place this Iron Mine in Ballard or Carlisle County, Kentucky. Schultz (*Travels*, II, 96) mentions the Iron Banks, fifteen miles below Fort Jefferson, which he locates near the mouth of Mayfield Creek. If La Mine de Fer was the Iron Banks, it was, accordingly, in Carlisle County, Kentucky.

[44] The Ohio River. In the early eighteenth century, the French gave the name Oüabache (Wabash) to that part of the Ohio below its junction with the Wabash. Above the Wabash, the Ohio was called La Belle Rivière.

[45] The Tennessee River, named Kasquinempos for the Kakinonba Indians living near it. Other forms of the name given by Hodge (*Handbook*, I, 644) are Casquinambeaux, Casquinampo, and Kaskinenpo. The Tennessee was also called Rivière des Cheraquis by the French.

[46] Identified by Charles Upson Clark as Grand Tower, Illinois. *Voyageurs, Robes Noires, et Coureurs de Bois* (New York, 1934), p. 367.

were so high that they had overflowed the banks in a great many places.

Three of our comrades crossed in a boat to the other side of the Missicipy, where they landed and fastened the boat to a tree at the edge of the water; and after they had separated in order to look for game, each in his own direction, or to kill birds, one of our comrades named Polonois perceived—from a distance in a little sunken path in which he was walking—two bears coming toward him, one behind the other. He hid behind a tree, and when the bear got quite close he fired his gun at its head. His gun was loaded only with shot; yet by the greatest luck in the world he struck it in both eyes. Stunned and nearly blinded, the bear kept turning round and round, without knowing where it was going; and our comrade had time to reload his gun with a bullet. With this he fired a second time, and this shot killed it. Those of us who had heard him fire the two shots went to him. We were very much surprised and at the same time delighted at such a lucky hunt; and after cutting the bear up in pieces we carried it to our longboat. This helped us subsist for seven or eight days, for the bears from the banks of the Missicipy are as fat as beeves and very good to eat. (At the right time I shall have more to say about them, noting the manner in which they are taken. It is a very dangerous kind of hunting.)

Each day we were expecting provisions from the Illinois because, several days earlier, we had met a priest across from the Écorts-à-Prudhomme who was going down to the sea to call on M. d'Hyberville; but, after learning from us that M. d'Hyberville had sailed back to

France, the priest changed his plans; and before he went back up to the Illinois—M. Le Sueure having declared to him our need of food supplies—he helped us out of his, as much as he could, even stinting himself in order to accommodate us. M. Le Sueure had besought him to send us a boat with food, telling him that we would wait for it at Cape St. Anthoine, as we were so weakened from lack of food that we did not have the strength to row farther. He had left at once, having promised us to row night and day in order to arrive as quickly as possible at the Illinois, from where he would send us some provisions. He did not go back on his word; and the minute he got there, he started a boat downstream filled with all kinds of provisions. It reached us after twenty-two days, in the time of our greatest need. On that occasion few people were in our longboat, as most of our men had gone off in the woods to find something on which to subsist. The Reverend Father Limoges [47] came in that boat with four Frenchmen to paddle him.

As soon as the Reverend Father got out of the boat, M. Le Sueure wished to compliment him as a mark of appreciation; but the Reverend Father said that, before paying him any compliments, we should give succor to the sick. To which M. Le Sueure told him that, thank God, he was the sickest one and that all his men were well, which very much surprised the Reverend Father and the four Frenchmen who had come with him.

When we got back to our longboat, we were delighted

---

[47] Joseph de Limoges, S.J., who had arrived at Cahokia in the Illinois Country on March 9, 1700. He came all the way downriver to Fort Mississippi, arriving by May 28, 1700. Delanglez, *French Jesuits*, pp. 27-28 ff.

to find such an abundance of things to eat. After we had taken them from the rowboat to our longboat, each man threw himself upon them. The Reverend Father thought that we were going to eat so much that we would get sick; and he was very much astonished that each of us did not eat one fourth pound of meat and just as much of a kind of flat cake or pie. But we evened things up by drinking quite a deal of the wine from Spain.

After resting in that place for three days to regain our strength, we left and went six leagues upstream, on the left, where we found Cape St. Cosme.⁴⁸ Then eight leagues upstream on the right we found the mouth of the Rivière des Illinois.⁴⁹ The Cascassias ⁵⁰ had just settled in this place two years before. Inland no more than two leagues from the river there is a small barren island that is opposite the mouth. Three leagues above, on the left side of the Missicipy, we found La Petite Rivière de la Saline,⁵¹ [so named] because there are two springs of salt water. Here is where the French and the Illinois come

⁴⁸ Chart No. 6 in War Department, *The Middle and Upper Mississippi River* (Washington, 1935), p. 42, shows a Cinque Hommes Cr. flowing into the Mississippi from Perry County, Missouri. The name of this creek looks like a folk development from St. Cosme, and as such is supported by the chart of Captain Philip Pittman, an engineer with British forces in Mobile. His chart gives Cap cinque homme and below it St. Come. See "A Draft of the River Mississippi from the Balise up to Fort Chartres," in Pittman, *The Present State of the European Settlements on the Mississippi* (Cleveland, 1906, but first published in London, 1770).

⁴⁹ Not the Illinois River, but an anachronism for the Okaw or Kaskaskia, in southwest Illinois. The Kaskaskia tribe of the Illinois Indians did not settle on this river till 1703, according to John Francis McDermott, *Old Cahokia* (St. Louis, 1949), pp. 4, 10. Okaw is a shortened form of "aux Kaskaskia."

⁵⁰ One of the Illinois tribes. They moved from the Illinois River proper in 1700 and first settled on the site of southern St. Louis, opposite the Tamaroa or Cahokia. From there they moved to the Okaw River. McDermott, *Old Cahokia*, pp. 4, 10.

⁵¹ Below St. Genevieve, Missouri. Christian Schultz visited the area in 1808, saw forty-six salt kettles in operation, and reckoned the position of Salt Creek as ten miles below St. Genevieve. *Travels*, II, 73–74.

to get their salt. In this place there is at present a settlement of Frenchmen, of whom we shall speak hereafter. We spent several days hunting deer in this place, where they are numerous, as these animals are fond of salt.

Then we advanced eight leagues upstream and found a small river on the left called Maramecq.[52] By way of this river the savages go to a lead mine located fifty leagues from the bank of the Missicipy. Upstream eighteen leagues from there, we found the village of the Illinois,[53] on the right side of the Missicipy, upon the bank of the stream. We headed in under sail, firing ten or twelve canister shots, at which the savages were greatly surprised, and they were even more surprised at seeing our longboat, since they have only small canoes made from the bark of trees, which come to them from Canada, and a few pirogues like those in the Lower Missicipy. When we got off the boat, they approached us, along with more than thirty Canadian traders who had come to barter for pelts. The French that were living among the Illinois armed themselves and gave an agreeable reception to M. Le Sueure, whom they had already seen in Canada. Also in the village were three French missionaries, among them one named M. Berger,[54] the grand vicar of Monseigneur the Bishop of Kébecq, with two other priests

[52] The Meramec River, in Missouri.

[53] Cahokia, Illinois. Citing this passage from Pénicaut, McDermott (*Old Cahokia,* pp. 4, 11–12) gives June 25, 1700, as the date the Le Sueur party stopped here. Old Cahokia had been established in 1699.

[54] Jean Bergier, a priest of the Séminaire des Missions Étrangères, Paris, according to Clarence Walworth Alvord, *The Illinois Country* (Springfield, Ill., 1920), pp. 117, 497. McDermott (*Old Cahokia,* p. 10) gives Marc Bergier as the grand-vicar of the Bishop of Quebec.

AND CALUMET

settled in the village, named MM. de Bouteville [55] and
de St. Cosme.[56] There were also two Reverend Jesuit
Fathers, namely, the Reverend Fathers Pinet [57] and
Limoges. The savages sang their calumet of peace to
M. Le Sueure, who gave them substantial presents. We
remained seventeen days in that village. Here four of
our Frenchmen left us and went off to Canada. In their
place we took five others, among them a man named
Chapongas,[58] who served us as interpreter, speaking the
languages of all these nations very well.

In front of this village of the Illinois is an island that
screens the entrance to it. There is no more than a small
arm of the Missicipy by way of which one approaches.
All around the village there is a very large prairie, beyond
which are mountains that make a very pretty vista.

After embracing all the persons of our acquaintance
that accompanied us to our boat, we left and ascended the
Missicipy six leagues higher and found on the left the

[55] This missionary priest, also of the Séminaire des Missions Étrangères, Paris,
arrived at the Tamaroa, in the Illinois Country, in the fall of 1699. Delanglez,
French Jesuits, p. 23.

[56] Jean François Buisson de St. Cosme supervised the building of the Tamaroa
mission, which was officially started by May 22, 1699. (McDermott, Old Cahokia,
p. 9.) He, too, was of the Séminaire des Missions Étrangères, Paris.

[57] Pierre Pinet, S.J., first gathered the Tamaroa and Cahokia tribes of the Illinois
Indians about a mission first known as Tamaroa, established about 1698. Father
Pinet died in June, 1702, on the west bank of the river near the site of St. Louis,
opposite Tamaroa, whence he had moved following the jurisdictional dispute between
Jesuits and missionary priests over the Tamaroa mission. See Hodge, Handbook,
I, 185; Delanglez, French Jesuits, p. 27; and McDermott, Old Cahokia, p. 11.

[58] This may be a dit name, i.e., a nickname, not necessarily jocose, likely to become a part of the surname or supplant it. In the 1752 census taken by Macarty, a
certain J. B. Chaponga is listed; and a Joseph Forel dit Chaponga was at Kaskaskia in
March, 1739. See Natalia Maree Belting, Kaskaskia under the French Regime
(Urbana, 1948), p. 93.

41

mouth of a very big river named the Missoury. This river has a frightfully strong current, especially in the spring, when it reaches its crest; for in passing over the islands where it overflows it uproots trees and sweeps them away. This is what causes the Missicipy, into which it rushes, to be all covered in springtime with floating trees and causes the water in the Missicipy at that time to be badly muddied by the water from the Missoury, which flows into its water. The source of the Missoury has not been discovered up to the present, nor has that of the Missicipy. The savages settled on the bank of the Missoury [told us that twice a year the caravan of the Spaniards crosses the Missoury] [59]—namely, in the month of August, when the waters are low, and at Christmas upon the ice—when they go to the mines. I shall not speak of the customs of those dwelling on the banks of the Missoury, as I have not gone up the Missoury River at all.

Having passed opposite its mouth, we went six leagues up the Missicipy and found the embouchure of the big Rivière des Illinois [60] on the right bank of the stream. By way of this river people go to Canada. Opposite its mouth

[59] ". . . nous dirent que la Caravane des Espagnols passe deux fois l'annee le Missoury." Supplied from Spofford, p. 67. Only Clermont has dropped this important passage. Margry (*Découvertes*, V, 409) made an awkward attempt to patch up the sentence. François Bouet's "Carte de la Louisiane et du cours du Missisipy sur la Relation d'andré Penicaut" uses this passage as a legend marked on the Missouri River northwest of the Padoucas villages and north of the headwaters of Riviere du Nort (Rio Grande), adding the words ". . . pour aller chés les Indiens au trafic de la poudre d'or." Also, Delisle's "Carte de la Louisiane," 1718, carries a similar legend, marked on the Missouri northwest of the Padoucas' ten villages: "Vers ce lieu au rapport des Indiens les Espagnols le passent à gué sur leurs chevaux le Missouri allans traiter avec des Nations Situées vers le Nordouest d'ou ils aportent du fer jaune cest ainsi quils lexpriment [*sic*]."

[60] The Illinois River proper, and not the Okaw, which Pénicaut has already called Rivière des Illinois.

is the beginning of a prairie, the most beautiful in the world and very extensive. Continuing our route upstream, we found the Rivière-aux-Boeufs [61] on the left, eighteen leagues higher up. There are two sheer cliffs, to right and to left of its mouth. We went on for half a league up this river and made camp on one of its banks. Four of our men went hunting and killed a buffalo bull and a cow within half a league of the spot where we were camped. Directly one of the three hunters came to get men to carry this game to our camp, which gave us a great deal of pleasure, hungry as we were; for during the whole day we had labored without taking more than a little nourishment. When this meat was cooked, we ate a portion of it while emptying several bottles of brandy, which greatly restored us.

I had not yet paid much attention to the physical composition of buffaloes, which are quite different from our cattle in France. They have low horns, black and very short, a big beard of hair under the jaw, and a forelock falling in their eyes, which makes them frightful. Their coat is wool finer than our sheep's wool.[62] They have on their back a quite massive hump, which begins above their shoulders and tapers to the hind quarters. The first rib in front is a cubit higher than the others of the back; it is three fingers wide; this is where the hump begins. Buffaloes are wide in front and get narrower and narrower

---

[61] Drawn on Delisle's "Carte de la Louisiane" as the most prominent river on the west side of the Mississippi between the Missouri and the Moingona (Des Moines). The Buffalo River in Missouri carries the right translation and has a corresponding position, but, for size, the Cuivre River, just below the Buffalo, has a strong claim.

[62] From the very beginning of French exploration up the Mississippi Valley, the French ministry had had great hopes of developing a textile industry with buffalo wool.

toward the rump. They have quite massive heads and very short necks and are a third bigger than cattle in France. They are very vicious, especially when the cows are calving. When you hunt buffalo, you must get downwind; in this way you can get very close to them; if you don't, they catch your scent a quarter of a league away and flee.

In this place there are a great many wolves, much smaller than those in France, having a rather blackish coat with long, fine hair. Here, too, one sees tigers [63] and, above all, foxes of an extraordinary beauty, for their fur is colored like silver. All these animals flee away to quite a distance the minute they catch sight of people.

Having departed from there, we found in the Missicipy, thirty-five leagues upstream, a mountain that is almost in the middle of the river, ever so little to the right; for this reason we named it La Montagne-qui-trempe-à-l'eau. [64] On the right, sixty leagues upstream from there, we found a prairie charming in its beauty and grandeur, along the edge of which runs a small stream that falls into the Missicipy. We named it Rivière de Mongona, [65] from the name of a savage nation living on its banks. A league above the place where it flows into the Missicipy, we came to rapids intersected by cascades. These rapids extend for

[63] The puma or mountain lion, called *tigre* or *tigre américain* by the French. McDermott, *Glossary*, p. 142.

[64] I cannot find a survival of the name of this particular Montagne qui trempe à l'eau, which means Soaking Mountain, the Mountain that soaks in the water. McDermott gives "the mountain that stands in the water" (*Glossary*, p. 144). The name survives for a different mountain as Trempealeau Mountain, in Trempealeau County, Wisconsin.

[65] The Des Moines River, separating Missouri and Iowa. The Indians whose name was transferred to the river as Moingona are given as Moingwena by Hodge, *Handbook*, I, 929.

seven leagues, over which, after putting our goods and
ammunition out on the ground, we had to pull our longboat by hand. After being in the water for seven leagues
we came to a seven-league stretch of navigable water;
but at the end of these seven leagues we again suffered the
same inconveniences of finding another seven leagues of
low water and rapids, where we had, first, to unload our
longboat all over again and [then] take to the water and
draw it along for seven leagues more.

To the left of these rapids are open prairies extending
for ten leagues from the bank of the Missicipy. The grasses
on these prairies, which are like sainfoin, come up no
higher than one's garter at most. On these prairies there
is an infinity of every kind of animal. When we had
passed beyond these rapids, which had tired us very much,
we found lead mines to right and left which are to this
day called Les Mines-à-Nicolas Peraut,[66] from the name
of the person who discovered them. Twenty leagues from
there, upstream on the right, we came to the mouth of a
large river named Oüisconsin.[67] Opposite the mouth of
the Oüisconsin are four islands in the bed of the Missicipy
and a mountain opposite on the left, quite high and half
a league long. People go by this river as far as the portage
at the Baye-aux-Renards,[68] which is sixty leagues from
the Missicipy River. That bay is within four leagues of
Lake Mescican. This is the route the French take on their

---

[66] Nicolas Perrot, a *coureur de bois* and interpreter, was sent with M. de Saint-
Lusson to Sault Ste. Marie in 1671 to take possession of the area and to discover
mines. Schlarman, *From Quebec to New Orleans*, pp. 46–47.

[67] The Wisconsin.

[68] The position given as "four leagues from Lake Mescican [Michigan]" indicates
Green Bay, commonly called Baye des Puans. The Wisconsin-Fox River route passed
through several lakes in east Wisconsin called Fox Lakes.

way to Canada when they are returning from the Cioux.

Ten leagues above the mouth of the Oüisconsin, on the same side, we came to the beginning of a great prairie, which extends for sixty leagues along the bank of the Missicipy, on the right side. This is called La Prairie-aux-Ailes.[69] The remote parts of this prairie terminate in mountains that make an agreeable vista. Opposite La Prairie-aux-Ailes, on the left, there is another prairie that faces it, called La Prairie de Paquitanet,[70] which is by no means so long. Twenty leagues above these prairies we found Lake Bon Secours,[71] which is seven leagues in circumference and one league across, the Missicipy flowing through it. To right and left of these banks are more prairies. Upon the one on the right side, at the edge of the lake, a fort built by Nicolas Peraut bears his name to this day. At the end of the lake is Isle Pelée,[72] so named because there is not a tree on it.

On this island the French from Canada set up their fort and trading center when they come to traffic in pelts and other merchandise; here, too, they spend the winter because game is very plentiful in the prairies on both sides of the river. As early as September one gets his supply of meat by hunting and puts it close to his hut on

[69] A translation is Winged Prairie.

[70] Delisle's "Carte de la Louisiane" shows a "R. Paquitanet," but on the east side of the Mississippi River.

[71] Either Lake Pepin, which Pénicaut does not mention even though he had to pass through it, or a part of the twenty-mile-long stretch still called Lake Pepin. Delisle's "Carte de la Louisiane" shows a "R. de Bon Secours" whose waters flowed into that stretch; and Chart No. 50, in War Department, *The Middle and Upper Mississippi River*, p. 130, shows Pepin Harbor of Refuge, on Lake Pepin, in Pepin County, Wisconsin. Harbor of Refuge is a translation of Bon Secours.

[72] The translation is Bald or Barren Island, but neither name appears on charts in War Department, *The Middle and Upper Mississippi River*.

46

a kind of high scaffold after it has been skinned and gutted, so that the great cold between September and the end of March keeps it from spoiling during the entire winter, which is very severe in that region. During this season you step out of doors only to go to the water, where you have to break the ice each day; and your hut is ordinarily at the edge of the water, so that you won't have to go far. When spring comes, the savages come to this island bringing their merchandise, which consists of every kind of pelt, such as beaver, otter, marten, lynx, pekan,[73] and all other kinds of pelts. Bear skins are commonly used by the savages and the Canadians to cover their canoes.

Often there are savages who rob the French-Canadian traders: particularly the savages of one village made up of five different nations distinguished by their names, namely, the Cioux, the people of the main village; the Mententons; the Mencouacantons; the Ouytespouy; some other Cioux of the soil.[74] Going on for three leagues above this island, we came to the Rivière Ste. Croix [75] on our right, at the mouth of which a cross is erected. Eight leagues upstream we found the Saut de St. Anthoine, which one can hear two leagues away. It is a fall of the

[73] The fisher, which belongs to the weasel family.

[74] Cioux des terres. This particular tribe of Sioux may be the Sioux of the Prairies or Sioux of the Meadows; or Cioux des terres may be an error for Cioux sédentaires, a name for the Santee Sioux. See Hodge's long list of Sioux tribes in *Handbook*, II, 1141. The Sioux are the Dakota Indians. The Mententons are the Mantantonwan, who lived at the mouth of the Minnesota River (*ibid.*, I, 819). The Mencouacantons are the Mdewakanton, a subtribe of Dakotas living on Mille Lac, Minnesota, when Le Sueur arrived in the area. (*Ibid.*, I, 826–28.) The Ouytespouy are the Oujatespouitons, another band of Dakotas. Hodge gives Ouyatespony, which he ascribes to Pénicaut, citing *Minnesota Historical Society Collections*, II, pt. 2, 6, 1864. Hodge, *Handbook*, II, 174.

[75] The St. Croix River is the boundary between Wisconsin and Minnesota.

47

entire stream of the Missicipy, which drops perpendic-
ularly for sixty feet, making a noise similar to thunder
rumbling through the air. At this place rowboats and
longboats have to be picked up and carried above before
one may continue his route on the Missicipy. This we did
not do; for, after gazing for some time at this drop of the
whole Missicipy, we returned a quarter of a league below
the Saut de St. Anthoine to a stream that empties into
the Missicipy from the left, which we named Rivière St.
Pierre.[76] We then made our way through the mouth of
this river and ascended it for forty leagues and found another river on the left, which empties into Rivière St.
Pierre. We entered this and named it Rivière Verte [77] on
account of clay that, loosened from the copper mines,
dissolves and turns the water green. One league up, upon
this river, we found a point of land one fourth of a league
from the woods; upon this point M. Le Sueure decided
to have his fort built, as we were unable to go higher on
account of the ice and it was already the last day of September, when winter has already set in, which is quite
severe in that region.

Half of our men hunted while the others worked on
the fort. We killed four hundred buffaloes, which were
our provisions for our winter. We put them on scaffolds
within our fort after skinning, gutting, and quartering
them. Also, within our fort we made some huts and a
storehouse to hold our merchandise. After bringing our
longboat within the enclosure of the fort, we spent the
winter there inside our huts.

While we were first at work on our fort, seven French

---

[76] The Minnesota River.   [77] Now named the Blue Earth River.

traders from Canada made their way to it. They had been robbed and entirely stripped of their clothes by the Cioux, a nomadic nation that lives altogether from hunting and thieving. Among these seven persons was a Canadian gentleman who was acquainted with M. Le Sueure. M. Le Sueure knew him at once and had clothes given to him as well as to all the others, for they needed them too. Furthermore, they remained with us for the entire winter at our fort, where we had no food except our buffalo meat, not even having salt with which to eat it. In the beginning, for the first two weeks, we had trouble enough getting accustomed to it: we had diarrhea and fever and became so squeamish that we could not taste it; but little by little our bodies became so accustomed to it that after six weeks there was not one of us who did not eat more than ten pounds of it daily and drink four bowls of the broth. When we got used to that kind of food, it made us quite fat, and there were no more sick among us.

Chapter 3

The Year 1701

M. Le Sueure discovers a red copper mine on the Rivière Verte
—How the savages hunt bears—MM. de St. Denis and de Bienville lead a detachment up the Rivière Rouge—Fort Mobile
established

HEN SPRING came, we went to work at the copper mine; this was at the beginning of April of that year. We took with us twelve workmen and four hunters. The location of this mine was about three quarters of a league from our fort. In twenty-two days we took from this mine more than thirty thousand pounds of ore. We selected only four thousand pounds of the finest of it, which M. Le Sueure, who was well informed in such matters, sent to the fort; later, it was shipped to France. I have not learned what the results were. That mine is located in the beginning of a very long mountain that is on the bank of the river. Boats can go right up to a point underneath the mine. The stratum where the ore is found is a green clay that is a foot and a half thick. Above, there is dirt as solid and as hard as a rock, which is black and charred, like a coal, from the fumes coming from the mine. We scratched the copper with a knife. There is not a tree on this mountain. If this mine proves to be good, a fine business can be made of it, since the mountain contains more than ten unbroken leagues of the same formation. According to our observations, it seems that during the finest weather

in the world there is always a fog on this mountain.
After twenty-two days of work we returned to our
fort. Here pelts were brought to us for barter by the
Cioux, of the nation of savages who had robbed the Canadians that had made their way to our fort. They had
more than four hundred beaver robes, which are made
of nine skins stitched together. M. Le Sueure bought
these as well as many other pelts, consuming a week in
bartering with the Cioux. He compelled their chiefs to
take up lodgings with savages near the fort. They had
trouble making up their minds to do so, because this
nation, which is very populous, is always on the move,
living only from hunting, and because, after they have
lived in one place for a week, they have to hunt ten
leagues away from there if they are to subsist. They
have, however, one settlement where they gather fruits,
which are quite different from the fruits of the Lower
Missicipy River, such as cherries, which grow in bunches
just like our grapes in France; *atoquas*,[1] which is a fruit
resembling our strawberries, but bigger and square
shaped; artichokes, which resemble our truffles. Also,
there are more different species of trees than in the Lower
River, such as the wild cherry tree, the maple, the red
maple,[2] the cottonwood,[3] which is a tree that grows so
big that some are five fathoms in circumference. As for
the trees named maple and red maple, they are gashed at
the first of March. Into the gash is put a tube that catches
the juice, which passes through the tube and drops in a
vessel set below to catch it. The sap of these trees runs
freely for three months, from the first of March to the

---

[1] Canadian-French *atoca,* cranberry.   [2] *La plaine.*   [3] *Le liere.*

end of May. The juice that trickles from these trees is very sweet. To preserve it, people boil it until it becomes syrup; and if it is boiled too long, it turns to brown sugar.

The cold is even more severe in these regions than it is in Canada. During the winter we spent in our fort, we heard trees snap like the reports of guns—split by the rigor of the cold. Ice is as thick as the fresh water in the river, and snow piles up there to a height of five feet on the ground. All this ice and snow melts ordinarily in the month of April, which causes the Missicipy to overflow in springtime.

With the beginning of winter in this region—that is, in the month of September—bears climb into hollow trees and hide. Here they remain six or seven months without going outside, nourishing themselves solely by licking their paws during the winter. When they go inside the trees, they are extremely thin; and when they come out after the winter is over, they are so fat that they have half a foot of back-fat. Bears hide almost always in the cottonwood tree or the cypress, as these trees are usually hollow.

Wishing to kill a bear, a person leans a tree against the tree the bear is in,[4] so that it mounts to the hole the bear went through. He climbs up the leaning tree and throws pieces of blazing dry wood through the hole in the hollow of the bear tree, forcing the animal to come out to keep from being burned; and when he starts through the hole in the tree, he backs out as a man would do. As he comes climbing down, he is shot with a gun.

[4] If I have knowingly improved any part of Pénicaut's French text, it is this passage giving the Indian method of forcing a hibernating bear from a hollow tree. English, which only grudgingly admits the *de* possessive of the French, cannot show the tautology of the original.

This is a very dangerous kind of hunting; for, although wounded sometimes by three or four shots from a gun, this animal still will not fail to charge the first person he meets, and with one single blow of tooth and claw, he will tear you to pieces instantly. There are bears as big as coach horses and so strong that they can very easily break a tree as big as one's thigh. The nation of the Cioux are great bear hunters: they use bear for food and traffic in bear skins with the French-Canadians. The commodities we deliver to them, we sell to them at a high price— tobacco especially, which is tobacco from Brazil, for as high a rate as one hundred crowns [5] for eight pounds. Two small bone-handled knives or four lead bullets are at the rate of ten crowns when exchanged for their merchandise of pelts, and so on.

At the beginning of May we launched our longboat and loaded it with that green clay we had taken from the mines and with the pelts acquired by our trading, of which we took away three boats loaded. M. Le Sueure, before leaving, held a council with M. d'Éraque,[6] the Canadian gentleman, and with the three big chiefs of the Cioux, three brothers. M. Le Sueure told them that, as he had to go back down to the sea, he besought them to continue in complete peace with M. d'Éraque, whom he was leaving as commandant of Fort Huilier, with twelve Frenchmen. M. Le Sueure gave a substantial present to the three brothers, the chiefs of the savages, exhorting

[5] The French *écu*, crown, is reckoned by McDermott (*Glossary*, p. 95) as worth sixty cents.

[6] A certain M. Darrac, an officer from Canada, was ensign in Chateaugué's company at Mobile. Bienville to Pontchartrain, February 25, 1708, in Rowland and Sanders, *MPA*, III, 121.

them not to forsake the French. After this we got into the boat—the twelve of us chosen by M. Le Sueure to go down to the sea with him.

When departing, M. Le Sueure promised M. d'Éraque, and the twelve Frenchmen remaining with him to guard the fort, to send him some ammunition up from the Illinois as soon as he got there, which he did; for upon arrival he sent a boat loaded with two thousand pounds of lead and powder, with three of our men to take them. We remained several days at the Illinois,[7] leaving after we had got the food supplies necessary for the trip down to the sea. On the way down, we spent the night at each of the villages that we mentioned above when describing the trip upstream. We landed at the post commanded by MM. de St. Denis and de Bienville. They informed us that M. d'Hyberville had reached Biloxi more than a month before.

MM. de St. Denis and de Bienville gave us an account of the trip they had made up the Rivière Rouge with a detachment of twenty-five men, to search out the Spaniards in the direction of Mexico by way of this river. They told us that while we were at the mines they had gone seventy leagues above the point at which the Rivière Rouge empties into the Missicipy and that seventy leagues up they had found a nation of savages named the Nassitoches, who had sung the calumet of peace to them. During the three days they spent there they inquired of their chiefs whether they had any information as to

---

[7] ". . . aux Illinois," which is equivalent to a place name. Cf. "aux Alibamons" as a substitute for Fort Toulouse. Both the Tamaroa mission and Cahokia across from present-day St. Louis, as well as the settlement on the Kaskaskia River, were spoken of as "aux Illinois."

where they could locate the settlement of the Spaniards. One of their chiefs, named Le Chef Blanc, escorted them overland with six of his savages as far as the village of the Cadodaquioux,[8] one hundred leagues from the Nassitoches; [9] and when they got there they asked the Cadodaquioux where the Spaniards could be found; but these savages replied that the Spaniards no longer lived in their village, none having returned during the more than two years they had been gone. This compelled MM. de St. Denis and de Bienville to return to their fort.

While we were still at M. de Bienville's fort the three persons whom M. Le Sueure had instructed at the Illinois to take a boat loaded with ammunition up to M. d'Éraque at Fort Huilier arrived at M. de Bienville's fort.[10] They greatly surprised M. Le Sueure when they informed him that the boat they were taking had split and they had lost it with all the ammunition opposite La Mine-à-Nicolas Peraut.

MM. de St. Denis and de Bienville issued an order at once that a boat be loaded with more ammunition and supplies, commanding the men to make all haste possible in order to reach Fort Huilier in a short time. As for us, after unloading our longboat and unloading from our rowboats the pelts we had bartered from the Cioux, we accompanied M. Le Sueure on a quick trip by longboat

---

[8] The Kadohadacho Indians—the name meaning "Caddo proper"—lived on the Red River and lakes in northwest Louisiana. Hodge, *Handbook*, I, 638–39.

[9] The Natchitoch Indians, living near the site of Natchitoches, Louisiana, were a tribe of the Caddo confederacy. After a failure of their corn crop, St. Denis settled them with the Acolapissa on Lake Pontchartrain in 1705. Hodge, *Handbook*, II, 37.

[10] The mss. show confusion in this sentence. I have used the reading in Parkman, p. 89.

down to Biloxi. Here we found M. d'Hyberville arrived, still busy having the ships unloaded.

After we had rested for a week, M. d'Hyberville had two longboats loaded with provisions and took thirty men and one pilot with him, and we went to take soundings off Isle Massacre,[11] following up M. de Sauvol's report to him that a good anchorage for ships would be found there. This was in fact found to be true. At the east end of Isle Massacre, where there is a small island off shore [12] forming a crescent-shaped harbor, thirty ships could be sheltered. In getting in, one runs right along the ground, all mud, of Isle Massacre.[13] The channel to it and all adjacent waters were sounded and found to be good. We then went from Isle Massacre to a bay five leagues wide [14] that is only two leagues distant from Isle Massacre. We entered this bay and went as far as a river that is nine leagues up into the headwaters of the bay, into which it empties. We ascended it for one league and found a river that empties into it on the left side, and a league farther, still another river that also empties into

[11] Dauphin Island, at the mouth of Mobile Bay.

[12] Now Pelican. The harbor described here, which was perhaps the most commonly used anchorage in all Louisiana from 1702 till 1717, was on the Gulf side of Dauphin Island. With the years the sands have changed, but Pelican Island, a chain running in an arc from Sand Island toward Dauphin, protects Pelican Bay, which is roughly equivalent to the old port. A French settlement, called Massacre or Dauphine, grew up on the southeast shore of Dauphin Island. The houses faced Pelican Bay.

[13] "Pour entrer dedans, l'on joint en passant le terein tout vase de lisle Massacre." (Spofford, p. 92.) This sentence appears ambiguous to me: I can't be quite sure whether "le terein . . . de l'isle Massacre" means the shoreline or the bottom. I let *vase*, "mud or slime," determine the sense as bottom. The penman of Parkman, p. 90, seems to have been puzzled too, and he omitted "tout vase," giving ". . . et pour entrer dedans l'on joint en passant l'isle massacre de fort pres." See Du Sault's chart, facing p. 206.

[14] Mobile Bay.

it. The first river we got to we named Rivière St. Martin [15]
and the second Rivière-à-Boutin.[16]

Twelve leagues upstream [17] we found a settlement of
savages named the Mobiliens. They were not surprised at
seeing us, because they had already learned that we had
built a fort at Biloxi. They wanted to make preparations
to sing the calumet of peace to M. d'Hyberville, but he
told them that for the moment he did not have time to
stop. He gave them several presents, anyhow, and left
next day to go back down the Rivière de la Mobile. He
took one of their chiefs with him to show him a spot on
high ground, six leagues below their village on the right
side going downstream. He told the chief he would order
a fort to be built here and would have all the French come
here to live. We then went down the river to the bay.
On our way back to Fort Biloxi, two leagues from the
Rivière de la Mobile we found a stream named Rivière-
aux-Chiens; [18] one league below, on the right, we found
another named Rivière-aux-Chevreuils; [19] and still a
third, two leagues from Rivière-aux-Chevreuils, which
we called Rivière-aux-Poulles.[20] From there we went directly to our fort, where the illnesses were becoming fre-
quent on account of the summer heat. This compelled

[15] Identified by Hamilton (*Colonial Mobile*, p. 36) as either Bayou Marmotte or
Bayou Chateauguay, which in American horse-and-buggy days became One Mile
Creek and Three Mile Creek respectively. They were very close to downtown Mobile.

[16] Probably Chickasabogue, according to Hamilton, *Colonial Mobile*, p. 36.

[17] Up the Mobile River. The early French gave the name Mobile to the Tombigbee,
as well as to the river below the fork of the Alabama and Tombigbee.

[18] Dog River, entering Mobile Bay on the west side.

[19] Deer River, on the west side of Mobile Bay. On the British Admiralty Chart,
A.D., 1771, it is called "Buck R." Hamilton reprints this chart in *Colonial Mobile*,
p. 210.

[20] Rivière-aux-Poulles [*sic*] is now Fowl River on the west side of Mobile Bay.
It makes Mon Louis Island. The name was once translated as Chicken River.

M. d'Hyberville to speed up the construction of the fort on the Mobile. After this, he sailed back to France with M. Le Sueure. He had had the clay from the copper mine put into his ship in order to have it assayed in France,[21] but we have not yet received any news of that.

After the departure of M. d'Hyberville, M. de Boisbrian took sixty men and left for the Mobile to erect the fort on the spot [22] that M. d'Hyberville had marked before his departure. During that time, M. de Sauvol, the commandant at Biloxi, who had fallen sick, died there.[23]

M. de Bienville, who was with M. de St. Denis at the fort on the bank of the Missicipy, came down to the sea and took over the command of Fort Biloxi in the place of M. de Sauvol; and noticing that lack of water was the cause of the illnesses, he worked as fast as possible to move all the merchandise and the munitions from Fort Biloxi to the fort on the Mobile, where M. de Boisbrian, who was there, had already got the fort and the warehouses ready to hold everything securely. M. de Bienville then came to the Mobile [24] and had the work on the fort con-

[21] In the 1870's the Reverend E. D. Neill reported that no one had located Le Sueur's copper mine. But he cites Featherstonhaugh (I, 2, 301–305) as saying that Le Sueur's claim had no credit with him, for the seam contained only a "silicate of iron of a bluish-green color." E. D. Neill and A. J. Hill (eds.), "Relation of M. Penicaut," in *Collections of the Minnesota Historical Society*, III (1870–80), 11–12.

[22] Twenty-Seven Mile Bluff, where the new French capital of Louisiana, Fort Louis de la Louisiane, was established. Commonly called Fort Louis de la Mobile, it was the first settlement of Europeans in the present area of Alabama and the second settlement in all the province of Louisiana, which at first did not include the Illinois Country. The name finally contracted to La Mobile.

[23] On August 21, 1701, according to Rowland and Sanders, *MPA*, II, 9 and note.

[24] ". . . à la Mobile." I cannot tell whether to translate "to Mobile" or "to the Mobile." At this stage of the narrative the river is the better choice, since the post had not been fully developed; still, Pénicaut may have meant the little town, for he was writing years after the name La Mobile had developed for the town.

cluded, both on the lodgings for the *habitans* [25] and on the fortifications.

This fort was sixty toises [26] square. At each of the four corners there was a battery of six pieces of cannon which, protruding outside in a half circle, covered the sector in front and to right and left. Inside, within the curtains, were four fronts of buildings fifteen feet back from the curtains behind them. These buildings were to be used as chapel, as quarters for the commandant and the officers, as warehouses, as guardhouse. So, in the midst of these buildings there was a *place d'armes* forty-five toises square. Barracks for the soldiers and the Canadians were built outside the fort, to the left, one hundred and fifty steps away, on the bank of the Rivière de la Mobile. [27] During the winter we were kept busy putting the finishing touches to all these buildings.

[25] Not inhabitants, but settlers; sometimes the word means farmers.

[26] The *toise* is approximately 6.4 feet.

[27] Only a marker at Twenty-Seven Mile Bluff shows that the capital of a great part of the United States—the province of Louisiana—was located here. No building remains, and trees and brush have reclaimed France's colonial capital on Rivière de la Mobile.

Chapter 4

The Year 1702

M. d'Hyberville arrives in Louisiana—M. d'Éraque comes down from Fort Huilier—Cause of war with the Alibamons—Strange festivals of the Mobiliens—M. de Bienville leads a war party against the Alibamons—M. de Boisbrian leads a detachment against the Alibamons

NEAR THE beginning of spring in the year 1702, M. d'Hyberville arrived in Louisiana. He anchored at Isle Massacre; and as soon as he got there he came on to our fort upon the Mobile, which he found to be constructed very well; and two days later he sent workmen from Mobile to Isle Massacre to labor upon the construction of several warehouses to hold the goods he had brought with him in the two ships from France. He had several barracks built there, too, to house the soldiers that were to remain to guard the merchandise.

Several days later, M. d'Hyberville came to this island and named it Isle Dauphine; and, from that time, too, Isle Surgère took the name Isle-aux-Vaisseaux [1] because it is the first approach-to-land that one finds for ships on arriving in the country. He then returned to Mobile and organized several detachments to ascend the Rivière de la Mobile in search of the chiefs of the savage nations of the neighboring region. For guides they took some Mobiliens, who led the way, some directing our men toward

[1] Ship Island, off Biloxi, Mississippi.

the Alibamons, a savage nation off toward Carolina, others toward the Chactas and Chicachas, who are savages in the direction of the Illinois. The chiefs of these nations, with others from the area close to us—the Mobiliens, the Tomez,[2] and the Gens des Fourches [3]—came all together to our fort one month later and sang the calumet of peace to M. d'Hyberville. Before sending them away, he gave presents to them all. He made them understand through an interpreter that they should come freely to our fort to barter their provisions and merchandise with the French and that they would be well pleased if they did. After this they went home quite satisfied.

During this time M. d'Hyberville sent a *traversier* [4] loaded with munitions and provisions to M. de St. Denis, the commandant of the fort on the bank of the Missicipy. There they found M. d'Éraque, who had got there with the twelve Frenchmen that had remained with him at Fort Huilier. A few days later M. d'Éraque came in the *traversier* to Mobile, where M. d'Hyberville was. He paid

[2] The Tohome Indians, speaking a Choctaw dialect, lived on the west side of the river eighteen to twenty miles north of Fort Louis de la Mobile.

[3] The translation is People of the Forks, who were, by inference, the Naniabas, since several times, in giving the names of small tribes close to the fort, Pénicaut mentions the Mobilians, the Tohome, and a third tribe, which he twice calls Gens des Fourches and once the Naniabas. The Naniabas lived on a bluff on the Tombigbee, just above its fork with the Alabama River. Their name seems to survive in Nanna Hubba bluff, which is in the right location. The Naniabas were almost certainly a Choctaw tribe. Swanton (*Indian Tribes of the Lower Mississippi Valley*, p. 32) says they were sometimes called Gens des Fourches; but he may be making the same inference from Pénicaut that I have made. *Gens,* "people," was commonly used by the French in naming Indian tribes because in naming themselves or their neighbors Indians themselves used "people" as a part of the names. Cf. Bayogoula, from *báyuk-ókla,* "bayou people." Hodge's *Handbook,* II, 1056, lists seventy-nine tribal names beginning with the word *Gens,* even a Gens de la Fourche du Mackenzie, which is not the one in question.

[4] A freight boat or ferryboat of light draft.

his respects to M. d'Hyberville and reported that, after M. Le Sueure had left him at Fort Huilier, promising to send him some ammunition and food supplies from the Illinois, and he had waited a long time without receiving news of them, he had been attacked by the nation of the Mascoussins and Renards,[5] who killed three of our Frenchmen that were working in the woods two gunshots away from the fort. When these savages withdrew he had been compelled—after burying the goods he had left, seeing that he lacked both powder and lead—to abandon the fort and go down to the sea with his men. At Oüiscon-sin he had met M. Jusserot,[6] a prosecuting attorney from Montreal in Canada, with the thirty-five men he had brought along to set up a tannery at Oüabache.[7] He had gone with him down to the Illinois,[8] where he found the boat sent him by M. de Bienville; and in this boat he had come to M. de St. Denis' post the day before the *traversier* got there; and from M. de St. Denis he had learned of the arrival of M. d'Hyberville and had taken advantage of the facilities of the *traversier* to come and pay his respects to him and at the same time to offer him his services. M. d'Hyberville showed him a good many honors and then pressed him to remain at Mobile. And then M. d'Hyber-ville went to Isle Dauphine to inspect the warehouses in which the goods had been stored. He also inspected the

[5] The Mascoutens and Foxes, both Algonquian tribes living on or near the Fox River, were strategically located near the Wisconsin–Fox River portage; both were enemies of the French. Hodge, *Handbook*, I, 472–73, 810–12.

[6] Charles Juchereau de St. Denis, or St. Denys, not to be confused with Louis Juchereau de St. Denis, one of the heroes of this book.

[7] On the Ohio River (Oüabache), at the site of Cairo, Illinois. Adams (ed.), *Dictionary of American History*, III, 182.

[8] Almost certainly Cahokia, which like other Illinois settlements was given the common place name "aux Illinois."

62

barracks built for the soldiers guarding the warehouses. During this time the Spaniards came and built a fort which they named Passacol,[9] twelve leagues from Isle Dauphine, on the mainland some thirty leagues east of Mobile. As we were at peace at that time and it was on their land, we did not judge it proper to oppose them; but we shall see hereafter that that fort was the cause of a war we had with the Spaniards over a period of two years.

After he had given all necessary orders and said goodby to our officers, M. d'Hyberville sailed back to France in the month of June.

Just a few days after [10] he had gone, M. de Tonty,[11] the governor at the Illinois, came with some Canadian merchants to Mobile, believing he would find M. d'Hyberville there. He paid his respects to M. de Bienville, our governor, with whom he remained for some time.

During this time five of our Frenchmen asked M. de Bienville for permission to go among the Alibamons [12] and traffic for poultry and other food supplies that they

[9] Pensacola. The memory or the information of the author is faulty: the Spanish post at Pensacola had been built three months before Iberville attempted to bring his ships into the harbor on January 27, 1699. See Iberville's log for January 26–28, Margry, *Découvertes*, IV, 142–43.

[10] ". . . apres son depart," Parkman, p. 100. Clermont, p. 92, has "peu de jours avant son depart," which is not logical.

[11] Henri de Tonti, "of the Iron Hand," the companion and lieutenant of La Salle. His loyalty to La Salle is still one of the most moving experiences a reader finds in following the history of the Mississippi Valley. A change in Crown policy toward the fur trade accounts for his leaving his Illinois post and coming downriver; he died at Fort Louis de la Mobile in the yellow-fever epidemic of 1704.

[12] The Alibamu Indians, whom the ethnologist Swanton calls a stinkard element of the Creek confederacy. (*Indian Tribes of the Lower Mississippi Valley*, p. 33.) De Soto met the Alibamu in Mississippi, but before the French arrived on the Coast they had moved to the forks of the Coosa and Tallapoosa rivers, which form the Alabama River just north of Montgomery, Alabama.

needed. They took the opportunity of leaving with ten
Alibamons who were at our fort on the Mobile and
wanted to go home. On the way they stopped at a village
five leagues from our fort, where three different savage
nations were assembled and holding their festival. They
were named the Mobiliens, the Tomez, and the Naniabas.[13] They do not have a temple, but a hut to which they
go and claw. In their language clawing [14] is a kind of invocation of their Great Spirit. As for me, who have seen
them several times, I believe it is the devil they are invok-
ing, since they issue forth from this hut with the fury of
men possessed and then make magic such as perambulat-
ing the straw-filled skin of an otter dead for more than
two years. They make much more magic which would
appear unbelievable to the reader; that is why I do not
wish to dwell on it; I would not even mention it if I had
not been a witness to it—I as well as many other Frenchmen who were there with me. The ones that do these kinds
of tricks—whether magical or otherwise—are esteemed
very highly by the other savages. During their illnesses
the savages put much faith in their treatments.

At the beginning of September they have a festival
in which they show themselves, in a way, to be like the
ancient Lacedaemonians: on the day of this festival they
flog their children till the blood comes. The whole village

[13] Margry (*Découvertes*, V, 427) gives Namabas. See note 3, in this chapter.

[14] ". . . une cabane où ils vont ongler; ongler en leur langage est une espèce
d'invocation à leur grand Esprit." The word *ongler* is puzzling. Margry (*Découvertes*,
V, 427) let the first entry of *ongler* stand; but he apparently thought Pénicaut had
written a bad form of *jongler*, "make medicine." Accordingly, Margry gives:
"Jongler, en leur langage, est une espèce d'invocation de leur grand Esprit." *Ongler*
may indeed be Pénicaut's form for *jongler* or may be no more than a phonetic
representation of an Indian word. I have chosen to take it as a forced verb-form in
French, meaning "scratch" or "claw," which is certainly more primitive.

is at that time assembled in the big square. All must come there—boys, girls, old and young, down to the very youngest—and if some child is sick, the mother is flogged in the place of the child. After that, they engage in dances that last through the night. The chiefs and the old men exhort the flogged ones, telling them that they have been flogged to teach them to have no fear of the evils their enemies can do to them and to teach them to be good warriors that would never cry out or shed tears even in the middle of the fire, supposing that their enemies should cast them into it.

Our five Frenchmen, having rested while watching this festival, went off with the ten Alibamon savages, who led them to a point ten leagues from their village. They told our Frenchmen to stay at this place, as they were going to their village in advance to notify their chiefs to come and receive them on the morrow and escort them to the village. But while the Frenchmen were asleep, the Alibamons came in the night without noise, took possession of their weapons, and killed four of them, the fifth escaping. As he was escaping, jumping into the water to swim the river, one of the savages tomahawked him in the shoulder. Several days later, he came to our fort, having dressed his wound along the way with pine rosin, which he had chewed before applying. That is the cause of the war that we later carried on with the Alibamons for more than seven years.

Therefore, M. de Bienville immediately notified the nations living close to our fort—the Mobiliens, the Tomez, the Gens des Fourches, the Chactas, and others—and they came and combined their eighteen hundred war-

riors with the seventy Frenchmen that we were. As officers of this expedition we had MM. de Bienville, de St.
Denis, de Tonty, who had served as captain in Canada.
The Mobilien savages served as guides. At the beginning
of September we set out, all together, to go against the
Alibamons; but after five or six days of travel most of
these savages abandoned us; and our Mobilien guides had
us wasting time along the way and daily were deserting,
too, because they were friends and allies of the Alibamons,
against whom we were leading them to war, so that after
seventeen days of march just a few savages remained with
us; and, having been badly guided by the Mobiliens, we
had not covered thirty leagues in eighteen days. M. de
Bienville, watching the desertion of the savages, who
were abandoning us daily, told our officers that it was
useless to attempt to go farther, as all the savages were
quitting us. He ordered the French to descend to our
fort on the Mobile, which we did in four days by taking a
straight route.

Several days after we returned to Mobile, M. de Bienville had ten boats constructed; and as soon as they were
finished, he had fifty of us Frenchmen embark in them,
together with our officers, himself being the superior.
And we departed secretly at night to conceal our move-
ment from the savages.

After several days of travel—when we were ten leagues
from the Alibamons' village and very close to the spot
where the four Frenchmen had been killed—we sighted
fire. Upon the river, two gunshots away, were fourteen
boats of the Alibamons, who were on a hunting expedition with their families. As it was broad-open daylight,

66

we went a quarter of a league below and for the rest of the day remained within half a league of the savages, in a place where our boats were concealed behind a hill. We placed six men on top of this hill to reconnoiter the position of their shelters, which we readily detected from that hill. We had to go higher up the river to get ashore opposite them.

When we saw that their fires were almost burned out and believed them to be asleep, M. de Bienville made us advance. We crossed a little hill and descended into a wood through which the road was quite bad. When we drew close to the shelters of the sleeping savages, one of our Frenchmen put his foot down on a dry cane, which cracked when it broke. One of the savages who was still awake shouted an alarm in their tongue, which made us keep still. In a little while the savage, hearing no more noise, lay down. Then we advanced; but the savages, hearing us move, leaped up, gave the *cri de mort,* and fired a shot from a gun which killed one of our men. Immediately their old men, their women and children escaped, and there were only the warriors, withdrawing last, firing several shots at us. We did not know whether we had killed a single one of them, as we could not tell where we were shooting in the dark. The savages having withdrawn, we remained at their shelters till daybreak. These we burned before leaving for the river, where we found their boats. The boats, together with the goods inside of them, we took back to our fort on the Mobile.

There we found ten savages from the Chicachas nation with one of their chiefs. They were awaiting M. de Bienville to ask him for a French boy, whom they would teach the savage language at their village. M. de Bienville gave them little St. Michel,[15] fourteen years old, the son of M. St. Michel, the harbor master of Rochefort. They took him away with them. They had also been given some presents.

A few days later, M. de St. Denis, who had straightway returned to his post on the bank of the Missicipy, sent word to M. de Bienville that the savage nation named the Bayagoulas had been defeated by the Tinssas, who had burned their village, so that the Bayagoulas that escaped had come seeking refuge at a place two gunshots from his fort, where he had given them a location on which to build some huts.

At the beginning of December, M. de Boisbrian, wanting to go on a raid against the Alibamons, asked M. de Bienville for forty men. He set out with five boats and the food supplies necessary for the trip. Going up the Rivière des Alibamons, seventy leagues upstream on the left side he came upon six Alibamon boats, which made him believe that there must be Alibamons off hunting in the vicinity. He sent a French soldier with a Canadian to reconnoiter, in order to try to locate their huts. From a distance our men were able to see their camp on the bank of a creek. They returned as fast as possible to warn M. de Boisbrian. He quickly led his men up close to them

[15] This child was one of the six cabin boys that Iberville left in Louisiana to study Indian languages so that they could serve as interpreters. Living in Indian villages, they were innocently trained by the Indians to act as cultural spies for the French. The St. Michel child had already been left with at least one tribe whose language he had learned. "J'ay aussi envoyé avec le chef des Chicachas le petit Saint-Michel," wrote Iberville in the log of his third voyage, "qui parle assez bien l'Oumas, qui est la mesme chose que le Chicachas, à quelque chose près." Margry, *Découvertes*, IV, 521. Entry for March 16, 1702.

without making any noise. At once he had us fire a volley. All the savages were killed, only women and their children being spared; they were taken away as slaves to Mobile along with their boats loaded with their game.

The Mobiliens, our neighbors six leagues away and allies of the Alibamons, saw us pass with these slaves on our way back to Mobile. They came to M. de Bienville and asked him for them, begging him to kindly give them to them, as these captives were their kin. M. de Bienville granted their request. This act of generosity on M. de Bienville's part caused the Mobiliens later on to unite with us in the wars we carried on against the Alibamons.

Chapter 5

The Year 1703

M. de St. Denis leads a detachment against the Chetimachas
savages—M. de Chateaugué leads another war party against the
Alibamons—The notorious deceit of the Chactas nation

AT THE beginning of this year, M. de St. Denis sent a letter to M. de Bienville informing him that M. de St. Cosme, a missionary priest, had come from Canada with three Frenchmen as far down as the Natchez [1] and had set out from the Natchez to visit him at his post. While M. de St. Cosme was on his way downstream and camped on the bank of the Missicipy to pass the night, a party of eight savages of the Chetimachas nation [2] went to the village of the Baya-goulas to make war upon them; they missed the Baya-goulas and, going back enraged, came across M. de St. Cosme, the priest, sleeping on the bank of the Missicipy with the three Frenchmen and one little slave who were with him. The Chetimachas murdered them all,[3] with the

[1] Jean François Buisson de St. Cosme may have been the father of the Natchez chief, St. Cosme, who a generation later led his tribe in the massacre of the French at Natchez in 1729. Writing from St. Domingue, where the deported Natchez chiefs were slaves, Bienville mentioned by name only St. Cosme among the enslaved Natchez he saw. (Bienville to Maurepas, at Cap François, January 28, 1733, in Rowland and Sanders, *MPA*, III, 581, and n. 1.) According to Surrey, a manuscript in the Bibliothèque Nationale identifies the Natchez chief St. Cosme both as Grand Soleil of the Natchez and as child of the missionary. *Calendar of Manuscripts in Paris Archives*, I, 477.

[2] Their territory extended from the site of Donaldsonville, Louisiana, along Bayou Lafourche as far as Grand Lake.

[3] Near the Mississippi entrance to Bayou Lafourche. Delanglez says that the exact date of the murder has not been established, but that the murder was known by January 1, 1707. *French Jesuits*, p. 63.

exception of the little slave, who escaped and brought the news to M. de St. Denis. M. de St. Denis further stated to M. de Bienville that the death of these Frenchmen must be avenged. Acting on this information, M. de Bienville instructed him to come down to Mobile, where they would confer about this. As soon as M. de St. Denis received M. de Bienville's reply, he came down to Mobile, where they decided to alert the nations of the Oumas, the Chaoüachas [4] and the remnants of the Bayagoulas near M. de St. Denis' post.

He went back and a few days later assembled a war party of these savages, two hundred men, with ten Frenchmen; and after loading twenty boats with the necessary provisions they went all in a body as high up as the entrance to the Rivière des Chetimachas,[5] which M. de St. Denis had them ascend at night to within three leagues of their village. The Chaoüachas, our guides, who knew the terrain well, made us hide in that place during the day. When evening came, two of our savages with one Frenchman reconnoitered the village. The Frenchman and the two savages came back at midnight to inform us that on the shore of a lake they had located huts filled with Chetimachas savages who were there to catch fish. We set out at once without making a sound and in the dark got close to their huts and lay on our bellies till

[4] The Chawasha Indians, a small Muskhogean tribe living on Bayou Lafourche. In 1718 they moved to the Mississippi. When the Indian conspiracy to murder all the French in Louisiana became known after the Natchez Massacre, the nervous French at New Orleans incited Negroes to attack the Chawasha village. This destruction of the little Chawasha tribe was an attempt to forestall any alliance between Negroes and nearby tribes of Indians. See Swanton, *Indian Tribes of the Lower Mississippi Valley*, pp. 30 31.
[5] Bayou Lafourche.

71

daybreak. Then our savages gave the *cri de mort*, and so did we, which terrorized the Chetimachas; and as they tried to flee, we fired into them, killing fifteen and taking forty prisoners, as many men as women and children. Several of the wounded escaped. We tied our prisoners' hands behind their backs and made them move off ahead of us for the return trip.

Among these prisoners we held one of the savages that had killed M. de St. Cosme, whom he had struck six times with arrows. Irons were put on his hands and feet. We took all these prisoners to Mobile to M. de Bienville, who had the murderer of M. de St. Cosme bound to the wooden horse and his head broken with a blow of a stick. His scalp was taken and his body thrown into the water. M. de Bienville then had it proclaimed among all the savage nations friendly to us that they should make war on the Chetimachas and the Alibamons and that he would give them ten crowns for the scalp [6] of each enemy slain or for each enemy brought back alive.

During this time, twenty-four itinerant traders from the Illinois reached Mobile, bringing merchandise in pelts. [While these Illinois traders were at Mobile, M. de Chateaugué, brother of M. de Bienville, made up an expedition of forty Frenchmen and these twenty-four Illinois traders, who volunteered to go with him to war against the Alibamons.] [7] They loaded eight boats with the necessary provisions, embarked, and ascended the Rivière des Alibamons. A week later, they ran into a war party of sixty

---

[6] The bounty was roughly six dollars per scalp.

[7] Supplied from Spofford, p. 120. Clermont, pp. 104–105, contains copyist's errors, which are reflected in Margry, *Découvertes*, V, 435.

Alibamons on their way to fight the Chactas. Our men encountered them, but killed only fifteen of their men because they were moving along deployed through the woods. The others fled back to their village and raised an alarm; therefore M. de Chateaugué, who had planned to surprise them in their village, was compelled to retire.

During the same time, thirty-five chiefs of the nation of the Chicachas savages came to Mobile, asking to speak with M. de Bienville. They told him they had come to beg him to mediate for peace between them and the Chactas, another savage nation with whom they had been at war for a long time. They had been forced to go a long way round to get to Mobile, because half way between their village and Mobile, on the most direct route,[8] is the village of their enemies, the Chactas. M. de Bienville, who would have asked for nothing better than to mediate for peace, assigned them M. de Boisbrian with twenty-five Frenchmen to convoy them to the Chactas' village, in an effort to accommodate them.

When they got there, the Chief of the Chactas came to speak to M. de Boisbrian. The Chief made him come into his hut, and in his language, in which M. de Boisbrian was passably proficient, he said privately: "Where are you going with those Chicachas? Are you going to get yourself burned at their village the way a little French boy [9] was burned whom M. de Bienville gave them last year to learn their language?"

---

[8] The direct route to the Chickasaw villages, which lay between the headwaters of the Yazoo and Tombigbee rivers, was by way of the Tombigbee, if by water, or through eastern Mississippi and southwest Alabama, if by land. Either route would have taken the Chickasaws through hostile Choctaw territory.

[9] Little St. Michel.

M. de Boisbrian, being greatly surprised, replied that he did not know that and that he did not believe the Chicachas spiteful enough or treacherous enough to have dared to burn the little French boy that had been given them; that, furthermore, he had come to mediate peace between them, so that they might live in harmony in the future.

"I'll make peace with them," this chief of the Chactas told him, "if they will bring your little French boy back here. Therefore, believe me: go no farther," added this chief of the savages, "but send two of those Chicachas to their village instructed to bring back your French boy; and if they do not bring him back to you within one month, you will know from that that I have told you the truth."

The chiefs of the Chicachas, to whom M. de Boisbrian then went to speak, assured him on their part that the little French boy was alive, and they consented for two of their men to be sent to fetch him. They sent these off at once, ordering them to make all possible haste.

The Chief of the Chactas said something else to M. de Boisbrian: "Permit us to put these Chicachas in one of our huts; for if the others do not bring back your little French boy, these will belong to us and as our enemies they will have to die, since they then will be your enemies, too."

The chiefs of the Chicachas further agreed to stay in a hut while awaiting the return of the little French boy, who they insisted was alive.

The month had almost slipped away, and still the two Chicachas who had gone to their village for the little

French boy did not return. On one side, the Chief of the Chactas said to M. de Boisbrian each day: "You see that those Chicachas whom you sent to fetch your French boy are wicked men: they don't dare come back because they have burned him, just as I told you."

On the other side, the chiefs of the Chicachas, who were shut up, said to him, "They had our comrades killed on the way there, or they would have come back."

One must admit that, however clever an officer may be, he is utterly perplexed by an issue so equivocal and at the same time so dangerous as that one, when he is as far away as M. de Boisbrian was—fifty leagues from the settlement of the French, who at that time were still no more than a handful of people in Louisiana—in the middle of a village of a populous savage nation of more than twelve thousand warriors—and also doubtful of being able to discover which side is in the right.

The time fixed for the return of the two Chicachas and the little French boy had elapsed; every appearance of justice seemed to be on the side of the Chief of the Chactas, who each day pressed M. de Boisbrian for a decision. I do not believe that M. de Boisbrian's prudence has ever appeared better than on this occasion; for after warning his men to get ready to leave on the morning of the next day, he sought the Chief of the Chactas in his hut and said to him: "I am sick and tired of waiting for the return of the two Chicachas, who do not bring back my French boy. This convinces me that you have told me the truth—that they are wicked men; and since they have deceived us, do whatever you want to do with those in the hut; I leave them to you upon this condition—that your chiefs and all your nation shall always be friends of the French. Tomorrow I am going with my men back to Mobile."

The Chief of the Chactas promised him—in the name of all his nation—that they would always be friends of the French. The next day he had provisions given to M. de Boisbrian and his men, and he convoyed them for more than two leagues before he left M. de Boisbrian,[10] wishing him a good journey. M. de Boisbrian returned to Mobile quite satisfied with having bound the most dreadful nation of all the savages to be friends of the French. With the French they have never been at war.

During this same time M. de Bienville received a letter from M. de St. Lambert,[11] informing him that M. Jusserot had died at Oüabache, where he had set up a fort and a tannery. In this letter M. de St. Lambert asked for instructions about what M. de Bienville wanted done with the fort and the merchandise that the late M. Jusserot had accumulated. M. de Bienville sent him his reply by a boat in which six workmen went to build boats for him and

[10] According to Hamilton (*Colonial Mobile*, p. 55), Boisbriant returned wounded to Mobile after escorting Chickasaws through Choctaw territory, either on this or some other occasion. Pénicaut may have been guided by the art of fiction rather than by historical facts.

[11] M. de St. Lambert de Mandeville was second in command at the Oüabache post, on the Ohio River, and attempted to run the tannery after the death of Charles Juchereau de St. Denis. (Adams [ed.], *Dictionary of American History*, III, 182.) But which St. Lambert? There were two brothers called, in various documents, De St. Lambert de Mandeville and De Mandeville de St. Lambert. By July, 1706, the brother who was ensign in the company of Vaulezard had died, and Bienville had appointed the other brother to fill the vacancy in the company. (Abstract of Letters from Bienville to Pontchartrain, in Rowland and Sanders, *MPA*, II, 29.) Dunbar Rowland (*ibid.*, n. 2) identifies the surviving brother as François de Mandeville, Sieur de Marigny. If Rowland's identification is correct, the St. Lambert at the tannery on the Ohio is either the remote ancestor or the remote uncle of the splendid Creole gentleman Bernard de Marigny. See King, *Creole Families of New Orleans*, pp. 10–23.

to bring down river all the peltries and the thirty-five persons who were with him. These six men that M. de Bienville sent to M. de St. Lambert, reaching the village of the Yasoux on their way up the Missicipy, found M. Davion [12] there, a missionary priest who had come from Canada to the Yasoux to try to convert them to the faith or at least to baptize their infants. Several times he had been in danger of being murdered by this nation, one evening particularly, when his zeal induced him to go into their temple and knock down their idols and break them in pieces. Afterwards he returned to his hut carrying the remaining idols, which he had not been able to break. There he found Brunot, a small boy who waited on him. M. Davion told him to take refuge with the French because the savages were coming next day to kill him. And they did not fail to rush there to kill him when they had seen the destruction he had wrought among the idols in their temple. But their Grand Chief, who loved that priest, made them go away and kept them from killing him or the little boy either, so that M. Davion is still alive, by the very special grace of God, and is Monseigneur the Bishop of Kébecq's grand vicar for Louisiana.

The next day the six men departed from the Yasoux, where they had spent the night, and some time afterwards arrived at Oüabache. They presented M. de Bienville's letter to M. de St. Lambert; and when they finished the boats, they loaded them with more than twelve thousand

[12] Antoine Davion left his Tunica post, near the site of Fort Adams, Mississippi, and made Mobile his headquarters after 1708. "He left Louisiana in 1725, and died of gout among his kinsmen in France, April 8, 1726." See John Gilmary Shea, *Catholic Church in Colonial Days* (New York, 1886), p. 553.

buffalo hides, which they brought down to M. de St. Denis' post. M. de St. Lambert then came down to Mobile with thirty men, leaving the others at the fort with M. de St. Denis.[13]

At the end of this year ten Chicachas arrived at Mobile, bringing that little French boy whom the Chief of the Chactas had told M. de Boisbrian they had killed and burned. The Chactas had used that deceit to avoid making peace with the Chicachas, while tricking M. de Boisbrian. Unable to discover the truth, he had delivered to them the thirty Chicachas they had been holding in their village, whom they killed after he left.

Here is cause to admire the wisdom of God, who destroys the schemes of men that appear to be even the most prudent for their greatest good; for if M. de Boisbrian had conciliated the Chactas with the Chicachas when he was there to make peace between them, according to his orders and his intention, these two nations—our two neighbors and the most dreadful in all Louisiana, since they can by joining forces put as many as sixteen thousand warriors on the warpath—would have had the power to destroy our colony in its infancy; [14] whereas, by the grace of God, and contrary to our intentions, the two nations remaining at war with each other, as it happened, we have always been at peace with them, especially with the Chac-

---

[13] Louis Juchereau de St. Denis.

[14] In November, 1729, both Choctaws and Chickasaws were involved in the great conspiracy to destroy all the French in Louisiana. The Choctaws, however, took no part in the massacre, although they appear to have been committed. The Natchez actually struck before the appointed day and thus seized all the French booty at Natchez. Angered, the Choctaws then joined the French and took an active part in the Natchez war. The Chickasaws never again became really friendly to the French. Twice they defeated Bienville and impressive forces under him.

CHOCTAW WARRIORS AND NATCHEZ CHIEF. From Bushnell, "Drawings by A. DeBatz."

tas, who are the more powerful of the two nations and the one living closer to Mobile.

After the Chicachas had been placated as well as they could be with words, they were sent back to their village; and little St. Michel, who already spoke the language of these savages quite well, was kept at home.

During this same time there arrived two Frenchmen of the three that M. de Bienville had sent up the Rivière de la Madelaine [15] to discover the nations that were in that area. They reported to us that they had been more than a hundred leagues up into the territories of seven different nations they had found and that, at the last nation, one of their comrades had been killed and eaten by those savages, who are cannibals. That nation is named Atacapas.[16]

[15] The Sabine River now, the boundary between Louisiana and Texas. Delisle's "Carte de la Louisiane," 1718, based in great part on data furnished by Father Le Maire, shows "Petite R. de la Madelene" leading north to the Red River area, between the Ainais and Adaie.

[16] The Attacapa were a separate linguistic family living in southwest Louisiana and across the Texas line. The name Attacapa, not to be confused with Capa (Quapaw), means "cannibals," from Choctaw *hatak*, "man," and *apa*, "eats." Hodge, *Handbook*, I, 114.

Chapter 6

The Year 1704

Village of the Natchez described: customs of the savages, their temple, their religion, their funeral rites, their nobles, and their dances—The ship named "Le Pélican" arrives at the Isle Dauphine roadstead

AT THE beginning of this year M. de Bienville —having inspected the food in the warehouses and found no more than a four months' supply of flour—ordered M. de Béquancourt [1] to take the *traversier* with twenty men and go to Havana for food supplies. During that time he permitted fifty men, who had volunteered, to go into the woods and live from hunting or live among the savage nations friendly to us, with instructions to return when they heard the ships had come.

As I was young and passionately fond of rambling, I went with the group. We went in several rowboats, all keeping together, as far as the Baye de St. Louis,[2] where we had very good hunting and fishing, off which we lived. After a few days I proposed to twenty of my comrades, the youngest ones, that we go back up the Missicipy together and visit some of the nations along the bank of the river. I was acquainted with all these nations because on my own account I had ascended it three times already

---

[1] Given as Sieur de Beccancourt in Abstract of Letters from Bienville to Pontchartrain, 1706 (Rowland and Sanders, *MPA*, II, 29). Bienville reports that Beccancourt has died and that he has given to Chateaugué the command of Beccancourt's ship on a trip to Vera Cruz.

[2] St. Louis Bay, on the Mississippi coast.

—the first time with M. de Bienville as high as a point opposite Lake Pontchartrain, the second with M. d'Hyberville as high as the Tinssas, and the third with M. Le Sueure up to the Saut de St. Anthoine—and because, too, I had learned their languages tolerably well during the five years I had been in Louisiana, especially Mobilien, the principal one, which is understood in all the nations.

So, without saying anything to our other comrades, some twenty of us set out with three boats and one kettle. We ascended as high as the Soupnatcha,[3] where we found the Biloxis, a small nation that earlier lived close to the first fort we had after we arrived in the country. M. de St. Denis had since made them come to that place and settle because, by having them nearer to his fort, he would sometimes get food from them with which to subsist the more easily in his establishment. After spending the night in their huts, we set out again next morning. We took some small supplies of food stuffs that they gave us and carried our boats overland to a point half a league from there, where the Missicipy is, and embarked upon it.

When we got to Bâton Rouge, we went ashore to hunt. We entered a forest, some ten of us who were together, the others staying with the boats to watch them and to keep fire burning. Beyond the forest into which we had entered we found a prairie. Never in my life have I seen such great numbers of buffalo, harts, and roes as there were on that prairie. We killed five buffaloes, which we skinned and cut up in order to carry some to our comrades who had stayed with the boats; and as there was fire burn-

---

[3] I cannot locate this stream or spot, which should be in Plaquemines Parish, east of the Mississippi River.

ing we broiled some of it on spits and boiled some, too, in our kettle. Our comrades made some shelters on the bank of the Missicipy while we went for the rest of our buffaloes, which we transported in our boats. We felt so well off at that place that we remained more than ten days. Some of us went hunting every day, especially during the evening, in the woods where one commonly finds bustards and turkeys coming to roost in the trees; so we changed our menu from time to time.

Time did not drag for us except at night; for, young as we were, we had in our own group elected a leader whom we obeyed and who made us stand sentry duty two at a time when night came. One of these sentries was given a position half a gunshot beyond the other, who watched over those asleep under the shelters. Each man took his turn of an hour at sentry duty. Furthermore, prayers were strictly held morning and night.

When ten days had passed, we cooked what we had left of the meat, put it in our boats, and set out for the Oumas, who are another savage nation friendly to the French, dwelling on the bank of the Missicipy thirty leagues from Bâton Rouge. They received us very well indeed, giving us abundantly of their food supplies. Here we remained only six days, after which we left to go to the Natchez,[4]

[4] The tribe got its name from the name of the main village. There were several villages along St. Catherine's Creek, near the present city of Natchez, Mississippi. Hodge (*Handbook*, II, 35–36) classifies the Natchez as a Muskhogean tribe, that is, related to Choctaws and Chickasaws. But Swanton (*Indian Tribes of the Lower Mississippi Valley*, p. 9) makes up a separate linguistic group, of Natchez, Taensa, and Avoyel. The tribe became widely known after Chateaubriand published two novels about them, *Atala* and *Les Natchez*. What Pénicaut writes about them in this chapter ultimately influenced Chateaubriand, through Charlevoix's *La Nouvelle France*.

who are the nation that has seemed to me the most courteous and civil along the banks of the Missicipy.

At noon three days later we got there and were received with every possible mark of cordiality and affection. Everybody in the village was happy because it was the opening of a dance festival, a description of which I shall give. We remained for a very long time in their villages, where we all but forgot M. de Bienville's instructions because of the amusements we had.

The village of the Natchez is the most beautiful that could be found in Louisiana. It is located one league away from the bank of the Missicipy. It is beautified by very pretty walks which nature, and not artifice, has formed there. Around it are flower-adorned prairies, broken by little hills upon which there are thickets of all kinds of fragrant trees. Several little streams of very clear water issue from beneath a mountain visible for two leagues across the prairies and, after watering them in many places, they gather up into two big creeks which encircle the village, beyond which they unite in the form of a small river which flows over very fine gravel and passes on by three villages separated one from the other by half a league and then, two leagues away, flows into the Missicipy. The water in it is very pleasant to drink, being cold as ice in summer and tepid in winter.

Formerly this village had a missionary named M. de Montigny,[5] one of the four that had come from Canada.

---

[5] François Jolliet de Montigny, of the Séminaire des Missions Étrangères, in Paris. His mission was at the Taensa, but he served the Natchez too. Shea says he sailed back to France with Iberville in May, 1700, being disturbed over the jurisdictional dispute between missionary priests and Jesuits. *Catholic Church,* p. 541.

But he did not stay there a long time: being unable to make any progress, he proceeded to France.

In this village one finds every amenity conducive to association with this nation, which does not at all have the fierce manners of the other savages. All the necessaries of life are here, such as buffaloes, cows, hinds, harts, roes, chickens and turkeys and an abundance of geese. There are also fish in abundance, all kinds of them; there are carp weighing more than twenty pounds, which are of an exquisite taste. As for fruit, there is more than in any other place in Louisiana. They have many cherries, which grow in bunches like our grapes in France; they are black and have a touch of bitterness, but are excellent in brandy, in which they put many of them. In their woods everywhere are many peach trees, plum trees, mulberries, and walnuts. They have three kinds of walnut trees: [6] there are some that bear nuts as big as one's fist; from these they make bread for their soup. But the best are scarcely bigger than one's thumb; these they call *pacanes*.

Beginning with the first of May, their prairies are flecked with every sort of flower and fragrant grass. Here grow multitudes of strawberries as big as one's thumb and of an exquisite flavor. In their woods they have a grape that grows as a vine arbor; the stem clings to trees and grows round and round them. This grape is small and a little sour; a wine is made from it that will not keep more than a week or ten days.

This nation owns nine settlements, or villages; but the

[6] The French used *noyer*, "walnut," for hickory as well as for walnut trees. Sometimes they called the hickory *noyer blanc*, "white walnut." McDermott, *Glossary*, p. 108.

village where we were is foremost of them all and the most substantial because it is the residence of the Grand Chief; he is named Sun, which means noble. They are much more decently housed than any other savage nation. In front of their houses they have peach trees right in the open, which bear excellent peaches and make a pleasant shade for their houses.

Natchez men and women are very handsome and quite decently clothed. The women wear white linen dresses that hang from the neck to the feet, made almost like our *Andriennes* [7] of the ladies of France. They make this linen cloth from nettle bark and mulberry bark. They prepare the bark in the following manner: they soak it in water for a week; they put it out to dry in the sun for a long time; and when the bark is quite dry, they beat it until it becomes tow; then they put it through the laundering process and wash it three or four times until it is white. Then they spin it and make it into linen cloth, which they use according to their needs.

The men wear deer skins made like our jackets, which hang halfway down their thighs. They have *braguets* and leggings under them, which cover them from the feet to the hips. They have rather handsome faces, and so do their wives. Their speaking voices are quite pleasing, as they do not speak so strongly from the throat as the other savages. The dress of the girls is different from that of the women: girls wear only *braguets,* which are made

[7] When Terence's comedy *The Girl of Andros* was revived at the Théâtre-Français with the title *Andrienne* in 1703, a costume worn by an actress in that play was soon imitated, the style being called *Andrienne*. Andriennes must have been worn by French colonials, or Pénicaut—in Louisiana from 1699 to 1721 and blind when he did return to France—would hardly have used the word.

like those little taffeta aprons that the young ladies in
France wear over their skirts. The *braguets* worn by the
girls, which are commonly made from a fabric of white
thread, cover only the forepart of their nakedness, from
the waist to the knees. They tie them at the back with
two pieces of tape, to the ends of which they hang tassels
that drop down behind. In front, fringes are sewed to
the hem of the *braguets* until the girls reach puberty,
when they take the dress of a woman. The girls are
courteous and love the French very much. We found it
fascinating to watch them dancing during their festivals,
when they put on their most beautiful *braguets,* and the
women their pretty white dresses, all of them bareheaded,
their long black hair hanging to their knees and as low as
the heels of many of them.

Here is how their dances are arranged: women dance
with men, and boys with girls. They always dance twenty
or thirty together, as many boys as girls. A married man
is not permitted to dance with the girls nor boys to dance
with the women. After they have lighted a great flam-
beau, which is commonly the dry trunk of an old pine
tree, which blazes up, lighting the public square of the
village, and another in front of the house of the Grand
Chief, the master of the dance, at the head of some thirty
men and women, commences the dance at sunset to the
sound of a little drum and the cries of spectators; and each
one dances in turn till midnight, when the men go to their
homes with their wives, turning the area over to the boys
and the girls, who dance from midnight till broad daylight. The dances are repeated time and again, each one
dancing in turn; they are danced just about like the new

cotillion in France. With this difference: when a boy has danced in that region with the girl at his side or in front of him, he is permitted to escort her beyond the village and into one of the thickets out on the prairie, where he dances with her another cotillion *à la Missicipyene*. Afterwards they go back to the village square and take their turn dancing as before. Thus they continue their dances till broad-open daylight, so that in the morning the boys in particular are like disinterred corpses, on account of the loss of sleep as well as the exhaustion caused by dancing with the girls.

I should not be at all surprised if these girls are lustful and devoid of restraint because their fathers and their mothers and their religion teach them that, when they leave this world, they have to cross over a narrow and difficult plank before they can enter their Grand Village, where they claim they go after death, and that in the Grand Village will be only those who will have made merry indeed with the boys—they will pass easily across this plank.

From the tenderest age, what detestable lessons are instilled in them—supported by the liberty and the idleness in which they are maintained! For until they are twenty or twenty-five, girls do nothing else, their fathers and mothers being obliged to keep their food always ready for them and, furthermore, according to their tastes and their demands, up until the time they are married.

If by these wretched prostitutions they become pregnant and give birth to children, their fathers and mothers ask them whether they wish to keep their babies. If they answer that they do not and that they cannot suckle them, the poor little unfortunate newborns are strangled outside the huts and buried, without the slightest stir. But if a girl wishes to keep her baby, it is given to her and she suckles it.

When a boy agrees to marry a girl, they go into the woods together; and while the boy goes hunting, the girl makes a hut of foliage in the woods and builds a fire close to the hut. When the boy returns from the hunt, having killed a buffalo or a deer, he brings a quarter of it to the hut, and then together they go after the remainder. On getting back to the hut, they roast a piece of the meat and eat it for their supper. And the next day the two of them carry this game to the village, to the house of her father and mother. They notify her parents, giving to each a piece of the game, which they carry into their house. The boy and girl dine with the father and mother, and he afterwards takes her away to his hut as his wife, where she remains with her husband. After that, she is no longer permitted to go to the boy-and-girl dances or to have commerce with any man other than her husband. She is obliged to do the housework. Her husband can repudiate her if he learns that she has been unfaithful to him, up until the time she has a child by him.

It is usually the Grand Chief who proclaims the dance festival, which goes on for a week or ten days, more or less, throughout all the villages of his dominion. These festivals are commonly held when the Grand Chief needs food supplies—meal, beans, and other such things—which are put in a pile at the door of his house on the last day of the festival. This Grand Chief rules over all other chiefs of the eight other villages. He sends his orders

to them by two of his thirty flunkies, who are called hire-
lings, in their tongue *tichou*.[8] Also, there are many servants that they call *ouchil-tichou*, who serve him for various purposes. The chiefs of the other villages send him
whatever is obtained from the dances in their villages.
His house is large enough to hold as many as four thousand
persons.

This Grand Chief is as absolute as a king. His people,
out of awe, do not come close to him: when they speak
to him, they stand four paces away from him. His bed is
on the right side of his house as one enters. It is arranged
as four wooden posts two feet high set ten feet apart
lengthwise and eight feet apart crosswise. Upon bars extending from one post to another, planks have been put,
making a table-like structure which is quite smooth and
has the same length and width as the quadrangle of the
bed. The bed is painted red all over. Upon it is a mat made
of fine canes and a goose-feather bolster. For cover there
are deer skins for summer and buffalo skins and bear skins
for winter. Only his wife may sleep with him in that bed;
only his wife, too, can eat at his table. When he offers his
leavings to his brothers or to some of his kinsmen, he
pushes the dishes to them with his foot. When he rises
from his bed, all his kinsmen or several distinguished old
men draw near his bed raising their arms aloft and howl-
ing frightfully. This is how they pay their respects to
him; still, he does not deign to look at them.

It should be observed that a grand chief, a noble, cannot

---

[8] Given as *Tichon* by Margry, *Découvertes*, V, 449. The ethnologist Swanton
(*Indian Tribes of the Lower Mississippi Valley*, p. 100) follows Margry's *Tichon*.
But the mss. support *tichou*.

marry any one except a plebeian,[9] but that the children born to that marriage, whether boys or girls, are noble. If he happens to die before his wife, she has to be strangled so that she can accompany him to the other world. Likewise, a noble girl—that is, the daughter of the wife of a noble chief—when she wishes to marry may marry only a plebeian; and if, after marriage, she dies before her husband, he too will be put to death, so that he can accompany her to the other world. The children that issue from these marriages are considered nobles, or Suns.

The houses of these noble chiefs are built upon elevations and are distinguished from other houses by their magnitude. The Grand Chief sends these nobles to be chiefs in the villages subject to him whenever he needs them there.

Nobility among them is quite different from nobility among our Europeans, for in France the more ancient it is, the more it is esteemed. Their lineage, on the contrary, is considered noble only up to the seventh generation; furthermore, they derive their nobility from the woman and not from the man. When I asked them the reason for this, they answered me that nobility can come only from the woman, because the woman is more certain than the man about whom the children belong to.

In this village there is a temple highly esteemed among the savages for its magnitude: it may be thirty feet high and twenty toises square on the inside. The outside is round. The walls are a good three toises thick. It is built

---

[9] Natchez society was divided into three classes of nobility—*soleils,* nobles, and *considérés* (distinguished people)—and the common people or plebeians, who were called Miche-Miche-Quipy, which means stinkards, *puants.* See Le Page Du Pratz, *Histoire de la Louisiane,* II, 393–94.

out of walnut trees [10] that, at the butt end, are as big as one's thigh, and all of the same height. They are bent to a half circle at the tops by bringing their ends together. Next, canes—made and cut like our laths—are tied on, six inches apart, from bottom to top. The spaces between the laths are plastered up with mud, and the mud covered with straw; then still other laths are put up, which, like the first, are tied together at the top ends into a circle to hold the straw in place underneath. Then the whole is covered with mats, ten feet long and six wide, of quartered cane, just about like the wicker with which they cover the temple. They put new covering on it every year.

In this temple they keep a fire burning continuously. They say this fire represents the sun, which they worship. That is why they make a fire before the temple door every morning at sunrise and every evening at sunset. The wood with which they feed the ever-burning fire within the temple has to be oak or walnut from which the bark has been stripped. The logs must not be under eight feet and must be cut at the beginning of each moon. Four temple guards sleep in the temple, one in each corner, and keep the fire going continuously. If they should accidentally let it go out, their heads would be broken with wooden mauls that are always kept in the temple for that noble purpose. During each new moon they bring to the temple some presents of bread and meal, which become the gain of the temple guards. In this temple the three highest families of nobles are buried. In it is the image of a snake which they call the rattlesnake; in the region, snakes just like it can be seen, which have a kind of rattle on their

[10] Probably hickory instead of walnut, as the use indicates.

tails and a bite that is mortal. Also in this temple they have quite a number of little stone images which are shut up in a chest. They have a necklace, too, of fancy pearls that they have got from their ancestors; but all the pearls are damaged, having been bored with a hot iron. They put two or three of them about the necks of noble infants when they are born. They wear them until they are ten years old; then the pearls are put back in the temple. At all ceremonials of women chiefs, the chiefs wear this necklace around their necks until the ceremony is over; then it is carried back to the temple, where it is kept in a chest like a very precious relic. Morning and evening the Grand Chief and his wife go alone into the temple to worship their idols, for only these have the right to go there; and when they come out they tell the people waiting for them before the door a thousand lies—just as they have occurred to them.

It happened in our time that the Grand Noble Female Chief [11] died and we witnessed the funeral ceremonies, which were indeed the most horrifying tragedy that could be seen. It made us shudder with horror, me and all my comrades. She was a female chief noble in her own right; accordingly, as soon as she died, her husband, who wasn't at all noble, was immediately strangled by the first boy that she had borne him, so that he might accompany his wife to the Grand Village, where they think they go after such a fine beginning. Everything in the Grand Chief's

[11] A noble female chief among the Natchez was not the wife of the grand chief, but the grand chief's sister. Nephew succeeded uncle in the royal line, no matter how many sons the grand chief had. The important woman in the tribe was not the grand chief's wife, but his sister. Pénicaut's account may possibly suggest that this woman was the ruler of the Natchez. She was most probably the grand chief's sister.

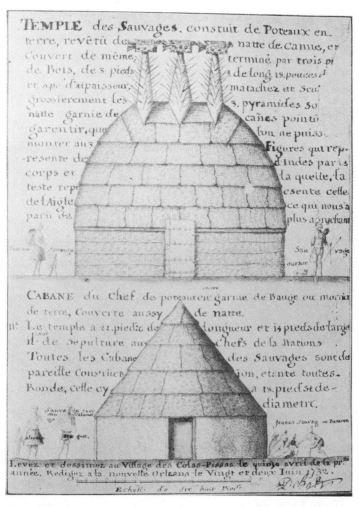

INDIAN TEMPLE OF THE TYPE BUILT BY THE NATCHEZ, SHOWING
CANE MATS USED AS SHINGLES AND SIDING. From Bushnell, "Drawings by A. DeBatz."

house was taken outside. As is the custom, a kind of triumphal chariot was made inside the house, and upon it were placed the Dead One and her strangled husband. A little while later, a dozen little infants that had been strangled to death were borne in and arranged about the Dead One; the fathers and mothers took them there by order of the Dead Female Chief's oldest child, who could then, as Grand Chief,[12] bespeak as many persons as he wished to have put to death, honoring his mother's funeral.

In the village square, fourteen scaffolds were erected, which they decorated with branches of trees and with linen cloth covered with paintings. Upon each scaffold was put a person who was to accompany the Dead One to the other world. On these scaffolds they are surrounded by their nearest of kin. Sometimes they are forewarned ten years in advance of their death; this is an honor to their kin. Usually they have offered their death while the Dead One was alive, out of the great love they bear her; it is they themselves who have spun the cord with which they are strangled. Then—dressed in their finest clothes, with a large shell in their right hand, and accompanied by their closest kinsmen (for example, if the father of a family is to die, his eldest son walks behind him carrying the cord under his arm and a *casse-tête* in his right hand, uttering a horrible scream called the death cry) —then all these unfortunate victims come down from their scaffolds once every quarter hour and, meeting in the middle of the

---

[12] Unless his uncle was dead, this young man was still only heir apparent. Pénicaut seems to have slipped into prematurity at this point, unless there really was a ruling female chief at this time among the Natchez. The law of succession as he explains it elsewhere in this chapter denies the possibility of a ruling woman.

square, dance together before the temple and before the
house of the Dead Female Chief; then they remount their
scaffolds and take their places once more. They are highly
respected on that day, and each one has five servants.
Their faces are painted all over with vermilion. As for me,
I believe their purpose was to hide their fear of death,
which was at hand.

Four days later they began the ceremony of the
Corpses' March. The fathers and mothers [13] who had
brought their children picked them up and held them out
on their hands. The oldest of these children did not seem
to be over three years old. They took their places to right
and left of the door of the Dead Female Chief's house.
The fourteen victims doomed to be strangled came and
took up similar positions. The chiefs and the Dead One's
kinsmen appeared there, likewise, in mourning—that is,
with their hair cut off. At that time they made such
frightful howls that we thought the devils had come out
of hell just to get to this place and howl. The unfortunates, doomed to death, danced while kinsmen of the Dead
One sang. When they started off, two by two, in that
grand funeral procession, the Dead One was brought
from her house, four savages carrying her on their shoulders as on a stretcher. As soon as she was brought forth,
the house was set on fire—that is the grand fashion with
nobles. The fathers with their dead children out on their
hands marched in front at intervals of four paces, and
after taking ten steps they dropped the children to the
ground. Those carrying the Dead One walked on top of

---

[13] These parents, having strangled their children to honor the death of a *soleil*,
were then eligible for promotion from the stinkard to the *considéré* class.

94

these children and three times marched around them. The fathers gathered them up then and fell back in line; and every ten steps they repeated this frightful ritual till they came to the temple, so that the children were mangled in pieces by the time that fine funeral procession got there.

While the Noble Woman was being buried inside the temple, the victims were undressed before the door; and after they had been seated on the ground, one savage sat down on the knees of each while a second savage behind him held his arms. Cords were put around their necks and deer skins placed over their heads, and they were made to swallow three tobacco pills each, with a drink of water to moisten them in their stomachs, which made them lose consciousness. Then the Dead One's kinsmen lined up beside these poor unfortunates, to right and left; and singing the while, each pulled an end of the cord about a victim's neck as a slipknot until they were dead. They were then buried.

When a chief dies, if his wet nurse is still alive, she has to die with him.[14]

[14] This description of the funeral rites of the Female Sun were plagiarized, possibly, by the Jesuit historian Father Charlevoix. It is, of course, conceivable that both Pénicaut and Charlevoix plagiarized a third source. With Pénicaut's account cf. Charlevoix's *La Nouvelle France*, Tome III, pp. 421–23. The passage is in a letter to the Duchess de Lesdiguières, dated "Aux Natchez, ce vint-cinquième de Décembre 1721." Charlevoix did seem to give credit to an individual: he says the funeral rites are taken "d'un voyageur, qui en fut témoin." Now, according to Pénicaut's own statement in this book, he left Louisiana for France in October, 1721, taking his manuscript with him, one may assume, if he had written it by that time. If Charlevoix actually acquired the funeral rites passage in Natchez in December, then Pénicaut must have left a copy of the completed chapters at Natchez. Of course, Charlevoix may have been using the literary device of letters in his journal, which he may have composed entirely in France after he returned and after Dartaguette-Diron lent him the copy of Pénicaut's manuscript.

Chateaubriand singles out Charlevoix as the chief source of his novel *Les Natchez;*

This nation follows this execrable ritual even to this day, in spite of all that has been done to dissuade them. Our missionaries have never been able to succeed in dissuading them: they have been able to do no more than get permission sometimes to baptize those poor little children before their fathers strangled them. Moreover, this nation is too stubborn in its religion, which humors the wicked inclinations of their depraved natures so that there has been no progress in converting them and in establishing Christianity among them.

We had tarried long enough in this village, and we were seized, as it were, with sadness and horror at having seen such a frightful spectacle; so we decided to leave two days later and return to Fort Mobile. After we had thanked them for the good treatment with which they had regaled us during our stay, they escorted us back to our boats. They vied with one another in providing us with food and invited us to come back as soon as we could. At the edge of the water we embraced them once more and departed. We came down to Bâton Rouge and spent the night. We were making a good deal of headway each day, because the currents in the Missicipy are very rapid when one is coming downstream.

In fourteen days we reached Fort Mobile, where we found a ship that had arrived from France, bringing us food supplies. This ship, named *Le Pélican*, was under the command of M. du Coudray.[15] He had brought

---

then, for the convenience of his readers, he puts at the end of his book the influential passage, which is the one Charlevoix lifted from Pénicaut. See [François René,] Vicomte de Chateaubriand, *Les Natchez* (Paris, 1882), pp. 4, 437–38.

[15] Identified by French as M. Ducoudray de Guimont. "Annals of Louisiana . . . By M. Penicaut," p. 95.

twenty-six girls from France. These were the first ones that came to Louisiana. They were quite well behaved, and so they had no trouble in finding husbands. They were in the care of a priest named M. Huet,[16] who remained in Louisiana as much to instruct the French as to convert the savages.

A little later, two companies of the garrison were relieved, and in their place other soldiers were left us who were not the equals of those that were going away, who were already well informed about the region.

The Reverend Fathers Dongé and de Limoges returned to France on *Le Pélican*.[17] M. de Bienville entrusted several bundles of letters for the Court to M. du Coudray, the captain of the ship.

[16] This priest is Father Alexandre Huvé, who came to Mobile in 1704 as curate when De la Vente was *curé*. He baptized the first Creole child born in Louisiana: Jean François, son of Jean le Can and Magdelaine Robert. (Mobile Baptismal Records, October 4, 1704.)

[17] On the *Pélican*, which had brought yellow fever to Fort Louis de la Mobile, sailed away the last Jesuits in Louisiana. (Delanglez, *French Jesuits*, pp. 34–37.) Having lost their jurisdictional dispute, the Jesuits were not to have further assignments in the Gulf area of Louisiana until Father Beaubois received a mission assignment in 1725, with the right to reside in New Orleans. Father Dongé, who had been living at Fort Mobile with Father Davion, died at sea, November, 1704. (*Ibid.*, p. 48.) Father Joseph de Limoges died January 30, 1704. Delanglez thought Father Limoges possibly sailed on *La Loire*, October 16, 1703.

Chapter 7

The Year 1705

The nation of Taoüachas savages comes to Mobile—M. Foucaut and two Frenchmen are killed by the Coroas; the outrageous cruelty of the Coroas toward their enemies—The Nassitoches come to M. de St. Denis' fort—M. de St. Denis' fort on the bank of the Missicipy is abandoned—M. de St. Denis leads a war party against the Chetimachas—The Apalaches come to Mobile

T THE beginning of this year, a savage nation named the Taoüachas [1] came to Mobile seeking M. de Bienville, to ask him for a place in which to settle. He assigned them a location a league and a half below the fort, where they remained as long as we maintained our establishment at Mobile. These savages are good hunters, and every day they brought us much game of all kinds. Besides their personal belongings, they had brought a great deal of corn with which to plant the fields that M. de Bienville gave them. They had deserted the Spaniards to settle in French territory because they had been daily exposed to raids of the Alibamons, and the Spaniards had not stood by them.

Some time afterwards three persons came to Mobile, sent by M. Davion, a priest staying at the Yasoux, with a letter that informed M. de Bienville about the death of M. Foucaut, [2] a priest, and of two Frenchmen named

---

[1] The Tawasa, grouped by the Spaniards with the "Apalachicola" tribes. Swanton reports that they were finally absorbed by the Alibamu. See *Indian Tribes of the Lower Mississippi Valley*, p. 33, and Hodge, *Handbook*, II, 704–705.

[2] Nicholas Foucault, according to Shea (*Catholic Church*, p. 545). He was a

MM. Dambouret and de St. Laurent, who had come down from Canada to visit M. Davion, the grand vicar of Monseigneur the Bishop of Kébecq. As this priest became sick on the way down, they hired four savages at the Coroas village to paddle their boat to the Yasoux. When the priest opened his chest to advance the four savages the agreed-upon wages, the savages noticed in that chest several articles that tempted them. This made them determine to murder the Frenchmen. And that same night, while the priest and the two Frenchmen were asleep, the savages broke their heads and then threw the bodies into the river.[3] Afterwards they took the boat and the articles of merchandise off to their village, which is not far from the Yasoux.

These savages, who are named the Coroas, are the most cruel of all the savages in Louisiana. They are forever off hunting or making war; and when they capture one of their enemies alive, they fasten him to a frame made of two posts eight feet high set five feet apart, tying his hands at the top and his feet at the bottom in the form of a St. Andrew's cross. The poor wretch is fastened up this way entirely naked, and the whole village gathers around him. In that place they have a fire burning in which they have put pieces of iron to get red hot—old

missionary priest who had come from Canada to the Arkansas, where he had not had successful relations with the Indians. When two sick Frenchmen arrived at the Arkansas village, Father Foucault decided to go down river with them and hired visiting Koroas as paddlers. Delanglez, *French Jesuits*, p. 33 and note.

[3] At the very time this murder was committed, Father Davion was on his way to visit Father Foucault at the Arkansas. Coming to the scene of the murder, Father Davion found "hats, plates, and the altar which was still set up, and a few papers written by M. Foucault"—the "débris of this disaster." Father Davion buried the bodies. His letter, quoted by Delanglez, dates this murder as in "the last days of July, 1702." Delanglez, *French Jesuits*, pp. 33–34 and notes.

gun barrels, spades, or axeheads, and other such things. When these get red hot, they rub his back with them, his arms, thighs, and legs. Then they ring the skin on his head even with his ears and tear it off him. They fill this scalp with burning coals and refit it to his head. They stick the ends of his fingers into their lighted pipes and draw on them. And they tear out his nails. Thus they torment him until he is dead. These savages reside on the bank of the Missicipy four leagues from the Yasoux.

During that same time, the Colapissas,[4] who dwelt on the bank of the Taleatcha,[5] a little river four leagues from the shore of Pontchartrain, came to the shore of that lake and settled at a place named Castein Bayouque.[6]

Six months later, the Nassitoches, who had abandoned their settlement on the Rivière Rouge, came seeking M. de St. Denis at his fort to ask him for a place in which to settle and for help with food because the rain[7] and the overflow of the waters had rotted all their grains. I was then at M. de St. Denis' fort, where M. de Bienville had sent me; so, after M. de St. Denis had welcomed these poor destitute savages the best he could, he commissioned me to escort them to the village of the Colapissas, instructing me to commend them in his name to the Chief of the

[4] The Acolapissa, of Choctaw stock, who, according to Hodge (*Handbook*, I, 9), are sometimes given by early writers for Bayogoula and Mugulasha.

[5] Pearl River. Margry (*Découvertes*, V, 459) gives Talcatcha, which shows a misreading of the *e*.

[6] See Chapter I, n. 46. Margry (*Découvertes*, V, 459) has Castembayouque, which is a misreading.

[7] ". . . parce que la pluye et le debordement des eaux avoient poury touts leurs grains [*sic*]." Spofford, pp. 170–71. Margry, following the copyist's error in Clermont, has ". . . parce que la plage [*sic*] et le desbordement des eaux avoient pourri tous les grains." *Découvertes*, V, 459.

VICTIM ON THE FIRE-CADRE. From Antoine Simon LePage du Pratz, *Histoire de la Louisiane* (Paris, 1758).

Colapissas. The Colapissas received them cordially and located them next to their village. Here, on the shore of Lake Pontchartrain, they built their huts. Afterwards, the Colapissas and the Nassitoches were well linked together—till their separation, which I shall recount later on in the proper place. When I got back to M. de St. Denis' establishment, I gave him a report of the commission he had assigned me, and he was well pleased.

Some days afterwards, M. de Bienville wrote a letter to M. de St. Denis, ordering him to have all the munitions and all the merchandise at his establishment loaded on boats and sent to Mobile. Longboats came up there every day to load; and when the fort was entirely empty, we abandoned it and came to Mobile.

After a short while, M. de St. Denis, who was bored at being shut in with nothing to do at Mobile, organized a detachment, with M. de Bienville's consent, to make war on the Chetimachas. He took just fifteen Frenchmen with him and the necessary provisions in three boats. Leaving Mobile, we went to the village of the Colapissas and the Nassitoches, who were living together, where we engaged eighty of these savages to go with us. From there we ascended the Rivière des Chetimachas [8] to make an attack on the Chetimachas' village. But on the way we ran into twenty Chetimachas going on a fishing trip with their women and children. They fled as soon as they saw us. We killed several of them; the others escaped to their village and gave the alarm. This compelled M. de

[8] Bayou Lafourche, which led toward the main Chitimacha territory near Grand Lake.

St. Denis to retire downstream. We caught twenty of their women and children and took them away as slaves to Mobile.[9]

Some time later, because something had displeased him or because he objected to being shut in, M. de St. Denis went away with twelve Frenchmen to live at Biloxi.

Toward the end of this year, a savage nation named the Apalaches [10] came to Mobile to ask M. de Bienville for a place in which to settle. They had deserted the settlement they had in Spanish territory ninety leagues east of Mobile near the Rivière de Tolacatchina.[11] As they had often been pillaged by the Alibamons without ever receiving relief from the Spaniards, they had been forced to abandon their settlement and come and put themselves under the protection of the French. They were excellent Catholics; therefore, as soon as they came, M. de Bienville had them given food to live on and then had some

---

[9] Entries in the Mobile Baptismal Records show the Indian's inability to adapt himself to a life of slavery. Child slaves were sometimes baptized in agony, as subsequent notations prove. There is no doubt that these Chitimacha women and children arrived at Mobile. For example, on April 2, 1710, Father Huvé baptized a "Sitimachas" woman "dangereusement malade."

[10] The Apalachee Indians were a once-great Muskhogean tribe in Florida, north of Apalachee Bay. In 1703 they were struck a deadly blow by Governor More, of Carolina, who employed a company of Englishmen and 1,000 Indians against them. Two hundred Apalachees were slain and 1,400 taken off into slavery. (Hodge, *Handbook*, I, 67–68.) Pénicaut is describing a surviving remnant that came to the French at Mobile. The great Apalachee tribe has left its name in many places on modern maps; the little remnant left its name to the Apalachee River, next to the Tensaw, flowing into the head of Mobile Bay. There is ample evidence, in Mobile Baptismal Records, both of their Christianity and of their former association with the Spaniards. An entry for November 22, 1711, in Father Le Maire's hand, gives the chief of the Apalachees as Ouan—"c'est à dire Jean Appalache."

[11] Written Talacatchina on Delisle's "Carte de la Louisiane," 1718. It shows as the west river of the two flowing into the headwaters of Apalachee Bay and as the first river east of the "Apalachicolis." As next to the Apalachicola it should be the Ochlockonee, which enters the Bay on the west side; but as paired with the Aucilla, it should be the St. Mark's.

land assigned to them close to the Mobiliens and the Tomez, with seed corn for the first year. M. Huet,[12] one of our priests, has always taken good care of them, going among them quite often to preach and to administer the sacraments.

[12] Father Alexandre Huvé, who, Hamilton states, was inept at learning Indian languages. *Colonial Mobile,* pp. 126–27.

Chapter 8

The Year 1706

Dom Gusman, the Governor of Passacol, comes to Mobile: the welcome given him—Description of the Colapissas and the Nassitoches savages

T THE beginning of this year, Dom Gusman, a Spaniard and the Governor of Fort Passacol for the King of Spain, came to our fort on the Mobile to visit M. de Bienville, who welcomed him with the firing of cannon and the discharge of muskets of the garrison, who had been put under arms. During the four days that he stayed, he was entertained by M. de Bienville and all the officers of the garrison.

While he was at our fort, a French-Canadian named Boutin begged him to do him the honor of consenting to be sponsor of his child at christening, along with M. Le Sueure's daughter, the cousin of M. de Bienville.[1] This christening was celebrated with all possible pomp: the garrison, having been put under arms, fired three volleys from their muskets; Dom Gusman emerged from the chapel preceded by his valet, who tossed more than a

---

[1] Mobile Baptismal Records show Pénicaut's memory to be at fault about the year of this christening as well as about the identity of the godmother. The whole entry is worth quoting. "Ce jourdhuy dix neuf de Janvier [preceding entries show 1709] ont esté supplées les ceremonies du baptême a Narie [Marie] Marguerite Fille de Guillaume Boutin marchand a la Mobile et de Louise Marguerite Housseau sa legitime epouse. Le Parrein a esté Dom Joseph de Guzman gouverneur gñal de Pensacola et la mareine Demoiselle Marguerite veufve de M^r. Le Sueur." It is signed, "Joseph de Gusman [or Guzman], Messier [may be Mersier], F. Le Maire P. M. Ap."

thousand piastres [2] to all the soldiers of the garrison of the fort; and Dom Gusman requested M. de Bienville to set French prisoners free, which M. de Bienville agreed to do. Before he went away, he asked M. de Bienville for two carpenters, whom he took along with him to build two houses for him in his Fort Passacol. His departure, too, was celebrated with artillery and musketry and the beating of the drums of the garrison.

Several days after Segnor Dom Gusman had departed, M. de Bienville, seeing that the food supplies were fast diminishing and that no vessel was on the way to bring some, gave permission to several persons of the garrison to go hunting or to go live as best they could among the savage nations friendly to the French. When I heard that we were to be given this liberty, I proposed to several of my comrades, not to go back to the Natchez, but to go among the Colapissas, with whom I was acquainted. During the preceding year I had escorted the Nassitoches there to live with them on the shore of Lake Pontchartrain. I understood and spoke their language well and was even a friend of the chiefs of both these nations. So, after taking the three-day ration of food that was portioned out to us, we set out, twelve of us together in two boats, taking one kettle, which we were careful to put into one of our boats. We were provided with a good supply of powder and shot, which is absolutely necessary in that country. The oldest among us was no more than thirty and the youngest twenty-four. It was the beginning of May, and

---

[2] Roughly $1,000, as the Spanish piastre was worth about five livres or five francs. Spanish piastres circulated throughout Louisiana for years, particularly during the times when French paper money was deflated and French coins were scarce.

the weather was the finest that could be desired; therefore, we journeyed by easy stages, going ashore every now
and then to hunt.

On the very first day, we killed two deer, which we
carried to our boats. We roasted a part of the meat by
the water's edge, and there we built some shelters out of
green branches. We ate supper and spent the night under
our shelters. While watching over us, one of our comrades
kept the kettle boiling, which we had filled with the meat.
When day broke we had breakfast and set sail again. A
week later we reached the Colapissas and the Nassitoches.
That day we brought a great deal of game in our boats,
having killed it the same day near the spot where we had
spent the night. As we had had no more than two leagues
to travel between our last stop and the Colapissas, we had
hunted from morning till four in the afternoon, with
the intention of carrying game to our hosts as an arriving
present. And so in our boats there were six deer, eight
turkeys and as many bustards, killed that same day. When
we got to their village with all this, they embraced us,
the men as well as the women and girls, all being delighted
to see us come to stay with them. Then they started cooking the meats that we had brought. And after supper the
entire village began to dance, and danced far into the
night.

We had in our group a companion named Picard, who
had brought a violin with him. He could play it well
enough to have these savages do some figure-dancing in
step. They had us nearly dying of laughter, for the musi-
cal instrument had the whole village drawn up around
Picard; it was the most comical sight in the world to see

them open their eyes in amazement and every now and then cut the most comical capers ever seen. But it was quite another matter when they saw us dance a minuet— two boys dancing together. They would gladly have spent the whole night watching us and listening to the violin, had not the Chief of the Colapissas, fearing we were tired out, come to tell us that lodgings were assigned to us. All of them wanted to have us in their homes: the Chief of the Colapissas reserved the violin player to lodge with him; the most important men gave lodging to the others. For my part, I was lodged with the Chief of the Nassitoches. On my arrival, he had invited me to stay with him, and he led me away. I was the person that, acting for M. de St. Denis, had conducted this chief among the Colapissas the year before to live there with them. I knew him as one of the most honorable men among the savages of the region. Since that time, he had been indebted to me for saving his life, as I shall show later on.

I was not sorry that I was lodged with him, for in his house I received every possible favor. He had two daughters that were the most beautiful of all the savage girls in this district. The older one was twenty; she was called Oulchogonime, which in their language means the good daughter. The second was only eighteen, but was taller than her older sister. She was named Ouilchil, which means the pretty spinner.

I got up a bit late next morning because we had tired ourselves by dancing the greater part of the night. On getting up, I was surprised to see my host bring in a great platter of fish fricasseed in bear fat, and cooked very well. There was also some sagamité, which is a kind of bread that they make from cornmeal mixed with flour of little beans that are similar to our haricots in France. Just the two of us were to eat together, and I was surprised at not seeing his wife or his daughters; but half an hour later they came back together, bringing a big platter of strawberries, for as early as the first of May strawberries abound in the woods. That day they had put on their fine *braguets* of very white nettle-linen. I gave each of them a present of half an ell of brocade of white background woven with little flowers colored pink and green, out of which each could make a *braguet;* but their father did not approve and begged me to keep this material for the daughter of the Grand Chief of the Colapissas because that chief outranked all others in their settlement. He was absolutely determined that the younger daughter should give her piece of brocade back to me; but when I showed him another piece that I was saving for that purpose, he thanked me at great length and was beside himself with politeness, and the mother was, too.

At this time two of my comrades came in to see me, one of them being Picard, the violin player. As soon as my host's elder daughter saw him, she kissed him. I was not so sorry about this as I would have been if it had been the younger daughter kissing him. Picard ate a bit of fish with us; and, when my other comrades arrived unexpectedly, we all went together to the house of the Grand Chief of the Colapissas. When we got there, I embraced his daughter and also gave her a present of half an ell of the same material that I had given the daughters of the Chief of the Nassitoches, at whose house I was staying. I think the father and mother would gladly have given me all their possessions, they were so delighted with the present I had given their daughter. We then went into all the huts of the savages, one after the other, they vying with one another in entertaining us.

Afterwards, during the after-dinner hour, we went to see their methods of fishing. They pulled up their nets from the lake filled with fish of all sizes. These nets, actually, are no more than fishing lines about six fathoms long. All along these lines, numerous other little lines are tied a foot apart. At the end of each line is a fish hook on which they put a bit of sagamité dough or a small piece of meat. With this method they do not fail to catch fish weighing more than fifteen or twenty pounds. The end of the line is tied to their boats. They pull the lines up two or three times a day, and they always catch many fish when they do. Such fishing as this does not keep them from working in their field, for it can be attended to in less than half an hour. When they have pulled in all their fish, each person takes some fish home, and after it is cooked and seasoned with bear fat, as I have already said, they begin to eat it, each in front of his door in the shade of peach trees.

When the sun had sunk low and all had eaten supper, we danced, as on the evening before, quite far into the night. Their dances, like the ones I spoke of in the article on the Natchez, are conducted to the sound of a little drum. Our musician endeavored to keep time with the drum and the singers' voices. Although he made a most painful attempt that drew upon all his skill and caused us all to laugh out loud, he never was able to approximate their rhythm; and, as a matter of fact, their singing is more savage than the savages themselves. Although it is an incessant repetition, Picard could not get their pitch; but he made amends by teaching many of the girls in the village to dance the minuet and *la bourrée*.

Every day after dinner, which these savages usually have at eight o'clock in the morning, we would get together and then go hunting, and every day we would bring game back to the village, so that the savages were delighted to have us with them.

The Nassitoches are handsomer and have better figures than the Colapissas, because the Colapissas' bodies, men's and women's, are all tattooed.[3] They prick almost their entire bodies with needles and rub the pricks with willow ash crushed quite fine, which causes no inflammation of the punctures. The arms and faces of the Colapissas women and girls are tattooed in this way, which disfigures them hideously; but the Nassitoches, men as well as women and girls, make no use of such punctures, which they loathe. That is why they are so much better looking; besides, they are naturally whiter.

As for their religion, they have a round temple before which they appear morning and evening rubbing their bodies with white mud and lifting their arms on high; they mutter some words very low for a quarter of an hour. At the portal of the temple there are some wooden likenesses of birds; within the temple are numerous little idols, of both wood and stone, representing dragons, snakes, and some toadlike creatures, which they keep

---

[3] The French word is *piqué,* "pitted," which appears in the French name for a famous Natchez chief, Le Serpent Piqué, Tattooed Snake. His name is sometimes given as Tattooed Serpent, more often as Stung Serpent.

locked up in three chests inside the temple, the key being held by the Grand Chief.

When a savage dies, a kind of grave is prepared, or, rather, a platform raised two feet above ground, on top of which the dead man is placed. He is covered completely with mud, and, further, bark is put on top of that, for fear of animals or birds of prey; and down below is put a little jug filled with water together with a platter full of meal. Every morning and every evening fire is lighted beside the platform, and here they come and weep. The richest people hire women to weep beside the platform. After six moons, the body is uncovered; if the flesh is consumed, the bones are put in a little basket [4] and carried to their temple; if it is not yet consumed, the bones are taken from the flesh, and the flesh is burned.

They are rather cleanly with their food: they have an individual pot for each thing that they cook—that is, the meat pot is never used for fish. They cook all their food with bear fat, which is white in winter, when it is congealed, like lard, and is like olive oil in summer. It does not have a bad taste. They eat it with salad, use it in making pastry, in frying, and usually in everything they cook.

As for fruits, they happen to be few. They have, however, peaches in season that are even bigger than those in France, and sweeter; strawberries; plums; and a grape that is a bit sour and not so big as the grapes of France. There are also nuts which they pound into flour, using it

---

[4] ". . . dans un petit panier," supplied from Spofford, p. 190. The "dans un panier" in Clermont, p. 161, is the work of an officious hand, which has tampered with that manuscript in other places too.

with water to make pap for their children and mixing it with corn meal to make sagamité, or bread.

These savages have no hair on them whatever except the hair on their heads. The men as well as the women and girls remove the hair from their faces as well as from other parts of the body; they remove hair with shell ash and hot water as one would remove the hair from a suckling pig.

They have an unusual way to light a fire. They take a small piece of cedar wood, the size of one's finger, and another small piece of mulberry wood, which is very hard. They put them side by side between their hands and by spinning them together, like making chocolate froth, they make a little piece of fuzz come out of the cedar wood and catch fire. This can be done instantly.

When they go hunting, they go dressed in deer skins with the antlers attached. They make the same motions that a deer makes; and when the deer notices this, he charges them; and when he gets in good musket range, they shoot at him and kill him. With this method they kill a great many deer; and it should be acknowledged that in hunting buffalo as well as bear and deer they are more skilful than the French.

When winter came, we went out to the channel and into the woods to kill bustards,[5] ducks, and wild geese [6] that are much bigger than the geese in France. During that season unbelievable numbers of them are attracted to Lake Pontchartrain, and there they stay along the lake shore. Every day we brought back some of them,

---

[5] *Outardes,* "bustards," was the French name for common Canadian geese.

[6] *Oyes sauvages,* snow or blue geese. Clark, *Voyageurs,* p. 345.

which we roasted inside the huts, where good fires were kept burning on account of the cold. The cold is not, however, so long or so severe as in the Upper Missicipy.

In this way we spent the greater part of the winter. As far as I was personally concerned, I was just as happy there in winter as in summer, for, to keep myself busy whenever I returned from hunting, I would sit close by the fire and teach my host's daughters to speak French. They made me die of laughing, with their savage pronunciation, which comes entirely from the throat, whereas French is spoken solely from the tongue, without being guttural.

Chapter 9

The Year 1707

M. de Noyant arrives at Isle Dauphine with three ships—A
ship from Martinique runs aground at Isle Dauphine—The Isle
Dauphine settlement is begun

AT THE beginning of the year 1707, in the
month of February, M. de Noyant,[1] a commander, arrived at Mobile. He came on the
ship named *L'Aigle*. Besides that one, he had
brought two other small vessels. This relief came in the
nick of time; for there was no food at Mobile, and the
garrison there was living entirely off game brought in by
the neighboring savages.

M. de Noyant had brought two priests with him from
Paris: one, a great preacher, was named M. de la Vente; [2]

---

[1] Identified by Hamilton as Bienville's uncle. Since Bienville's sister married a De
Noyan, this identity has the implication that she married her first cousin. See
Colonial Mobile, p. 28, and p. 58. Bienville's nephew came to Louisiana; two of his
sons were active during the last years of French Dominion. One of them, Jean
Baptiste Noyan, was married to the daughter of the great Creole patriot Lafrénière.
Both he and Lafrénière were executed by General O'Reilly October 25, 1769. See
King, *Creole Families*, pp. 173–81.

[2] Henri Roulleaux de la Vente was given possession of the parish church at Fort
Louis de la Louisiane (Mobile) September 28, 1704. The record of the impressive
ceremony of his induction as parish priest is still among the Mobile Baptismal
Records. I saw also a typescript of it when I examined the Records. Hamilton
published it in *Colonial Mobile*, p. 417. Father De la Vente soon allied himself
with the scrivener La Salle in a violent attack upon the honesty and morals of
Bienville. It was their accusations that Dartaguette investigated when he supplanted
La Salle as commissary. The life of this missionary priest at Mobile must have been
very unhappy, for his letters or reports show more bitterness than *caritas* toward
Bienville as well as some others. I do not doubt that he had cause, for Bienville was
a formidable opponent supported by kinsmen and other men dependent on him.
Perhaps Father De la Vente was in poor health most of the time. In October, 1710,
he returned to France critically ill. See Shea, *Catholic Church*, p. 552.

and the other was M. Le Maire,[3] who had been vicar of St. Jacques de la Boucherie. There were also several families of expert craftsmen and a great many materials for working the fields, such as millstones and other similar things, and above all a great supply of wine, brandy, and salted meats, which were stored in the warehouses.

Immediately M. de Bienville ordered that savages be sent to all places where we had gone to subsist, to notify everybody to return to Mobile. As soon as we learned the news, we became quite melancholy over it; but we had to make up our minds to leave. The savages, too, were distressed, for they really loved us, the girls in particular, who were very sorry to see us leave, among them the ones Picard had been teaching to dance to the tune of the violin. Before we left, they gave us a present of several deer skins, which proved quite serviceable to us on our way down the Missicipy, as it was very cold. Also, they furnished us with provisions for four days. After embracing them we got into our boats and left to go down to Mobile, which we reached three days later. We greeted MM. de Bienville and de Noyant and gave them an account of our pleasant stay among the Colapissas. This pleased them; but what pleased us, too, was to behold the provisions that had come for us and to find wine in the lot, which we had not had among the Colapissas.

[3] Father Le Maire, a missionary priest, did not come with De la Vente, but later, on the *Coventry*, in the winter of 1705. He was the most scholarly churchman in the Mobile area during the years covered by this book. He wrote letters about the geography of the country. His observations greatly influenced the cartographer Guillaume Delisle. (See the full title of Delisle's map, 1718, given in the bibliography.) He served the Spaniards at Pensacola for a while and studied Spanish while there. He served as pastor of Dauphin Island and made observations about the settlement there. He left the colony about 1720. See Delanglez, *French Jesuits*, pp. 56, 72–73; Shea, *Catholic Church*, pp. 549–50.

The wine consoled us for the loss of the favors of their girls.

The number of priests having increased, a larger presbytery than the one they had had was built to the left of the fort; [4] it was located on a height from which the priests could see all the surrounding country.

During that time MM. de Bienville and de Noyant sent two French-Canadians overland to carry letters to the Cascassias Illinois, because M. de Bienville wanted to know how far it was by land. They were given two Mobiliens as guides. They left Mobile and went to the Chactas, sixty-two leagues from Mobile; then they passed through the Chicachas, who are fifty leagues beyond the Chactas. From there they reached the Oüabache River, which they crossed on a little raft; and thirty-three leagues above it, they found the Cascassias Illinois, [5] from whom they returned after a six-months' trip, coming back by way of the Missicipy. As soon as they reached Mobile, [6] they delivered the Reverend Jesuit Fathers' letters to M. de Bienville and told him that it was only one hundred and ninety-five leagues by land, whereas by way of the Missicipy it was four hundred leagues. The Cascassias Illinois nation is Catholic. Three years earlier, [7] these savages had abandoned the settlement they had on the shore of Lake Pinthouy, [8] sixty leagues up the Rivière des Illinois above

---

[4] Fort Louis de la Mobile, at Twenty-Seven Mile Bluff.

[5] On the Okaw or Kaskaskia River, in southwest Illinois.

[6] In Parkman, p. 185, the remainder of this paragraph comes just before the last paragraph in this chapter.

[7] After a temporary settlement on the site of southern St. Louis, the Kaskaskia tribe of the Illinois confederacy moved to the Okaw River in 1703. McDermott, *Old Cahokia*, pp. 4–11.

[8] This seems to be a copyist's error for Pimitoui, i. e. Lake Peoria, Illinois.

its embouchure at the Missicipy, and settled on a small river that bears their names to this day—two leagues from the bank of the Missicipy, on the right side going upstream, and forty-three leagues this side of the Rivière des Illinois. This nation is highly civilized; we shall have something to say about them later.

M. de Noyant returned to France two months after he had come.

A few days afterwards, we went to Passacol [9] with M. de Chateaugué to carry back to the governor of the fort the flour he had lent us the year before. On our way back from Passacol—when we were approaching Isle Dauphine in our *traversier*, towards Petite Isle de Sable, [10] which is the outer island—we observed from a distance what appeared to be a small merchant ship. M. de Chateaugué had us sail toward the place to find out whether it was Englishmen. Approaching nearer, we saw that it was some people signaling us to help them. M. de Chateaugué had the *traversier* close up to calling distance. Then we heard them shouting distinctly enough in French for us to have pity on them and to please come and save their lives. At once—not doubting that they were Frenchmen—we went to them and aided them.

They had run aground on the point of this island, where they had been driven by a storm that had battered them for ten days without surcease. More than half of their men had perished and fallen into the sea. They had been completely dismasted; the prow of the ship had been smashed by the violence of the storm. They had had to throw all their cannons and their ammunition overboard.

[9] Pensacola.   [10] Sand Island, in the Gulf south of Dauphin Island.

For four days they had not eaten. They were so carried away with joy when help arrived—contrary to every expectation—that they kissed the ground when they reached Isle Dauphine, to which we carried them in our longboat. M. de Chateaugué immediately had them given something to eat, but only a little at a time, for fear that much would make them sick.

The captain of the ship, M. de St. Maurice, was from Martinique. From Martinique he had set out in his ship to engage in trading at Havana and Vera Cruz, where he had sold his merchandise very well; but on the return trip he was becalmed for eighteen days. As his food supplies were about to fail him, certain ones of the sailors—as among such men there are always some who live like heathen—instead of imploring the aid of heaven, began to blaspheme and utter curses against God. They hurled overboard a little wooden image of St. Anthoine with a stone tied to his neck. *St. Anthoine* was the name of the ship, under the protection of this saint, to whom the master of the ship had dedicated it. The very next day, they had the storm I have just reported, which caused more than fifty of those blasphemers to perish; they were the cause of the loss of the ship [and of the riches they had gained by trading at Havana, which was a substantial amount. To lighten the ship they had to throw this into the sea.] [11] That was what M. Maurice, the commander, told M. de Chateaugué, and what I heard—just as I report it. He still had forty thousand piastres, which he said could be found at the bottom of the ship's hold, in the sand. He begged M. de Chateaugué to accept this as

[11] Supplied from Parkman, pp. 183-84.

thanks for saving his life and the lives of his men. He had forty-five men left, the greater part of whom were more dead than alive when we took them over to Isle Dauphine, for they hardly had the strength to stand. M. de Chateaugué sent for the forty thousand piastres and for everything else that could be salvaged from the ship. These things were brought to Isle Dauphine; but M. de Chateaugué would accept none of them: he gave back to M. Maurice all his money and his personal belongings and would not permit anyone to accept anything, telling M. Maurice that he would need to buy a small ship in which to return to Martinique. This did not happen quickly, and he was compelled to stay a long time with us at Mobile, where we took him and his men in our *traversier*.

This same year several families that lived at Mobile asked M. de Bienville for permission to settle on Isle Dauphine, which M. de Bienville granted. They had houses built there [12] and cultivated gardens. They brought their livestock and their poultry. With the course of time this proved to be a great help to ships from France that came in to the roadstead off this island.

[12] On the southeastern part of the island, facing the harbor, now Pelican Bay. At that time Dauphin Island was much longer than it is today. The western half is now cut away and is called Petit Bois Island. For a while, the Petit Bois half was called Massacre, presumably because the skeletons from which came the name Massacre were originally found toward the western end.

Chapter 10

The Year 1708

M. Dartaguet arrives in Louisiana—M. Dartaguet sends M. d'Éraque to the Illinois to make peace among the savages—The Alibamons along with other savages attack the Mobiliens and are pursued by M. Dartaguet—The bold exploit of two Frenchmen

OWARDS THE beginning of this year, in the month of February, M. Dartaguet,[1] the Intendant-General of Louisiana, arrived with his brother on board the ship that was named

[1] This is the prominent French gentleman to whom Pénicaut dedicated this book, calling him Dartaguiette Diron. He was made *ordonnateur*, commissary-general, of Louisiana on June 30, 1707, replacing Nicholas de la Salle, who was only a scrivener acting as commissary. (Surrey, *Calendar of Manuscripts in Paris Archives*, I, x.) His first duty in Louisiana was to investigate charges against Bienville. He left Louisiana in 1711 and returned to France, where he became one of the original directors of the Company of the West, September 12, 1717. (*Ibid.*, I, vii.) I have seen no evidence to show that he ever returned to Louisiana, in 1717 or at any other time. He was certainly in France, as receiver, or collector, of the taxes of the district of Auch, when Pénicaut dedicated his manuscript to him in 1723. I do not know his given name: he is called Dartaguette-Diron and Diron-Dartaguette. Since Pénicaut's dedication was flattery that might gain Dartaguette's support of a Crown gratuity for Pénicaut, the author had cause to be accurate in giving the relationships of three persons belonging to the Diron-Dartaguette family. So far as I know, this relationship has never been settled, for some historians have given two Dartaguettes, brothers, and others have given three, a father and son among them. (See Elizabeth McCann, "Pénicaut and His Chronicle," p. 289, n. 2.) Miss McCann states that the three Dartaguiettes (the spelling of the name varies) were brothers and that the one who returned to Louisiana in 1717 was the one to whom Pénicaut dedicated his manuscript: Bernard Diron Dartaguiette. But Bernard Diron was a "cadet de la compagnie de Mr. Chateaugué" when he served as godfather on March 16, 1709, signing the Mobile Baptismal Records as Bernar Diron [*sic*]. Again on August 10, 1710, he signed the Records, this time as Diron, but is identified by the priest's entry as Bernard Dartaguette. When the *ordonnateur* is mentioned, he is identified as M. Dartaguette the *ordonnateur* or commissary. Since a cadet, in the sense used above, means a young nobleman or young man of good family who has

La Renommée, of which M. de Chylay [2] was captain. A few days after M. Dartaguet reached Mobile, he reviewed the entire garrison and asked all the officers and soldiers whether they were pleased with the country. All of them told him that they were quite happy there. In like manner he called together all the French residents living in the neighborhood of the fort and asked their opinion about the country. All of them told him that they had found the soil and the climate just right for growing grains and everything in abundance, and even finer than in France if they could get horses and plows with which to till the fields. When M. Dartaguet returned to France he gave a report about this, and horses and plows were later sent.

A little while afterwards, M. Dartaguet and M. de Bienville took sixteen men in some boats to Lake Pontchartrain and went by the Rivière Choupicatcha [3] down to Biloxi, where they visited M. de St. Denis. He welcomed them to the very best of his ability. After they had stayed for several days and the savages had carried the boats to the Missicipy, MM. Dartaguet and de Bienville came there together, along with M. de St. Denis, and went back up the Missicipy River as high as Cannes Brûlées. [4] M. Darta-

volunteered for military service in hope of a commission, Bernar Diron-Dartaguette could hardly have been the same man as the *ordonnateur.* It is possible that he was the *ordonnateur's* son. But I believe he was the same Diron-Dartaguette that later became inspector-general of troops in Louisiana. This is the brother mentioned in this same sentence in Pénicaut's account. A third brother, easily identified, is yet to enter this narrative.

[2] Given as Sieur Deschilais, the captain in command of the *Renommée,* in D'Artaguette to Pontchartrain, July 6, 1707. See Rowland and Sanders, *MPA,* III, 73.

[3] To go from Lake Pontchartrain by way of Bayou St. John (Choupicatcha) to Biloxi appears to be strange navigation. Dartaguette and Bienville should have gone through the Rigolets, if taking the normal course.

[4] The translation is Burnt Canes, a name for a clearing. Reynolds gives the site of

guet found the banks of the Missicipy very pleasant; often he went ashore and made his way quite far into the country in order to acquaint himself with the soil, which he found very good and fertile everywhere. At length, after going ashore at a place called Pointe-aux-Chesnes,[5] they had a big hunt for deer and bustards and returned to Mobile.

A few days afterwards—having got information that some French-Canadians living among the Cascassias Illinois were inciting the savage nations in the environs of this settlement to make war upon one another and that the French-Canadians themselves were participating in order to get slaves that they afterwards sold to the English— MM. Dartaguet and de Bienville dispatched M. d'Éraque [6] with six men in a boat with letters for the Reverend Jesuit Fathers and presents for the savages to induce them to make peace among themselves. When M. d'Éraque reached the Cascassias Illinois, he delivered the letters to the Reverend Jesuit Fathers and forbade the French-Canadians to engage in further warfare with the savages or to incite them to war. He then addressed the savages, urging them in the names of MM. Dartaguet and de Bienville to live at peace with other savages, and then gave them the presents MM. Dartaguet and de Bienville had

Cannes Brûlées as the present town of Kenner, in Jefferson Parish. "Louisiana Place Names of Romance Origin," p. 90.

[5] Still marked on maps as the southeast tip of Mississippi. Except for one clue to the identity of this point, it could be any Pointe-aux-Chesnes between Cannes Brûlées and Mobile; the name must have been common enough. But one Pointe-aux-Chesnes, the one in southeast Mississippi, has already been mentioned as a good place for hunting. See page 10.

[6] Apparently the same man that Le Sueur left as commandant of Fort Huilier, and the one called M. Darrac by Bienville. He was ensign in Chateaugué's company. See page 53.

instructed him to give them. Then he went upstream, as high as the village of the Caouquias Illinois,[7] where he gave the same prohibition to the Canadians and the savages, to whom he also gave sufficient presents to induce them to keep the peace. Afterwards he went among the Reverend Jesuit Fathers and the missionaries for foreign lands, delivering the gentlemen's letters, and besought them to send word to Mobile if the Canadians again started to stir up war among the savages, for which the punishment would be severe. From there he went up the Missoury River to address the nations on its banks and exhort them to peace; and, after giving them the presents that had been sent them, M. d'Éraque and his men returned to Mobile.

During the same time, two Mobilien savages who had married among the Alibamons and were living among them with their families, discovered that the Alibamons, who were the Mobiliens' enemies as well as ours, had invited the nations of the Cheraquis, the Abécas, and the Cadapouces [8] to join them and make war on the Mobiliens, burn their villages and then the houses of the residents of our fort. The two Mobiliens came immediately down to Mobile to warn their kinsmen. MM. Dartaguet and de Bienville made all the residents of the neighborhood come inside our fort at once, bringing with them whatever valuable belongings they had. But the Ali-

[7] Across the Mississippi from present-day St. Louis. The Cahokia belonged to the Illinois confederacy. Pénicaut had visited them with the Le Sueur party in 1700.

[8] These three tribes were the Cherokees, living in northeast Alabama; the Creeks of the Upper-Creek town Abihka; and the Catawba, a Carolina tribe that spoke a Siouan dialect. Elsewhere Pénicaut calls the Catawba Canapouces. See Hodge, *Handbook*, I, 213–14, 245–47, and Swanton, *Indian Tribes of the Lower Mississippi Valley*, pp. 253–54.

bamons, noticing that the two Mobiliens that had married among them and lived among them were no longer there, suspected that they had come and warned us and that we would be on our guard. This was the reason the Alibamons did not come this time; nevertheless, when MM. Dartaguet and de Bienville heard this news, they came out of Fort Mobile and led a strong detachment to meet them. That was a wasted effort, for after they had gone more than ten leagues to meet the Alibamons and waited for them for four days, the food supplies grew short and MM. Dartaguet and de Bienville were forced to return to Mobile.

But six weeks afterwards—at a time when they were least expected—the Alibamons did attack the Mobiliens' village, which, however, they did not succeed in surprising as they had expected, because M. Dartaguet had instructed the Mobiliens to reconnoiter eight to ten leagues out upon their route; consequently, when the Alibamons did come—although with the other nations, their allies, they were more than fifteen thousand warriors—even with all these, they did nothing except burn some Mobilien huts six leagues from us and go home as fast as possible.

MM. Dartaguet and de Bienville took several officers and led a detachment from the fort that had been organized the minute the news about this had been received; but the Alibamons were already so far away that, after trying for quite a long time to overtake them, MM. Dartaguet and de Bienville were compelled to bring the detachment back to the fort.

M. de Chateaugué asked for sixty Frenchmen to take

toward Passacol, where, a savage had told him, several of these Alibamons had gone to pillage some settlements [9] in that direction. M. Dartaguet let him have the sixty, who were joined by some sixty Mobilien volunteers, the most fearless of savages, all armed with guns. Noticing that we were all quite determined, M. de Chateaugué made us quicken our pace; so, after proceeding for two hours, we descried a party of Alibamons that had become separated from the others who were going toward Passacol. A Mobilien guiding us had us take a road that cut across their way and we overtook them. We fired one round at them, killing thirty and wounding seven, who were dispatched and were scalped as well as the others that had been slain. Nine were taken alive; but the others fled with such speed that they never could be overtaken. This compelled us to go back to the fort, to which we brought our prisoners. Their heads were immediately broken.

A few days afterwards, the Chaqtos,[10] who were a nation disheartened by Spanish rule, reached Mobile with their women and children and begged MM. Dartaguet and de Bienville to give them a place in which to settle. They were assigned lands one league downstream,[11] on

---

[9] ". . . quelques habitations," which may mean farms, including improvements.

[10] The Chatot Indians, who had lived on the Apalachicola River. They were certainly not Choctaws, although of Muskhogean stock. The French nicely distinguished Chaqtos from Chactas (Choctaws). The spelling may vary in some respects, but never is the *o* sound missing at the end of Chaqtos or any other spelling of the name. English-speaking people later confused Chaqtos and Chactas. For this small tribe's history see Swanton, *Indian Tribes of the Lower Mississippi Valley*, pp. 32–33. In 1708 the chief of the Chatot was named Ouan, according to Father Huvé, who christened the chief's boy Ouan on December 24, 1708. Mobile Baptismal Records.

[11] An anachronism, for Pénicaut is reckoning the position of Choctaw Point as one league south of the present site of Mobile and doing so at a time in the narrative when the chief settlement was still at Twenty-Seven Mile Bluff.

the right side, on the shore of the bay, on a large cove about one league along the curve. To this day it is called Ance des Chaqtos.[12]

At this point I cannot keep from telling the exploit of two Frenchmen, which I believe the reader will not find unpleasant. The Governor of Passacol for the King of Spain sent to MM. Dartaguet and de Bienville asking for three or four of their best hunters to kill him some game. MM. Dartaguet and de Bienville sent him four, who went on a hunt in the woods in the neighborhood of Passacol. While two of these, named St. Michel and Moquin, were hunting in the woods, they were encountered by a party of Alibamons, who encircled them and caught them and afterwards took them eight leagues away, where they stopped to camp till the next day. When the Alibamons got to that spot, they asked the two Frenchmen what they had come to the neighborhood of Passacol to do. The two Frenchmen, who had a good understanding of the Mobilien tongue [13] in which the Alibamons had addressed them, replied that they had come to hunt game for the Governor of Passacol. Two of the chiefs of the party told them that they would take them hunting next day and see whether they were telling the truth.

And indeed the next morning the two savages gave their guns back to the two Frenchmen and took them hunting. Luckily for the two Frenchmen, they located

---

[12] Anse des Chaqtos means Chatot Cove or Chatot Hook. The folk of Mobile have irreparably changed it to Choctaw Point, although Choctaws never lived there.

[13] Mobilian, which is sometimes called Choctaw trade or Chickasaw trade language, was the lingua franca of Southern tribes. Many place names and tribal names in use today are derived from Mobilian.

a herd of buffalo, at which the two Alibamons in their eagerness fired at once; but the Frenchmen, who had not yet fired their shots, turned their weapons on the two savages instead of shooting at the buffaloes and killed them both. After scalping them, in keeping with the custom of war in that country, they went very far off and hid during the remainder of the day, carrying away the savages' two guns and everything they had on their persons. When the day ended, they walked all night, and three days later reached Mobile, where they gave MM. Dartaguet and de Bienville an account of what had happened to them; and, for proof, they exhibited the scalps and the guns of the two savages.

This deed will perhaps seem cruel of Frenchmen [to those who] [14] do not know the ways of savages. The only reason why the savages had refrained from killing those two Frenchmen at once was that they intended to keep them for burning with slow fire in their village, which is the treatment those nations usually give their enemies, as I have already reported elsewhere.

In this year M. Dartaguet had a little flat boat built, of around sixty tons, for the convenience of transferring goods from Isle Dauphine to Mobile.

[14] ". . . à ceux qui," supplied from Spofford, p. 217.

Chapter 11

The Year 1709

A new Fort Mobile is established near the Bay—M. La Vigne Voisin builds a fort on Isle Dauphine—Fifteen Chactas savages clash with fifty Alibamons

AT THE beginning of this year, Fort Mobile and the residents' settlement near the fort were so inundated by the overflow of the river that only high places were without damage.

MM. Dartaguet and de Bienville, seeing that, according to the accounts given them by the savages, we should often be in danger of such floods, decided to move Fort Mobile. They chose the place where we had located the Chaqtos savages—at the cove [1] on Baye de la Mobile, on the right. The savages whose grounds we were taking were given another place to live, two leagues below on our right side going down to the sea, on the bank of Rivière-aux-Chiens.

M. Pailloux,[2] assistant adjutant, went with our officers to this place, where it had been decided to have the fort built. He laid out the outer wall of the fort requisite for the interior and then the distances for the empty spaces of the cleared-off area outside the fort; also, beyond those

[1] Choctaw Point is the bayside edge of modern Mobile. The French were choosing the site of this city. L'Anse des Chaqtos, Choctaw Point, is south of the Bankhead Tunnel beneath Mobile River. The date of the founding of Mobile is commonly accepted as 1711.

[2] Jacques Barbazan de Pailloux, an officer who came to Louisiana in 1707. He held important commands at Mobile, Natchez, and New Orleans. See Rowland's biographical note, in Rowland and Sanders, *MPA*, II, 44.

distances, he assigned to the residents each family's location, giving them each a plot of ground twelve toises wide by twenty-five long. At the same time he marked the place for the soldiers' barracks. The residence of the priests was to the left of the fort and faced the sea. Work on this establishment continued through the whole year.

During that time, M. La Vigne Voisin,[3] a captain of St. Malo, arrived at Isle Dauphine, where he dropped anchor; then he came to Mobile to call on MM. Dartaguet and de Bienville; and after stopping there for several days he asked them to permit him to have a fort built on Isle Dauphine. This pleased them. He did not fail to have the work started as soon as he got there. At his fort he had embrasures constructed to contain cannon which secured the entrance to the harbor from all ships that might come there with the purpose of making a landing.

Also, at the place where the residents of the island lived, he had a very pretty church built. The front of the church faced the harbor where the ships were, and people in the ships could come there in a moment and hear Mass. This was the reason that several *habitans* of the environs of Mobile went to Isle Dauphine and settled. M. de La Vigne returned to France a month later.

This year a savage nation named the Oumas deserted their settlement and came to dwell on the bank of the Missicipy River near the Rivière des Chetimachas. Another savage nation named the Tonicas, among whom

[3] Probably the uncle of Jacques Esnould de Livaudais, pilot of the port of New Orleans, who founded the Creole family De Livaudais in Louisiana. Jacques had served his apprenticeship as seaman under his uncle, Lavigne Voisin, whom Bienville called a "famous corsair." Jacques's family came from St. Malo, and so did the La Vigne Voisin, a captain, mentioned by Pénicaut. King, *Creole Families*, pp 212–13.

M. Davion resided—the priest who had expected to lose his life for breaking their idols—went to settle in the location that the Oumas had vacated.

This year a party of fifteen Chactas who were on a bear hunt were encountered in the woods by a party of fifty Alibamons, their enemies. The Chief of the Chactas, named Le Dos Grillé,[4] a man of courage, was not in the least shocked by the number of Alibamons; and although he was straightway shot from a very long range, the bullet piercing his cheek, he drew out the bullet, which had lodged in his mouth, put it in his gun, and with that bullet killed the man that had wounded him. Instantly he drew his fifteen men together in a rather high spot, from which, each posted behind a tree, they killed more than thirty of the Alibamons, who did not dare resist further and fled, deserting their dead and wounded. The Chactas had only three men killed and three or four very slightly wounded. They brought the thirty Alibamon scalps to MM. Dartaguet and de Bienville at our fort and two deer they had killed on the way. As a reward for their bravery they were presented with gifts of merchandise and were given much powder and lead. The Chief of these Chactas had killed eight as his share, badly wounded as he was by the shot in the mouth.

Several residents of Mobile went this year to settle on the seashore at a place called Miragouin,[5] five leagues

[4] The translation is Broiled Back or Grilled Back. This chief may have got his name from the scars of wounds inflicted upon him during such torture as that inflicted by the Koroa on their captives. On the other hand, he may have had a reputation as torturer himself.

[5] Marked Miragouine on the detailed inset on Delisle's "Carte de la Louisiane," 1718. It was a place on Mon Louis Island, just north of Cedar Point. Here is an instance of a place named for a man or the man for the place. This spot on Mon

from Mobile going toward Isle Dauphine, one league above Rivière-aux-Poulles.

We spent the rest of the year improving the new fort we were building on the seashore. We set up two batteries outside the fort, each of twelve pieces of cannon, which faced the sea.

Louis Island was granted to a man named Nicolas Bodin, *dit* Miragouin, according to Hamilton (*Colonial Mobile*, pp. 154–55). Hamilton, thinking *Miragouin* to be a variant of *maringouin*, "mosquito," indulged in some light punning humor at the expense of Nicolas Bodin, the "mosquito" knight. But this place name, in my opinion, has no connection with *maringouin*, "mosquito." It is merely a variant of *miragoane*, which is the French form of Spanish *miraguano*, "a low palm of tropical areas." Miragoane is the name of a city and bay in Haiti. The entry for the baptism of Nicolas Bodin's child (Mobile Baptismal Records, January 22, [1719]) gives Bodin's name as Sieur de Miragouanne or Miragouonne. Hamilton himself knew another entry, for 1762, plainly denying the mosquito jest: it gives Louis Alexandre Bodin *dit* Miragoine.

Chapter 12

The Year 1710

Old Fort Mobile is abandoned—MM. de Rémonville and de Waligny arrive in the frigate "La Renommée"—Description of the Apalaches

HE NEW Fort Mobile on the seashore being finished and the living quarters built, all the furniture and merchandise were moved there in boats. Some raftlike structures were made, on which the cannon were put and, in general, all supplies and effects that were at the old fort.

Likewise, the residents carried their possessions at the same time to the dwelling place that had been given them very close to the new fort; and the old one was entirely abandoned. Several days after we were well established at our new fort on the seashore, a ship came and anchored at the Isle Dauphine roadstead. This was the frigate named *La Renommée*, commanded by M. de Rémonville,[1] who was captain of it.

The Sieur de Waligny,[2] an officer who had been a post adjutant from his youth, had come in that ship, bringing twenty-five Frenchmen to add to the garrison.

---

[1] This may be the same Rémonville who, after La Salle's failure, wrote a memorial urging the colonization of the Mississippi. Hamilton, *Colonial Mobile*, p. 29.

[2] Also spelled Valigny. A letter dated "At Marly, September 9, 1710," gives permission to a Sieur Jean Baptiste Valigny to go to Louisiana. (Rowland and Sanders, *MPA*, III, 155.) The Sieur Valigny who had a wooden leg was, in the opinion of Governor Cadillac, a quarrelsome blunderer who had held no higher office than master-at-arms. Lamothe Cadillac to Pontchartrain, Fort Louis of Louisiana, October 26, 1713, *ibid.*, II, 194.

The munitions and food supplies were unloaded and stored in the warehouses in the fort on Isle Dauphine, and troops assigned to guard them. Also, many people came and settled on the island. Something of a little town developed, as all the free persons settled there who came in the ships from France.

A while later, M. de Rémonville sailed for Vera Cruz, by order of MM. Dartaguet and de Bienville, to' trade merchandise there for flour and livestock, which we needed because the overflow that had occurred the year before had flooded all the houses of the savages and rotted the grain planted in the countryside; consequently, after that flood most of us were compelled to go into the woods and hunt buffalo and deer to keep ourselves alive.

M. Blondel,[3] a lieutenant of infantry, went with thirty soldiers to stay among the Chactas in order to subsist. The Sieur de Waligny went down Baye de la Mobile with twenty-five soldiers in the direction of Rivière-aux-Poissons,[4] taking, also, eight Apalaches savages with him that were quite good hunters.

These Apalaches are good Catholic Christians. They had been worn out with Spanish rule, under which they had lived for a long time and which they had deserted in 1705. Their village having been destroyed by the Alibamons, they had come and settled between the Mobiliens and the Tomez at a place that M. de Bienville had given them, together with the grains to plant their fields the

---

[3] Identified by Hamilton (*Colonial Mobile,* p. 67) as Philippe Blondel, who was later commandant at Natchitoches. He died at Natchitoches about 1721. Philippe Blondel belonged to Chateaugué's company on January 24, 1705. Mobile Baptismal Records.

[4] Now Fish River, on the eastern side of Mobile Bay.

first year; but the year we left the settlement at the first Fort Mobile, they followed us, and MM. Dartaguet and de Bienville assigned them a dwelling place on the bank of Rivière St. Martin, one league above us on the shore of the bay. The Taoüachas [5] were also given grounds on the river, extending down to one league above the Apalaches. They, too, had quit the Spaniards because of the wars of the Alibamons. They are not Christians like the Apalaches, who are the single Christian nation that has come from the direction of the Spaniards.

The Apalaches conduct divine service like the Catholics in France. Their big festival is St. Louis' Day. On the day before, they come and invite the officers of the fort to attend their village festival; and that day, with great feasting they regale all who come there, and particularly the French.

The priests from our fort go there and say high Mass, which the Apalaches hear quite reverently, singing the Psalms in Latin as is done in France and, after dinner, Vespers and the Benediction of the Holy Sacrament. On that day the men and women are dressed very decently: the men wear a kind of cloth overcoat; and the women wear cloaks and skirts of silk cloth in the French style, but haven't the least headdress, going bare-headed. Their hair, which is quite long and quite black, is plaited and hangs down their backs in one or two plaits, the way Spanish girls wear theirs. Those whose hair is too long fold it up to the middle of their backs and fasten it with a ribbon.

They have a church to which one of our French priests

[5] The Tawasa.

goes and says Mass every Sunday and every feast day. They have a baptismal font at which to baptize their infants, and at the side of the church a graveyard in which there is a cross. Here they are buried.

On St. Louis' Day, toward evening after the service is ended, they dress up in masks, men, women, and children. For the rest of the day they dance with the French who happen to be there and with other savages who come to their village on that day. They have cooked meat a-plenty with which to feast them. They love the French very much, and it must be confessed that the only thing savage about them is their language, which is a mixture of Spanish and Alibamon.

M. de Rémonville returned toward the end of the year with several sacks of flour; but he had not been able to do as much business as he would have wished, because the Governor of Vera Cruz would not permit him to engage in open trading. Some sacks of flour were sent to him out at the roadstead, with the command to go back at once.

A league from the fort, going toward the sea, M. de Bienville had a very pretty house built with a garden, which he had planted, and with extensive surrounding grounds, which he had plowed.[6]

[6] The French text of this paragraph, taken from Parkman, p. 211, is as follows: "Mᵣ. de Bienville fit batir a une lieue du fort du costé de la mer une tres belle maison avec un jardin quil y fit planter et baucoup [*sic*] de terres alentour quil fit cultiver." B. F. French's translation of this passage is as follows: "M. de Bienville has built himself a beautiful country house on the sea shore, about a league from the fort, which he has ornamented with a grove of orange trees, where he resides, most of the year, for his health." "Annals of Louisiana . . . By M. Penicaut," p. 106.

Chapter 13

The Year 1711

MM. Dartaguet and de Bienville send soldiers to the Illinois
to punish some Canadians causing disturbances there—Description
of the customs of the Cascassias Illinois: their religion, their weddings, their methods of hunting

T THE beginning of this year, several traders
from Canada came down from the Cascassias
Illinois with merchandise in peltries, which
they brought to Mobile to barter. They gave
letters to MM. Dartaguet and de Bienville from the Reverend Father Gabriel Marais,[1] a Jesuit, who requested
these gentlemen to send an officer with some soldiers to
put a stop to the disturbances caused by several Canadian
traders. Under the pretext of engaging in bartering there,
they were openly committing scandalous offences—de-
bauching the daughters and the wives of the Illinois and
dissuading them from being converted to our religious
faith. This hindered the propagation of the faith. Acting
on this information, MM. Dartaguet and de Bienville dispatched a sergeant up there several days later with twelve
men; I was one of the number.

When the sergeant got there, he left us with our boats
and went on foot to within two leagues of the bank of
the Missicipy, where the Cascassias Illinois settlement
stands. He delivered MM. Dartaguet's and de Bienville's

[1] Or Marest. After his second voyage to Louisiana, Iberville wanted to bring
this priest to the Biloxi area, having known him as chaplain of the Hudson Bay
expedition, years before. Delanglez, *French Jesuits*, p. 31.

letters to the Reverend Father Gabriel Marais, who advised him to wait till early next morning to surprise those Canadian rakes in their beds. During the night the sergeant sent us word to come on to the Illinois, bringing with us all our merchandise which was in the two boats in which we had come up there. We got there two hours before day; but, on account of a warning they had had or for some other reason, the Canadians had been gone since the day before, and we found none of them. Our sergeant was for staying among the Illinois for some time, either to wait for the Canadians or perhaps to carry out the orders given him, as food supplies were greatly diminished at Mobile. So, for four months we remained among the Illinois, living by exchanging merchandise for their food, which is very cheap among them.

The Cascassias Illinois are hard-working and skillful in tilling the fields. They plow them with a plow, which has not yet been done elsewhere in all the Lower Missicipy. They acquired a knowledge of the plow from the Reverend Jesuit Fathers more than sixty years ago, as early as the time they were residing near Lake Pinthouy.[2] The Reverend Jesuit Fathers had come there by way of Canada to get down to these Illinois and had converted almost all of them to the Catholic religion.

The region in which they are presently settled is one of the finest in all Louisiana and one of the best for fertility of the soil. Wheat grows there as fine as any in

---

[2] On Lake Pimitoui, now Lake Peoria, La Salle built Fort Crèvecoeur, on the south side "one mile from the end of the lake." On this lake, too, Tonti built the second Fort St. Louis, on the north side "one and one half miles from the lower outlet." (Alvord, *The Illinois Country*, pp. 81–82, 100.) Tonti's fort was called Fort Pimitoui as well as Fort St. Louis.

France, and all kinds of vegetables, roots, and grasses. Also, they have all kinds of fruits, of an excellent taste. It is among the Illinois that one finds the most beautiful prairies along the bank of the Missicipy; here they graze horses which they buy from the Cadodaquioux [3] in exchange for merchandise. On these prairies, too, they have a great deal of livestock, such as bullocks, cows, etc. Also at their settlement are many fowl of every kind; and, moreover, they have fishing in the stream,[4] and in the Missicipy River two leagues from their village, where they catch a great many fish; so they do not lack any of the necessities and comforts of life.

Near their village they have three mills to grind their grains: namely, one windmill belonging to the Reverend Jesuit Fathers, which is used quite often by the residents, and two others, horse mills, owned by the Illinois themselves.

The Cascassias Illinois women are very skillful: they commonly spin buffalo hair, which is as fine as wool off an English sheep. This wool is spun as fine as silk and is very white. With this they make materials which they dye in three colors, such as black, yellow, and deep red. Out of this they make dresses that are almost like the dresses of the women of Brittany or else like the dressing gowns of our ladies of France, which hang down to the floor—if to

[3] The Kadohadacho, or Caddo, Indians in northwest Louisiana had long been in contact with Spaniards north of the Rio Grande, from whom they had obtained horses.

[4] That is, in the small Kaskaskia or Okaw River on which they dwelt. Spofford, p. 235, is a little clearer than Clermont: ". . . et ils ont la peche dans la Riviere de leur nom qui passe proche leur Village et dans le fleuve du Missicipy a deux lieües de leur Village."

their collar a coif were sewed to cover the head.[5] They wear beneath their dresses a petticoat and a corset that comes halfway down their thighs. They sew with deer-tendon thread, which they make in this way: when the deer tendon is quite free of flesh, they dry it in the sun twice in twenty-four hours, and after beating it a little they stretch the tendon-thread as fine and as white as the most beautiful Mechlin thread, and it is still very strong.

The Illinois are quite fond of good eating and very often feast one another. Their favorite dish is the flesh of dog or tamed wolf, which they raise in their village.

The majority of the Illinois are Catholic Christians. They have in their village a rather large church in which there is a baptismal font. This church is quite clean on the inside. There are three chapels, the main one of the choir and two side chapels. They have a belltower, with a bell. They attend high Mass and Vespers quite regularly. The Reverend Jesuit Fathers have translated the Psalms and the hymns from Latin to their language. At Mass or Vespers the Illinois sing the stanzas in turn with the French that live among them; for example, the Illinois sing one stanza of the Psalm or the hymn in their language, and the French the following stanza in Latin, and so on with the remaining ones, and in the key in which they are sung in Europe among Catholic Christians.

As regards marriage among them, when a Frenchman or an Illinois has the intention of marrying one of their

[5] The French reading in Spofford, p. 236, is: "Elles Sen font des robes qui sont a peu pres commes les robes des femmes du Bretagne ou autrement comme les robes de Chambre de nos dames de frances [*sic*] qui trainent jusqua terre; au col des quelles seroit cousu une coeffe qui couvriroit la tete."

daughters, he sends a present in keeping with his means to the girl's brother, for neither father nor mother can give a girl in marriage if they have a boy; but upon the consent of the son, the girl's brother, the entire marriage agreement depends. Usually, then, the suitor sends to the girl's brother—oftentimes without having spoken to him—a present in keeping with his means. If the brother receives it and gives his consent, he invites his parents [6] to come to his house and asks their advice as to whether he will be doing the right thing if he gives his sister in marriage to the suitor who asks for her. If the parents speak of him as an honorable man, then the brother gives each parent a portion of the present sent him by the suitor; and this very same day the parents send the girl's brother a more substantial present than the one they have received. When the brother has received all the presents from his parents, he has them carried at once to the suitor's home; and the next day the suitor comes to pay his respects to the girl's brother and her father and mother. Together they go to the Reverend Jesuit Fathers' to have themselves written into the marriage register. Three banns are published on three consecutive Sundays or feast days; and they are afterwards made man and wife at Mass, as is done in France. Ordinarily the suitor is expected to give the wedding feast, at his home; but on the day before the wedding, each kinsman that intends to be there sends a piece of meat to the suitor; and next day, the day of the wedding, when the party leaves the church, the kinsmen escort the bridegroom and his wife to his home and there

6 ". . . ses parents," which could mean his kinsmen.

the wedding feast is given. It continues till about night, with dances in the local fashion.

If, on the other hand, the suitor who has sent the present is not accepted, his gift is returned to him that very day.

If Christian parents in France, at the time their near kinsmen are married, employed the same charity that these Catholic savages practise toward their kinsmen—in sending them, instead of a little present like the one they have received, another much more substantial, which serves to establish them in marriage and maintain them in their standard—one would not see in France so many poor families ashamed of having to beg. There would not be so many girls, even of good family, confined against their will in a convent, where most of them, by their grumbling and despair, call down the curse of heaven upon themselves and upon those who have forced them to enter the cloister.

In regard to their warfare, they are very brave and use both gun and bow. They are not without feeling for their prisoners, as the rest of the savages are. If they capture young children, they raise them up in their village, having them instructed in the Catholic religion by the Reverend Jesuit Fathers; if the captives are men that could injure them, or are old men, they break their heads.

Usually they hunt with the bow. When they have shot their arrows at a buffalo that flees, often taking away the arrows stuck in his body, they outrun him, they are so quick and nimble; and when they pass by the buffalo they tear the arrows from him on the run and use them again and again to shoot the same buffalo until he drops. For hunting bear and deer they use the gun. They have hunting grounds nearly eighty leagues long, where there is every kind of game in abundance. These grounds converge upon Canada.

After four months we went down to Mobile, where we no longer found M. Dartaguet. He had sailed back to France.

Chapter 14

The Year 1712

M. de la Mothe de Cadillac arrives as Governor of Louisiana
—M. de St. Denis sets out to ascend the Rivière Rouge—Strange
experience the author had among the Colapissas—M. de St. Denis
reaches the Nassitoches—His journey to Rivière du Nord—The
Assinaïs described

OWARD THE beginning of this year, M. de
la Mothe de Cadillac [1] and M. Durigoüin arrived at Isle Dauphine, the first to serve as
Governor-General of Louisiana and the second
as director-general, their expenses paid by M. de Croisat,[2]
to whom His Majesty had ceded the commerce of Louisiana. They came on the ship named *Le Baron de la Fosse*,
of which M. de la Jonquière [3] was captain. On this ship,
too, came M. Duclos as commissary-general.[4] M. de la

[1] La Mothe–Cadillac was made governor of Louisiana on May 15, 1710, but did
not arrive in the colony until June 5, 1713. (Surrey, *Calendar of Manuscripts in
Paris Archives*, I, ix, and Rowland and Sanders, MPA, II, 162–63 and n. 1.) This
caustic-tongued Gascon is better known nowadays for the automobile that bears his
name and for the small post he founded on the strait (*détroit*) between Lake St.
Clair and Lake Erie than he is for his six years as governor of all Louisiana under
the proprietary government of Antoine Crozat. It is true that he did little in
Louisiana that merits fame. Perhaps he was frustrated and sick. Certainly he was
in a bad humor all the time. Cadillac is interesting in Louisiana chiefly for his dislike
of the country and the people. Even after he was removed and sent back to
France his pen and his tongue continued the attack on Louisiana—at the very
time, too, when the Company of the West was advertising the colony as an
earthly paradise—until he was thrown in the Bastille for a period of cooling. Both
his letters and his reports from Louisiana are on a high level of the literature of
invective.

[2] Antoine Crozat held a monopoly of Louisiana from 1713 till 1717.

[3] Sometimes spelled Jonquières.

[4] From December 24, 1712, till November 12, 1716. (Surrey, *Calendar of Manu-*

Mothe brought his wife with him, his sons and his daughters, with their servants. There were also twenty-five Breton girls,[5] who had come of their own accord, and, in addition, a great supply of munitions and food, together with a great deal of merchandise, which M. Durigoüin, who was in charge of it, ordered to be stored both in the warehouses of Isle Dauphine and in those at Mobile.

M. de la Mothe had M. de Croisat's instructions to send detachments out both in the direction of the Spaniards, to sound them out over trade, and in the direction of the Illinois, to discover mines; and a few days after his arrival he sent M. de Jonquière, the captain of the ship, with M. Durigoüin,[6] the director, to Vera Cruz among the Spaniards to trade the goods he had brought from France for livestock, which we badly needed. But the Governor of Vera Cruz would not even hear of any trade; he merely had M. de la Jonquière given some food supplies and some livestock, which he sent to his ship out at the roadstead, along with the order to set sail immediately and go home.

During this time M. de St. Denis,[7] who was a very cou-

---

scripts in Paris Archives, I, x.) Duclos' experience in Peru and in Caribbean ports supposedly had prepared him to foster Crozat's trade with the Spaniards. Rowland and Sanders, *MPA,* II, 74–75 and note.

[5] Cadillac gives twelve as the number of girls that he and his wife had attempted to chaperone on the way across. (Lamothe Cadillac to Pontchartrain, Oct. 26, 1713, in Rowland and Sanders, *MPA,* II, 184). Bitterly he complains to the minister about the captain of the ship, the steward, and particularly about a half-pay captain named De Richebourg—all of whom had misbehaved either with or toward these girls, so that only three of the girls had found husbands between the arrival of the ship, on June 5, and October 26, 1713. One girl had died. Half-pay captain De Richebourg is accused, too, of corrupting Cadillac's wife's maid as well as the girls. (*Ibid.,* II, 184–85 and Cadillac's marginal notes.)

[6] Given as Sieur Dirigoin in an abstract of a letter from Sieur Dirigoin to Antoine Crozat, late October, 1713 (in Rowland and Sanders, *MPA,* III, 174–78). The letter tells of Dirigoin's inability to sell goods at Havana or Vera Cruz.

[7] Louis Juchereau de St. Denis.

rageous officer and venturesome man on war parties as well as in the discovery of mines, was summoned down to Mobile by M. de la Mothe. When he got there, M. de la Mothe engaged him to go to the Nassitoches and from the Nassitoches by land to Mexico among the Spaniards to sound out the freedom of trade in that direction.[8] M. de la Mothe made a contract with him in the name of the Company to stock him with ten thousand livres' worth of merchandise. We loaded five boats with it. He took also a passport from M. de la Mothe and twenty-two Frenchmen, of whom I was one. After he had embraced M. de la Mothe and M. Duclos, we got in our boats and rowed as far as Biloxi, where M. de St. Denis lived.

The day after we got there he sent me in a boat, with two Biloxi savages, to the Colapissas village [9] to get the Nassitoches and bring them with their families to Biloxi, so that he could then take them along with him to their old home on the Rivière Rouge. I was the person that had escorted them for M. de St. Denis to the Colapissas village five years before, so that they could live with the Colapissas. The night I got there, I was given a fine reception by the chiefs of the Colapissas and the Nassitoches;

---

[8] Pénicaut was apparently ignorant of the immediate cause Cadillac had for sending St. Denis overland to the Texas Indians and the Rio Grande. Father Hidalgo, a Spanish priest, had felt so frustrated by the withdrawal of the Spaniards from the east Texas area that he had written a letter in 1711 to the French priests of Louisiana, inviting the French to "pacify the tribes hostile to the Asinai [Texas Indians]." Although his letter seems treasonable, Father Hidalgo had believed that if the French approached the area and became a threat to Spanish interests the Viceroy of Mexico would send troopers back to the area. Thus Spanish missions could safely be re-established. The Hidalgo letter, after two years of traveling among Indians, came to Cadillac in May, 1713, according to Herbert E. Bolton, *The Spanish Border Lands* (New Haven, 1921), pp. 222–23. But see the date of Cadillac's arrival, n. 5 above.

[9] On the north side of Lake Pontchartrain.

but the morning of the next day, when I set out with the Nassitoches and their families, the Colapissas were seized with jealousy or, rather, with rage. Seeing that the Nassitoches women, too, were leaving and were going away with their husbands, they fell upon the Nassitoches with blows of guns, arrows, and hatchets and killed seventeen quite close to me without my being able to stop them. All I could do was save the Chief by keeping him behind me. They seized more than fifty women or girls—the others, men and women, having fled right and left into the woods, wherever they could. When night fell, they came like lost sheep and joined me on the shore of the lake. All that I could get together I took away to M. de St. Denis, who was greatly surprised at this grievous occurrence. He intended to take revenge for this at another opportunity and to make the Colapissas give back the women and the girls they had taken from the Nassitoches.

While waiting for the rest of the Nassitoches, we stayed for several days at M. de St. Denis' home, to which there must have come some thirty more. At last, after moving our merchandise from Biloxi to the bank of the Missicipy, we put it in our boats and set out for the Rivière Rouge. On our way upstream we paused at the Manchacq,[10] where we killed about fifteen buffaloes. Again on the following day we went ashore to hunt. We killed eight buffaloes and just as many deer. From there we went straight to the Tonicas' village, two leagues above the Rivière Rouge, to pick up there all the food supplies that we could. M. de St. Denis talked to the Chief of the Tonicas and by offering pay induced him to come with us, as

10 Bayou Manchac.

well as fifteen of his savages, the best hunters; this he gladly did.

So, all together we entered the Rivière Rouge,[11] the embouchure of which flows east into the Missicipy, coming from the northwest. After we had gone up it for eight leagues we found a river flowing into the Rivière Rouge on the right side going upstream; it is called Fourche des Oüachitas [12] because it forks before it flows into the Rivière Rouge. Four leagues from there, going upstream, we found a large prairie on the left side. Four leagues more upstream, one finds a river called the Saline.[13] Six leagues upstream on the left one comes to a small creek that flows down from a village four leagues from there. This village is called Toux Enongogoulas [14] in savage, which means Nation of Stones, and it is built at the foot of a chain of mountains running from north to south. The savages' huts are made like the Natchez' and roofed in the same way. They live in the same fashion, as they resided with the Natchez for a long time—until the wars they fought with each other forced them to leave and seek refuge in this place.

[11] The Red River, in Louisiana.

[12] Below its fork with the Tensas River, the Ouachita now takes the name Black River. Fourche des Ouachitas was named for a small Indian tribe in northeast Louisiana. Read, *Louisiana Place-Names*, pp. 47–48.

[13] Saline Bayou, separating Rapides and La Salle parishes, is in the right position for identification with the Saline.

[14] Parkman, p. 226, has Touxenongogoulas. Both Swanton and Hodge identify these Indians as the Avoyelles, belonging to the Natchez group of Muskhogean Indians. (Swanton, *Indian Tribes of the Lower Mississippi Valley*, p. 24; Hodge, *Handbook*, I, 118.) Professor Read (*Louisiana Place-Names*, p. 6) traces a form of the name, Tassenogoula, back to Choctaw *Tasannuk*, "flint," plus *okla*, "people." But Read got this form from B. F. French ("Annals of Louisiana . . . By M. Penicaut," p. 116). This is not Pénicaut's word, but apparently a poor transcription of the form Tassenocogoula in Iberville's log of the *Badine* (Margry, *Découvertes*, IV, 178–79).

Nine leagues higher up on the right side going upstream, one comes to a waterfall as wide as the river. Here
we found it necessary to carry our merchandise and our
boats above the falls; and one league upstream we found
another one, where we had to do the same thing. Three
leagues higher up, still going upstream, one finds a branch
of the Rivière Rouge extending for twelve leagues and
then flowing into a small lake, which is two leagues long
and a half league wide. On the right side of this lake are
very high rocky banks. Four leagues from the outlet of
the lake is a rocky mountain. Two leagues higher still, on
the left going upstream, one finds a lake eight leagues in
circumference and two leagues across, through which
this branch of the Rivière Rouge flows. Five leagues upstream, one finds a very high mountain on the bank of
the river, called Écort de la Croix.[15]

One league upstream one takes a branch of the river
on the left; at this spot we came upon the rest of the
Nassitoches, who had come overland and had got there
ahead of us. They had with them a savage nation of their
friends—some two hundred men without their women
and children. These savages were named Doustiony.[16]
After the loss of their grains, they had been unwilling to
go down to the Colapissas village with the Nassitoches.
For five consecutive years they had been wandering here
and there, living solely from hunting, fruits, and potatoes.
They followed us to the Nassitoches village, which is
nine leagues upstream on an island that the river forms
by dividing into two branches, flowing all around it.

---

[15] I have not found the modern name of this bluff.
[16] A Caddo tribe. Hodge, *Handbook,* I, 399.

When M. de St. Denis got there, he assembled the chiefs of the Doustiony and the Nassitoches and told them, in the presence of the Chief of the Tonicas, that they must sow seed in their fields, and that he was going to have grains distributed among them, which he had brought along for that very purpose; for henceforth there would always be Frenchmen living among them,[17] and in the future theirs would be the responsibility of feeding the Frenchmen who stayed there; therefore he exhorted them to work at the task unceasingly and informed them that they would have nothing to fear from other savages as long as they all stood closely united. Two or three days after we had rested, M. de St. Denis had some hatchets and picks given to the Doustionis and to the Nassitoches. They cut down trees for us and brought them to us so that we could construct two houses. We built these in their village—one to contain our merchandise and the other, the larger, to shelter us.

After a few days, M. de St. Denis made up his mind to try to locate the Spaniards with twelve Frenchmen, fifteen Tonicas and just as many Nassitoches, who came with us to serve as guides. Ten Frenchmen were left at the Nassitoches village to protect the merchandise. M. de St. Denis told them not to leave the village till he got back.

We went overland as far as the Assinaïs,[18] because

[17] This prediction proved relatively true; and St. Denis himself spent his middle years and old age as commandant at Natchitoches. He was always able to rule or lead the tribes around him. As Indian diplomat, he was without peer among the French, who as a nation were generally more suasive among Indians than the English were.

[18] The Hasinai, one of the leading Caddo tribes. Hasinai means "our own people." For the name Hasinai, the Yatasi used a word that developed into Tejas, or

the river above the Nassitoches is choked with obstructions of wood.[19] After we had traveled for twenty-two days we reached the Assinaïs. On this journey we had lived off the ends of our guns, that is, from the hunting we did when we stopped from time to time for that purpose. We were using for a mark [20] an ear of corn and a strip of buffalo skin.

As soon as the Assinaïs saw us, they were greatly astonished: they had never seen Frenchmen—only a few Spaniards who are miserable people that go quite naked and are a mixture of savages and Spaniards, although for more than five years, however, they had not seen any—not since they had left their village. They sang their calumet of peace to M. de Bienville,[21] which lasted three days, and when it was ended, M. de St. Denis gave them presents to persuade them to serve us as guides in the search for the Spaniards. In their village we found a woman named

---

Texas. Accordingly, the Hasinai are the Texas Indians. (Hodge, *Handbook*, I, 179–83). Hasinai is the Indian name of the Caddo confederacy.

[19] ". . . remplie d'embarras du bois." The great raft beginning above Natchitoches made Natchitoches the head of navigation on the Red River. The raft was over fifty miles long.

[20] The word *marque* in this sense puzzled both Margry and B. F. French. Margry (*Découvertes*, V, 499) wrote "pour marque (?)." French apparently took the word *marque* as a copyist's aberration from *manger* as noun. The French text (Spofford, pp. 254–55) reads as follows: "Nous avions pour marque un Epy de bled et un Morceau de peau de boeuf." B. F. French ("Annals of Louisiana . . . By M. Penicaut," p. 118) gives this translation: "Our rations consisted of an ear of corn, and a piece of buffalo meat." But *marque* is only a mark of identification used by the French to distinguish their own Indian companions, particularly scouts, from strange and potentially dangerous Indians they might see along the way. However the ear of corn was used as a mark, the strip of buffalo skin was probably worn as an arm band. Cf. a similar use of *marque* in Dumont de Montigny's *Mémoires*, II, 99–101.

[21] At first view, Bienville seems to be an error for St. Denis, since Bienville was not present. Still, it is quite possible that the Indians sang, before St. Denis, a calumet to his superior officer, Bienville, *in absentia*. Parkman, p. 230, may have the correct reading: "Ils chanterent leur calumet de paix qui dura trois jours," omitting the name of the French chief so honored.

Angélique, who had been baptized by Spanish priests on a mission to their village. She spoke Spanish, and as M. de St. Denis too spoke that language fairly well, he made use of her to tell the Assinaïs chiefs to let us have some guides for hire. They gave us four Assinaïs as guides, with whom we set out. We had not obtained a big supply of food from the Assinaïs, simply because we didn't find any there; therefore, it was again necessary for us, on this entire journey, to live off the ends of our guns; but, in spite of want and fatigue, we overcame all these troubles in the hope we had of being well repaid by making this exploration. We made one hundred and fifty leagues of route living in this manner, and after a month and a half of travel we reached their first village, named by the Spaniards Il Presidio del Norte.[22] We called it Rivière du Nord Village because it is located on the bank of the Rivière du Nord.

As soon as we got there, a Spanish captain of cavalry came and talked to M. de St. Denis to find out what he wanted. M. de St. Denis told him that he came as representative of the Governor of Louisiana to open trade with the Spaniards. This captain, who was a man of common sense, said that he was unable to give him the answer until he had first sent one of his cavalrymen with a letter to the Governor of Caoüil [23] to learn the answer and that M. de

[22] This Spanish military post was named San Juan Bautista. The name commonly given to this presidio was El Presidio del Norte, which comes from the old name of the Rio Grande: El Río Grande (or Río Bravo) del Norte. Hence the French name for the post, altered slightly to Rivière du Nord Village. According to Ross Phares, the presidio was located two leagues below the river. (*Cavalier in the Wilderness* [Baton Rouge, 1952], p. 53.) Margry incorrectly gives il Presidio del Porto. *Découvertes*, V, 500.

[23] Coahuila—not the modern state, but a town. On Delisle's "Carte de la Louisiane," 1718, Caouila is marked as a place in Nouveau Royaume de Leon, southeast of

St. Denis could stay with his men in the village until the answer came back. He had lodgings given to the soldiers and took M. de St. Denis off to lodge at his house, along with Jalot,²⁴ his valet-and-surgeon, and me. We went for a full six weeks without receiving any reply from the Governor of Caoüil because the Governor of Caoüil had sent to the Governor of Paraille,²⁵ another little town thirty leagues away, to get the answer and at the same time to find out his opinion about the matter. These two towns are sixty leagues from Rivière du Nord Village. Money is coined in both of them. Each of them may very well be three fourths of a league in circuit.

The Governor of Caoüil sent an officer with twenty-five cavalrymen to the village where we were, with the order to escort M. de St. Denis to Caoüil. M. de St. Denis went to Caoüil to talk to the Governor, being accompanied only by his valet Jalot. On setting out, M. de St. Denis told us to wait for him at this village, to which he would send us news of himself and his instructions. In this spot we remained for one month. I continued to lodge at the captain's, and our soldiers at their hosts', until we received orders from M. de St. Denis to go back to the

Parral. This old town of Coahuila may be the same place as Monclova in the state of Coahuila. Phares (*Cavalier in the Wilderness*, pp. 61 and 65) says St. Denis was later taken to Monclova, the capital of Coahuila; and he gives the governor's name as Don Gasparanya. Map No. 38, "Mexico," in *American Atlas* (Philadelphia, 1823), shows a "Pres. de Monclova or Coahuita [*sic*]."

²⁴ Médar Jalot, who was an early surgeon on the confines of Mexico. Mobile Baptismal Records show several persons by the name of Jalot living at Fort Louis de la Mobile.

²⁵ Parral was, according to H. E. Bolton (*Rim of Christendom* [New York, 1936], p. 20 and p. 246), the capital and residence of the governors of the kingdom of Nueva Viscaya. Margry (*Découvertes*, V, 501) has "Pavaille (?)" because the penman of Clermont wrote an *r* resembling a *v*.

Nassitoches, because the Governor of Caoüil, after examining his passport, had decided to send him to the Viceroy of Mexico, three hundred leagues from the village where we were. It was not until the following year, however, that he left Caoüil to go to Mexico.

As for us, after getting our orders, we had to make up our minds to leave. It was not without sorrow that we left Rivière du Nord Village. The Spanish girls there were very agreeable and were very much nettled at seeing us leave. Before I departed I expressed my great thanks to the captain at whose house I had lodged along with M. de St. Denis. He was named Dom Pedros de Vilesca.[26] He had two daughters; the elder, who was named Dona Maria, was afterwards married to M. de St. Denis upon his return from Mexico. I shall give an account of his *galante* story in its proper place. So, we departed with much sorrow and little food for the road we had to travel. We were two months getting back to the Assinaïs village, because we often had to stop to kill game, as we had nothing else to live on.

When we reached the Assinaïs we remained several days so that we could rest and get food supplies. At the time we got there, very few savages were in their village; the others had gone away to wage war against another

[26] The commandant at the Presidio del Norte was Captain Diego Ramón. And not the commandant, but his son Diego, was father of the seventeen-year-old girl here called Doña María. Natchitoches, Louisiana, records give her name as Emanuelle Sanche de Navarro, but this is the writing of Frenchmen, for there is no autograph. This young Spanish heroine, reared at an outpost of Spain, could not sign her name. She may indeed have been called María in her own family when Pénicaut knew her. Perhaps all girls in her family were given María as a part of their names, in honor of the Virgin Mary. Four of the five daughters later born to St. Denis and Emanuelle Sanche de Navarro had Marie in their names. See Phares, *Cavalier in the Wilderness*, pp. 50–55, 116.

savage nation named the Kitaesches.[27] These savages make war quite differently from those along the bank of the Missicipy, for they all go on horseback, armed with a quiver made of buffalo hide, filled with arrows, which hangs slung over the shoulder behind their backs. They have a bow and in their left arm a small shield of buffalo hide with which they ward off arrows. On their bridles they use no other bit than a horsehair rope which passes through the horse's mouth. Their stirrups are held up by a horsehair rope that is tied to four folds of doeskin, which serve them for a saddle. Their stirrups are merely small boards, three inches wide and five inches long, upon which they put their feet to mount the horse and to hold themselves upon his back.

The day after we arrived at their village they came back from the war. They were one hundred and fifty men, armed and mounted as I have just told. They sat a horse perfectly well. They brought back two prisoners with them of the six they had captured. They had eaten four of them on the way back. They placed these two prisoners on the main square, their hands tied behind their backs, in the middle of a guard of twelve savages, for fear they might get inside one of their huts; for the way of the savages is such that if a prisoner, in escaping either by force or cunning, can get inside one of their huts, his life will be spared and he will henceforth be considered one of that nation.

One hour later two frames were erected in the meadow at the edge of the village. These frames are merely two posts fixed in the ground four feet apart and nine feet

[27] The Kichai tribe of the Caddo confederacy. Hodge, *Handbook*, I, 682–83.

high, on top of which a bar extends from one post to the other. To this they tied the prisoners—with a rope by the two wrists—suspended on the air. Sunken in the ground underneath was a stake with a hole in it, through which passed a rope that was tied to the two ankles of those unfortunates, whom they stretched as tight as they could in order to hold them spread out on the air, their feet coming down to only fifteen inches from the ground. For half an hour they kept them so, evening and morning —in the morning with their faces turned toward the rising sun and in the evening toward the setting sun, without giving them anything to eat the first day. Oftentimes the prisoner is further made to dance against his will. And the morning of the second day they tied them up again in the same way, their faces turned toward the rising sun.

All the men and women of the village congregated around the frames on which those poor, drooping men were tied. Each family lighted its fire and put a pot full of water in front of it to heat. And when the sun was risen, four of the oldest savages, each with a knife in his hand, made incisions in the arms, in the thighs, and in the legs of the suspended men, whose blood ran down their bodies and fell off the ends of their feet, being caught in plates by four old men.[28] They carried this blood to two other old men, who tended the cooking of it in two kettles; and when this blood was done, they gave it to their women and children to eat. After the blood had been eaten, the two dead men were untied from the frames and were put on a table, where they were cut up

[28] The part played by this venerable foursome and the ceremonial behavior in general suggest an underlying religious motive in this case of cannibalism.

in pieces, which were distributed to all the congregation of the village, each family of which put some in its pot to cook. While this meat was cooking, they engaged in dancing. Afterwards they returned to their places and drew this meat from their pots and ate it.

I was so sickened at seeing this execrable feasting that I was squeamish for three days, and neither my comrades nor I could eat until after we had quit those cruel cannibals.[29]

Their neighbors, with whom they wage war,[30] are the Aquodocez,[31] ten leagues south of their village; the Cadodaquioux, forty leagues north; and the Trois Cannes,[32] also to the north, one hundred leagues away. All these nations wage war on horseback, and in their stables each man keeps three or four horses.

On our way back after leaving them, we passed through the village of the savages named the Yatacez,[33] whom we persuaded to come and live with us at the Nassitoches, where we conducted them together with their women and

[29] Parkman, p. 238, gives a slightly different reading: ". . . que j'en fus degouté pendant trois jours et mes compagnons de meme que moy et n'eurent point de repos que nous neussions quittés ces cruels Antopophages [sic], c'est pourquoy nous partimes deux heures apres, nous nous étions informés quelles etoient les nations qui leur sont les plus proches. Ils nous dirent quil y avoit les Aquodocez. . . ."

[30] The Parkman reading, given in n. 29, does not identify these tribes as enemies.

[31] I cannot identify this tribe, which, being in this particular locality, must have been Caddo or Attacapa. Caddo identified themselves by giving their village name, their tribal name, or the name of the confederacy. This name sounds like Spanish Agua Dulce, the name of the Fresh Water Indians in Florida.

[32] Not a French name meaning Three Canes, but a phonetic representation, in French, of the name Tawakoni. This is another Caddo tribe. Margry (Découvertes, V, 504), apparently being suspicious of the name, alters the reading to a dubious "Nacanes (?)." But the Nacanes, or Detsanayuka ("bad campers"), were a division of the Comanche. (Hodge, Handbook, I, 388; II, 701–702). The Trois Cannes, called Tuacana by the Spaniards, lived on the Trinity and the Brazos rivers in Texas.

[33] The Yatasi, another Caddo tribe. Hodge, Handbook, II, 993.

children and their cattle loaded with their grains and their personal belongings. They are residing there at present, and since that time they have always dwelt in complete unity with the Nassitoches.

On arriving at the Nassitoches we found the twelve Frenchmen whom M. de St. Denis had made stay there to guard the merchandise we left behind. We announced to them that we had M. de St. Denis' instructions to wait for him at the Nassitoches along with them. The Tonicas left us at this place and went home to their village.

During this year M. de la Mothe had many houses built on Isle Dauphine, where more and more people were settling every day.

Chapter 15

The Year 1713

M. de la Loire arrives at Mobile—The author goes down to the Natchez—An English nobleman, come to suborn the savages, is captured on the Missicipy—The savages in Carolina start an irruption—The Emperor of the savages comes to Mobile—A fort is built among the Alibamons and they make peace with the French

OWARD THE beginning of this year, in the month of February, M. de la Mothe intrusted several packets of letters for M. de Croisat to M. de la Jonquière, who was returning to France. The Sieur de Waligny went back with him. In the month of April the frigate named *La Dauphine*, commanded by Captain Belanger, arrived here. It was loaded with merchandise and munitions and food supplies which M. Durigoüin ordered to be moved to the warehouses at Mobile and to those on Isle Dauphine.

MM. de la Loire, two brothers,[1] had come on the ship. They came as representatives of M. de Croisat to be clerks in charge of merchandise. Some days later Captain Belanger went back to France in his frigate.

After the departure of Captain Belanger, M. de la

---

[1] The older brother was Marc Antoine de La Loëre Des Ursins, and the younger was Louis Auguste de La Loëre Flancour(t). They both became important men in Louisiana. Alvord (*The Illinois Country*, pp. 194–95) and Belting (*Kaskaskia under the French Regime*, p. 17) give the spelling as La Loëre. Since both Alvord and Belting had worked with Illinois records, I do not doubt that they were familiar with autographs of both brothers, who served in the Illinois Country as well as at Natchez and other posts in the Lower Missisippi area. But La Loire is a common spelling in documents of the times.

Mothe sent MM. de la Loire to the Natchez, with twelve persons in two boats to take them there with their personal belongings, because it had been decided to establish a trading office there.

During that time I was still at the Nassitoches, waiting for M. de St. Denis; but, seeing that we were going to give out of food, I went downstream in a boat with six of my comrades to buy some food at the Natchez, where I found MM. de la Loire. They informed us that they had been sent as representatives of M. de Croisat to keep the trading office at the Natchez.

Among the Natchez I found some slaves who were of the Chaoüachas [2] nation. They had been captured by a strong party of Chicachas, Yasoux, and Natchez, who had been in the Chaoüachas' village under the pretext of singing their calumet of peace; but these treacherous men had, on the contrary, gone there to make war, and the very first thing they did was kill the Grand Chief and several members of his family. They took eleven persons prisoner, among them the Grand Chief's wife, whom they brought to the Natchez.

I did what I could to rescue them, but I was never able to accomplish anything with the captors. I was surprised to find three Englishmen there [3] who had come to buy these slaves. They were the persons who had incited the nations to war among themselves so that by this means they might find a good number of slaves to buy and take back to Carolina.

[2] The Chawasha, or Shawasha, who lived south of New Orleans on Bayou Lafourche.

[3] Charles Town slave dealers.

During this same time, M. de la Loire received an order from M. de la Mothe to arrest an English nobleman named Mestriou,[4] who had come into Louisiana to suborn the savages in the Missicipy area. At that time he was with two Englishmen at the Natchez. Therefore, after sending back the boat, which I had had loaded with flour to be taken to our men at the Nassitoches, I remained, with two of the Frenchmen who had come with me from the Nassitoches, so as to support M. de la Loire in the order he had received. We did not dare arrest this nobleman in the village of the Natchez because they would have been opposed to that; but, not doubting that he would go back down the river, we decided to go down ahead of him and waylay him. However, before leaving, M. de la Loire wanted to see him and try to discover his plans; and, having approached him politely, he asked him whether he had come to make some purchases among the Natchez. The nobleman replied to him frankly that he had come with other Englishmen to try to buy some peltries among the savages; that he would afterwards go along the lower stretches of the river, calling on the Colapissas, and from

---

[4] Mestriou is Pénicaut's attempt to write Mister Hughes. Price Hughes was a Welshman whose ambition was to establish an English colony on the Mississippi River, perhaps at Natchez, for which he had already chosen the name Annarea in honor of Queen Anne. Also, his plan was to cut French communications by river between Louisiana and Canada. From Margry (*Découvertes*, V, 507) Hughes's name has got into history as Master You, which Pénicaut did not write. In altering Pénicaut's name for Hughes, Margry may have been following the reports of other Frenchmen who had trouble with the name. Such a scholar as Father Le Maire wrote Yousse (Mémoire quoted in Vernon W. Crane, *The Southern Frontier* [Durham, 1928], p. 107). Bienville spelled it Yous (Bienville to Pontchartrain, Fort Louis of Louisiana, June 15, 1715, in Rowland and Sanders, *MPA*, III, 182, n. 1). The Parkman ms., p. 243 and p. 247, has two entries for Mister Hughes: Mestroon and Mestron [*sic*]. Albert James Pickett gives Hughes's name as Hutchey. *History of Alabama* (2d ed., Charleston, 1851), I, 227–28.

there on the Chactas, where he had a warehouse containing a good deal of merchandise in peltries; and that from there he would return overland to Carolina with other Englishmen who also were trading in other savage villages.

After M. de la Loire had left him and come up to us, I advised him to let this nobleman leave first in order to avoid making him suspicious of us and that when he was one day ahead of us I was sure we could catch up with him and get at him.[5] M. de la Loire trusted me. We let the nobleman get a day's start. The next day we went downstream with two boats—twelve men that we were—to overtake him. While going, we learned from some hunters that he was at the Tonicas' village,[6] where a calumet had been sung to him. This compelled us to go still lower downstream and wait for him at the Manchacq, where we came across the savage nation named the Tinssas, who had abandoned their dwelling because of wars that the Oumas were continually making on them. We persuaded them to come with us to Mobile, where they would be given lands to live on. This they accepted.

We went ashore near the place where these savages had stopped. We cautioned them to wake us when they saw a boat pass in which there was an Englishman. This they did not fail to do as soon as he had gone on. Their chief showed us the presents he had given them and told us that he had crossed to the other side of the river, where he had

[5] Parkman, p. 244, has a different version of this sentence, adding a detail or so: "Apres que M^r. de la Loire l'eut quitté et quil nous eut raconté cela nous changeames de sentiment en le laissant partir devant nous, nous luy laissames meme deux jours d'avance parceque nous etions bien assuré de le ratraper. Il s'arreta en descendant au village des Tonicas."

[6] The Tunica had moved from Yazoo River to Wilkinson County, Mississippi.

FLEUR DE LYS

gone ashore to spend the night. We got in our boats and
made the two chiefs of the Tinssas savages get in our two
longboats and guide us there. We crossed the river and
went where he was.

We found him sketching. He was very much surprised
to see us coming up to him with our guns cocked and even
more surprised when M. de la Loire told him that he had
an order to take him to Mobile. He replied that we were
not at war and there was no accusation to be made against
him and that if we expected him to budge we would have
to seize him as a prisoner of war. M. de la Loire, who had
been ordered to arrest him at whatever cost, told him that
he was arresting him in the name of the King and at the
same time he seized hold of him. He wanted to put up
some resistance, but that was useless. Then and there we
made him get into one of our boats. The fifteen Chactas
savages he had with him followed us off. At the same time
the Tinssas nation followed us downstream. We gave
them all of the merchandise that was in the Englishman's
boat. We took him without stopping to Mobile and delivered him to M. de Bienville, as M. de la Mothe was
away,[7] having set out for the Illinois. M. de Bienville saw
to it that the Tinssas were given the dwelling place formerly occupied by the Chaoüachas,[8] two leagues from
our fort.

[7] Bienville to the Minister, June 15, 1715, shows Bienville complaining that
La Mothe-Cadillac had slipped away from Mobile without saying where he was
going. Then came a letter from Cadillac telling Bienville that Cadillac was on
his way to the Illinois to test a silver mine located by voyageurs. He had seen several
samples taken from the mine. Rowland and Sanders, MPA, III, 181.

[8] An error for the Taoüachas, the Tawasa, who had been settled near Fort Louis.
The Chaoüachas lived on Bayou Lafourche.

162

Lord Mestriou stayed only three days at Mobile, where he was very well entertained during these three days by M. de Bienville. He was then given his liberty to leave and did leave alone with an English boy [9] and reached Fort Passacol, where he was again very well entertained by Segnor Dom Gusman for three days, after which he departed alone, because his little English boy had sore feet. But while he was trying to reach the Alibamons, he was captured by a party of savages named the Tomez, who were out hunting. They broke his head.[10] We didn't learn that till two months afterwards.

M. de Bienville sent home the fifteen Chactas who had rowed the boat used by the nobleman during his trip on the Missicipy. When they got back, these savages did not fail to spread the news throughout all their villages that the English nobleman had been seized by the French. Immediately the Chactas killed the English that were at their village and pillaged the warehouse they had there. All the other savage nations did likewise. Thus the evil that the Englishman had attempted to do to the French fell on them.

The savages were not satisfied just with killing the

[9] This English boy may be the interpreter that Bienville said was captured with Hughes. If so, he may have had the same sort of training that little St. Michel had among the Chickasaws. (Bienville to Pontchartrain, June 15, 1715, in Rowland and Sanders, *MPA*, III, 181–82.) Or he may have been some English boy ransomed from Indians by the French at Mobile and now permitted to leave for Carolina with Price Hughes. They went from Mobile to Pensacola, "Passacol."

[10] According to Crane (*The Southern Frontier*, p. 107), citing several French sources, the Tohome Indians had "often felt the scourge of the Charles Town slave-dealers." This murder of Price Hughes, whether a spontaneous act of revenge on the part of the Tohome or a political assassination prompted by the French, ended the life of the most capable frontiersman and Indian agent the English had on the Mississippi at that time.

English that were among them; for the Canapouces, the Abécas,[11] the Alibamon savages, who are on the frontier of Carolina—without ever being incited by the French, for we were then at war with them—went with a party of three thousand men and made an irruption in Carolina, where they pillaged several settlements and took many prisoners—English men and English women and a great many Negroes—whom they took off with them. Hearing of this, M. de Bienville had all these Englishmen ransomed, men, women, and children, purposing to send back to their homes all those that wanted to go back. During this time, M. de la Loire returned to the Natchez, where I accompanied him with five other Frenchmen.

Toward the end of the year M. de la Mothe came back from the Illinois with his detachment. All those who had accompanied him on this journey told us that a very rich silver mine had been discovered. I have never learned the exact place where it is located or why there has been such a delay in opening it. Although the Company got the news along with several casks of ore taken from this mine to be assayed and afterwards sent fifty miners to Louisiana for this purpose—for all that, work has not begun on it yet.

A few days afterwards, the twenty Frenchmen who had remained at the Nassitoches—having tired of waiting for M. de St. Denis and being without food supplies —went down to Mobile, bringing the merchandise that was there.

During the same time, the Grand Chief of all the sav-

[11] The Canapouces, also called Cadapouces by Pénicaut, were the Catawbas, a Siouan tribe. The Abécas were Upper Creeks from the town Abihka.

ages in the direction of Carolina, whom all those savages called their Emperor, came accompanied by all the other chiefs of those nations, seeking M. de la Mothe at Mobile; and they sang their calumet of peace to him.

The Grand Chief of the Alibamons with his other chiefs was also with him there. He begged M. de la Mothe to grant peace. They proposed to have a fort built in their village at their expense, the kind that would be suitable for French people. M. de la Mothe took him at his word and dispatched M. de la Tour,[12] a captain, with two lieutenants and one hundred men. When M. de la Tour got there, he chose a very high place on the bank of their river, at a distance of two musket shots from their village; and here he had them build a fort about fifty toises square, with quarters for officers and soldiers and a large magazine for munitions and food supplies. Since that time this fort [13] has always been maintained, well provided with troops and munitions, because this is the corridor leading to and from Carolina.

[12] A Sieur La Tour was married to Marie, the daughter of the explorer Le Sueur, according to Hamilton (*Colonial Mobile*, p. 123). Marie could not sign her name when she acted as godmother on May 30, 1709 (Mobile Baptismal Records). Hamilton believed that Le Sueur's son-in-law was the M. de la Tour who built Fort Toulouse, described by Pénicaut in this passage. Hubert to the Council, Dauphin Island, October 26, 1717 (in Rowland and Sanders, *MPA*, II, 250), mentions Sieur de La Tour, a lieutenant in command at the Alabamas. This builder of the fort may be M. de la Tour Vitrac, who was captain of infantry of the Mobile garrison (Minutes of the Superior Council of Louisiana, March 29, 1724, *ibid.*, III, 393). De la Tour Vitrac died before March 25, 1729 (Messrs. Périer and De la Chaise to Directors of the Company of the Indies, March 25, 1729, *ibid.*, II, 635). The Minutes of the Superior Council show that De la Tour Vitrac owned tar works and that there had been complaint about objectionable leakage of tar in shipping.

[13] Fort Toulouse, near present-day Wetumpka, Alabama. Fort Jackson was later built on the site of the French fort.

Chapter 16

The Year 1714

M. Rogeon, a director, arrives in Louisiana—Treachery of the Natchez, who murder five Frenchmen—The author's daring undertaking—The French are avenged upon the Natchez—Fort built in their village and named Roselie

AS EARLY as February of this year, the flûte named *La Dauphine* arrived at the Isle Dauphine roadstead, commanded by Captain Belanger. He brought M. Rogeon [1] and his son. M. Rogeon came to be director, replacing M. Durigoüin. Also on the ship was M. de Varène,[2] an officer, and a great deal of merchandise and munitions. After his vessel was unloaded and he had received a packet of letters from

[1] Pickett, too (*History of Alabama*, I, 229), gives Rogeon as the name of the director who replaced Crozat's director Dirigoin. A better spelling of the name may be Raujon, which appears in letters of both Duclos and Bienville written in 1716 (in Rowland and Sanders, *MPA*, III, 199) while Crozat still had his monopoly. By November, 1719, plans were made to send director Raujon back to France, with his accounts, in the protective custody of a ship's captain. Minutes of the Council of Commerce, Dauphin Island, November 14, 1719, *ibid.*, III, 280–81.

[2] M. de Varène was a young nobleman who scandalized his family in France, and some people in Louisiana, by eloping either with a married woman or with a woman he had married secretly, if at all. Minutes of the Conseil de Marine for January 2, 1716, signed by Louis-Alexandre de Bourbon, Count de Toulouse, and Victor-Marie, Le Maréchal d'Estrées, contain the details of the story. Director Raujon, too, had got himself involved with this woman after helping the couple elope on the boat. When Sieur de La Varenne [*sic*] went on to the Illinois Country, apparently to escape the scandal known on the coast (this is his complaint), Governor Cadillac saw to it that the slanders should follow him. (The Council Minutes are printed in *MPA*, II, 209–17.) By October, 1717, the young nobleman had either married or proved wedlock to the satisfaction of the Church at Mobile, for on October 3, [1717], was baptized Marie Jeanne, child of the Sieur de la Vareine (his autograph is devarene Apuril) and his wife Dame Anne Quentin—born in legitimate wedlock. (Mobile Baptismal Records.) There is only slight chance that the two men are not identical.

M. de la Mothe for the Company, Captain Belanger did not long delay in going back, taking M. Durigoüin with him.

A little later, M. de la Loire, the elder, came down from the Natchez to Mobile. On the way down, he had met a boat in which four Frenchmen were going up to the Illinois to engage in trading with the goods they had in their boat. When they got to the Natchez, these four Frenchmen hired four Natchez savages to help them take their boat as high as the Illinois, as the current on the Missicipy was very rapid at that time. They went together as high as Le Petit Gouffre.[3] Here in the night the Natchez caught the four Frenchmen asleep, murdered them, and after stripping them threw them into the river. Later during the night they went back home to the Natchez, where they divided the goods that were in the boat and carried them into their huts.

I was at the Natchez at that time; and no matter what precautions they had taken, I did not fail to notice this, having seen in their huts some of the merchandise that those Frenchmen had brought in their boat. I reported it to young M. de la Loire, with whom his brother had left me to guard the merchandise in the warehouse the French had at the Natchez; but we pretended to know nothing about this. A little later, M. de la Loire, the elder, arrived from Mobile with three boats loaded with merchandise and fourteen Frenchmen. Also there was an officer named M. de Varène, who was having some goods of his own taken up to the Illinois. Before leaving Mobile, M.

---

[3] Ten miles below the mouth of Bayou Pierre, Mississippi. Schultz, *Travels on an Inland Voyage*, II, 129-30.

de la Loire had been ordered by M. de la Mothe to go up to
the Illinois and pay back the merchandise the Illinois had
lent him to pay off the savages who had been with the
party exploring for mines. M. de la Loire remained at the
Natchez two weeks, getting food supplies for his men.
Several times while he was there, the Natchez plotted to
kill us; but, even though we knew nothing about this at
the time, we always kept ourselves well on our guard
because we had learned about the murder of the four
Frenchmen, of whose death we gave a pretense of ignor-
ance.

We asked the Grand Chief of the Natchez for eight
men for hire, to leave with us in two days. He had them
notified at once.

Before leaving, M. de la Loire had a good deal of trouble
in persuading his young brother to stay to guard the
warehouse of Company merchandise, for he saw the evident danger that he ran, which would have been still
greater than we thought if God had not protected us.
After embracing this young man, we left him at the
Natchez greatly distressed over our having to leave him
behind; and we went off with the eight savages the Grand
Chief had given us to help us row up the river. When we
got in our boats, that traitor of a Grand Chief instructed
his savages, quite loud and in our presence, to do whatever we told them and not to approach the river bank
if we should find any people on the bank signaling for
us to come to them, for fear they might be people that
would wish to do us harm or make an attempt upon our
lives.

During the evening of the first day after we had left

the Natchez to go up to the Illinois, and while we were camped on the river bank, one of the eight savages came and sat down close beside me and, after asking me for a pipe to smoke, which I gave him, he whispered to me in such a way that I alone heard him: "Where do you think you are going, Frenchman?" I replied: "To the Illinois." But, after thinking a moment, I inquired why he had asked me that question. The savage answered that his heart was weeping because we were to be killed the next day and that the chief named Le Barbu,[4] the most wicked of the Natchez chiefs, was waiting for us at Le Petit Gouffre with one hundred and fifty men to break our heads. This speech did not surprise me, because one of their petty chiefs, a friend of mine, had already warned me about it before we left their village, although he had not said it so plainly. I had already reported this to M. de la Loire, but we had not taken that first warning seriously enough to break off our journey. However, the second warning forced us to pay more attention.

We took counsel among ourselves and afterwards summoned the eight Natchez savages that were rowing us. To each of them we promised a substantial present if they would consent to tell us the truth, promising them at the same time never to make known that it was they that had informed us. All eight savages frankly declared to us that six leagues upstream, on the left bank—where boats are compelled to pass close to shore on account of a very rapid whirlpool eddying in the middle of the river —one hundred and fifty Natchez armed with guns were waiting for us, with Le Barbu at the head of them, and

---

[4] The Bearded One. Most Indians were without beard.

that we could not fail to perish though we were six times as many men. This avowal of eight persons, all assuring us of the same thing, compelled us to turn back.

M. de la Loire, the elder, was, beyond everything else, greatly perplexed about how he could withdraw his brother, who had remained at the Natchez village to guard the warehouse of Company merchandise. He talked to me about this, all the while appearing to me to be greatly depressed. I told him that if he would permit me I would go after his brother by myself and would bring him back with me or perish in the attempt.

After making our arrangements to do that, we set out at three o'clock in the afternoon in order to get to the landing at the Natchez village one hour before sunset, so that I could go to the village by daylight, as it was one league from the river bank. When we got to the landing, I told our men not to get out of the boats and to wait for me till midnight and that, if I did not return then, they could count on it that I was dead and all they would have to do then would be to leave.

I took my gun, my powder flask, and my bullet pouch and got out of the boat to head for the village. M. de la Loire came with me as far as the edge of the prairie. He embraced me, weeping, and told me that if I brought his brother back he would not be the only one that would show appreciation for such a great service and that all his family would always be under obligation to me. I told him nothing, except to wait for me till daybreak and, God helping, I would do all in my power.

When I was in the middle of the prairie, in sight of the village, several Natchez savages saw me from afar and ran to tell the Chevalier de la Loire (for so he was called) that a Frenchman was coming, for they had not recognized me at a distance. That young man came immediately to see who it was and, recognizing me, he ran to meet me and flung his arms about my neck, asking me why I had come back. I told him, for the moment, that I had got sick, and when I got inside his hut I requested him to send for the Grand Chief. When he came a moment afterwards, I told him that six Frenchmen had got sick in our boats, which was the reason we had turned back to the landing, and that on the next day we would have to have thirty men to carry our merchandise into the Company's warehouse [5] at his village. He replied to me that he would go and have them notified and that we had done the right thing to come back down the river because the Yasoux savages were no good and could have waylaid us to break our heads. I thanked him, telling him that he was right, although I well perceived all his treachery.

After he had gone, I told the Chevalier de la Loire that we had to think about a way to escape, even if we were guarded by three savages that were sleeping in the hut where we were sleeping. As soon as I told him that, the young man became greatly disturbed and every minute asked me if we would really be able to escape. To reassure him, I told him that he had only to leave things to me and we would certainly escape. We got ready for the attempt: I made him load his gun, [fill his horn with powder and his pouch with bullets, and made him put his gun] [6]

[5] Crozat's warehouse and merchandise at the Natchez.
[6] Restored from Spofford, p. 309.

by the head of his bed, so that he would have no trouble in locating it.

When I saw that the three savages who were spending the night in our hut were asleep, I was seized with an urge to stab them in the heart with my bayonet; but the young man restrained me, being absolutely opposed—for fear, he said, that there would be noise which would wake the other savages, all of whom were then asleep. So, I used this time to make him leave ahead of me, and after I had gently opened the door I told him to take the road through the prairie to the landing.

When I felt that he must be fully a league ahead, I double-locked the door from the outside, shutting the three savages up. I threw the key in a pile of ordure and began to run after him, my gun in my hand. At the edge of the woods, where I had told him to wait for me, I caught up with him. As soon as he saw me, he asked me if the savages had awaked. "They are all sleeping soundly," I told him; "so it is now safe for us to walk." Even so, we ran on for nearly a quarter of a league without stopping, so eager were we to get to the landing. Every now and then the moon would come out, and the Chevalier de la Loire would look behind him to see whether any one was following us.

At last, thank the Lord, we reached the end of the prairie, which is quite close to the landing. Here we found M. de la Loire, the elder, waiting for us with another person, who was on watch with him keeping a lookout for us. After embracing one another fervently, we got in our boats and made the eight savages go ashore. M. de la Loire gave a reward to each of the eight savages and a more substantial present to the one who had first warned me. As we were leaving, they asked us where we were going. We told them that we were going to Mobile and that they would see us again shortly.

As soon as we had gone, the eight savages we had left on the river bank went back home to the Natchez and notified the Grand Chief that the French had gone. The entire village immediately became alarmed over this; but the Grand Chief said absolutely that that could not be and that the Chevalier de la Loire and Pénicaut had gone to bed in their hut, with three savages; but the eight savages told him for the second time that the Chevalier de la Loire and Pénicaut had gone with the other Frenchmen. The Grand Chief got up instantly and went and knocked madly on the door of the Chevalier de la Loire's hut, and hearing the savages say that they were inside, that they could not open up, that they did not have the key, he had the door of the hut beaten in. He rushed to the Chevalier de la Loire's bed. Failing to find us, he ordered a rough handling for the three savages to whom he had given the responsibility of guarding us. They gave as their excuses that we must surely have been wizards and that they had not heard the slightest sound. He seized all the merchandise in the warehouse and the clothes left in the Chevalier de la Loire's hut.[7]

[7] The subsequent careers of the La Loire, or La Loëre, brothers are of ironical interest in connection with the episode just concluded. The younger brother, the more nervous of the two—Louis Auguste de La Loëre Flancour—served for a while as clerk at the Balize. In 1734 he was promoted to civil and criminal judge in the Illinois Country. He suffered three attacks of apoplexy and died suddenly, December 10, 1746, at Fort Chartres, and was buried under his pew at Ste. Anne.

The older brother—Marc Antoine de La Loëre des Ursins—went with Boisbriant as principal clerk at the Illinois. Wishing to return to France, he was moved to the Lower Mississippi. He was a director of the Company of the Indies and was a mem-

As for us, we arrived at ten o'clock in the morning opposite the village of the Tonicas, and here we went ashore. We found M. Davion here, a missionary priest, who embraced us all. He told us that he had believed that we were dead. Then he said Mass for us, to thank God for the mercy He had done to us. After Mass, we told him how everything had happened, for which he thanked God a hundred times.

While we were talking to him, we saw three Natchez arrive. They came representing the Grand Chief to incite the Chief of the Tonicas to put the missionary to death and all of us Frenchmen that were in the village, promising him that all the Natchez savages would unite with them later on to make war on the French, adding that it was much better to deal with the English, who let them have their merchandise cheaper. The Chief of the Tonicas —as level-headed a man as a savage could be, but incapable of treachery, a virtue very rare among savages— was quite astonished at such a speech. The first thing he wanted to do was have their heads broken. He wished to know M. Davion's feelings about this. M. Davion did not wish to permit it and advised him to send them back without doing any hurt to them, as M. de la Mothe would perhaps have been irritated by it. M. Davion wrote a letter to M. de la Mothe about the treachery of the Natchez and their wicked intention.

------

ber of the Superior Council on August 24, 1726. By the fall of 1729 he was back at the Natchez again. On November 28, 1729, the day of the great Natchez Massacre, he put up perhaps the doughtiest self-defense of all Frenchmen who were there, killing four Indians single-handed before he was slain. See Surrey, *Calendar of Manuscripts in Paris Archives*, I, xi; Alvord, *The Illinois Country*, pp. 153, 194–95; and Belting, *Kaskaskia under the French Regime*, pp. 17–20.

BUFFALO TAMER, CHIEF OF THE TUNICA, 1732. From Bushnell,
"Drawings by A. DeBatz."

When we got to Mobile we delivered this letter to him, at which M. de la Mothe was very much surprised. He decided to take vengeance for this as quickly as he could and to that end he ordered M. de Bienville, then King's lieutenant [8] at Mobile, to pick fifty soldiers and a like number of French residents (of whom I was one) to go with him and M. Pailloux,[9] major of troops; M. de Richebourg,[10] company captain; M. de Tissenet,[11] lieutenant; MM. de la Loire, the two brothers—as officers, together with the necessary provisions and food supplies for three months. With these we loaded several boats.

We set out then and ascended the Missicipy as high as the portage of the Cross of the Tonicas, where we found a letter enclosed in a little canvas bag. It was hanging on

[8] The equivalent of lieutenant-governor—second in command.

[9] Barbazan de Pailloux, who had built Fort Louis and laid off the town of Mobile on the present site.

[10] Captain De Richebourg was the first commandant in New Orleans when the town was being established. Gayarré has characterized him as an amiable and brave officer and gentleman with two faults: he was licentious with women; and he had an inordinate and intractable hatred of any display of philanthropy. He had fought several duels in France, perhaps with philanthropists, perhaps with outraged husbands. His cynicism was so great that his friends had to protect him as well as his potential antagonists, by giving a general warning against philanthropists within a radius of three miles of Captain De Richebourg. Otherwise he was amiable (Gayarré, *History of Louisiana*, I, 137-39). He was in command of soldiers escorting Spanish prisoners to Havana after the first capture of Pensacola and was treacherously captured by the Spaniards. De Richebourg left a "Mémoire . . . sur la Premiere Guerre des Natchez," published in B. F. French, *Historical Collections of Louisiana* (New York, 1851), III, 241-52. His account is a primary source and comparable to Pénicaut's.

[11] Charles Claude du Tisné (also Dutisné) helped establish the post at Natchitoches, explored the Missouri River, and twice served as commandant in the Illinois Country, in 1724 and 1729. He was wounded in the cheek by a Fox Indian and died in 1730. His son Louis du Tisné was one of several prominent French officers slain—most probably burned on the fire-cadre—by the Chickasaws following Pierre Dartaguette's premature attack just before the battle of Ackia in 1736. Alvord, *The Illinois Country*, p. 157 and note; Belting, *Kaskaskia under the French Regime*, p. 43 and note.

a branch of a tree that stood on the bank of the Missicipy and extended far enough over the river to be noticed, with this inscription in big letters fixed on the bag containing the letter: TO THE FIRST FRENCHMAN THAT PASSES BY. It was M. Davion, the priest, who had put it there. We took this bag and carried it to M. de Bienville. He opened the letter, in which it was stated that a Frenchman named Richard on his way downstream from the Illinois had been seized by the Natchez. After taking his merchandise, they had brought him to their village, where they cut off his feet and his hands and then threw him in a mudhole. After M. de Bienville had read this letter, he realized that the matter was more serious than he had believed. Previously he had made light of it and had looked upon it as a trifle, accusing us of getting scared; but when he read this letter I believe he really became frightened himself, for he changed the plan he had of proceeding directly to the Natchez and made us go ashore at the Cross of the portage of the Tonicas.

That was about three o'clock in the afternoon. He had twenty-five shots of canister and perriers fired, which we had brought along with us to let M. Davion know of our arrival. The wind, being contrary, kept them from being heard. After night fell, we fired the same number again. We spent the night in this place. Several sentinels were put on watch in the area about us. The next morning at daybreak we fired twenty-five more canister shots. That time the savages heard us and came to us to serve as guides and escort us to their village, where we went to camp on an island in the middle of their bay. We made a fort on this island, working at it without stopping for feast days and Sundays in order to fortify ourselves for fear of some irruption upon us by the Natchez, who are a very numerous and strong nation of more than twelve hundred warriors; and we were only one hundred men and a few *voyageurs* who had joined us.

When our fort was far advanced, M. de Bienville ordered M. de Tissenet to go with twenty men to the Natchez to talk with their Chief. He told the Chief that he came as representative of M. de Bienville, who was awaiting them at the Baye des Tonicas, so that they might come there and talk to him. And he returned the next day, having got their word that they were going to get ready to come down there; and, indeed, a few days afterwards they came, twenty-eight in number, among them several chiefs.

When we perceived them in the distance, we hoisted five flags inside the fort; all the drums were beat and a bell rung which we had brought along and put up on one of the houses inside the fort; much canvas was stretched with stakes and poles in the shape of tents within the fort—so that we looked like a small camp of more than six hundred men, which is considerable for savages.

As soon as they came within the fort, they were taken to M. de Bienville's hut; and when they had gone inside, they wanted to prepare to sing their calumet of peace and to offer the pipe to him. He refused it, at which they were so greatly horrified that they thought their last day had come. At the same time M. de Bienville sprang up from the place where he was seated and told them in a powerful voice that it was not their calumet of peace he wanted, but satisfaction for the five Frenchmen they had killed; that he meant to have the savages who had committed that murder or have their heads, and among them the head of the chief named La Terre Blanche. To this the chiefs replied that, to do that, they would have to send a boat to the village of the Natchez to inform the Grand Chief. M. de Bienville told them that they would do right or their heads would answer for it. All of them were placed under strong guard inside a hut, from which they went out only to answer their needs, each one attended by two fusiliers.

The boat they had sent off was not long in returning. Those who had been sent brought back the head of a man whom the Grand Chief had put to death for that purpose; he had not in the least been implicated in the murder of the Frenchmen. M. de Bienville made me come to ascertain whether it was the head of the chief named La Terre Blanche. After I had looked at this head I told him that it was not and that it was the head of the most feeble-minded person [12] among the residents of their village. He immediately sent for the young chief and angrily asked him if he was ridiculing him and told him that this was not the head of La Terre Blanche, which he wanted along with the heads of the murderers who had killed the Frenchmen. The young chief answered him that the Grand Chief, his brother, would have all the village perish before he would send him the head of the Chief of La Terre Blanche,[13] because he was the Grand Chief's nephew

[12] Bienville had demanded heads rather than scalps because on the heads the French would be able to see facial tattoo patterns, which at that time served for identification of slain Indians just as dental work and fingerprints now serve to identify the slain. See De Richebourg's "Mémoire," p. 245.

[13] It is impossible to tell whether Terre Blanche is the name of the village or

and the bravest of the chiefs he had in all his village. Then he added that in the hut inside the fort, among those who had come with him, we held four of those who were guilty of the death of the Frenchmen. M. de Bienville ordered them to be brought before him; and when he asked them why they had killed the Frenchmen, they brazenly replied that it was not true; however, they were given the lie by six other savages, who accused all four for the second time. Immediately M. de Bienville commanded them to be bound and taken outside the fort and their heads broken. This was at once executed with clubs. Among these four was a man by the name of Le Barbu, the most wicked of all the petty chiefs: he had treacherously committed a great many murders, and all the other savage nations dreaded him and for a long time had wished for his death. After M. de Bienville learned that these four savages had been put to death, he sent the others back to their huts and held counsel with the other officers about what remained to be done. It was decided that, inasmuch as the Natchez are established on the bank of the Missicipy, we needed to make peace with this nation. If we remained at war with them, they would not fail to cut off our trade with the Illinois, and on this account it was necessary to agree to peace with them upon the following terms:

---

name of the chief. Preceding entries of the name in this chapter have seemed to be the chief's name; but here "la teste du chef de la Terre Blanche" shows Terre Blanche to be the name of a village. Such ambiguity is present in the chronicles of De Soto's expedition in Florida, for the names of chiefs are often the names of villages. One cannot tell which is the primary use. Ethnologists still did not know whether there was really a White Earth (Terre Blanche) village at Natchez when Swanton wrote *Indian Tribes of the Lower Mississippi Valley,* published in 1911. See Swanton's note on p. 48. His source is the De Richebourg "Mémoire."

1st. That they would build a fort in their village, at their expense, on the spot that M. de Bienville would mark for them and in the manner that he would wish, with the necessary quarters and magazines within the fort for the convenience of the officers and soldiers that would stay there;

2nd. That they would return all the merchandise and clothes they had taken both from the Company's warehouse and the Chevalier de la Loire's hut;

3rd. That the chief named La Terre Blanche would never show his face in the village of the Natchez—upon pain of death if he was caught there.

After that had been decided in the council of officers, they sent for the young chief [14] and all the other Natchez who were in the hut. They were conducted into M. de Bienville's room, where he gave them a reading of the three articles proposed to them in the peace agreement. In the name of all, the young chief replied that he accepted these terms and that they would be faithfully carried out as soon as was desired; all the others said the same thing about it, and M. de Bienville immediately had them set at liberty.

The next day M. Pailloux, who was ordered to go with them to the village of the Natchez and announce the peace to the Grand Chief, asked M. de Bienville for

[14] ". . . ils envoierent chercher Le Jeune Chef," Parkman, p. 274. Although *jeune chef* may be no more than an age qualification, there is the possibility that the French gave this particular petty chief that proper name. De Richebourg specifies among the chiefs "un troisième frère, surnommé le Petit-Soleil." ("Mémoire," p. 245.) Secondary sources have carried his name as Little Chief, although *petit soleil* is the French commonly used for any one of the petty chiefs of the Natchez nation. B. F. French, who probably gave this name a start, translates the preceding passage about the young chief as "They were confounded at this reply, and the *Little Chief* lowered his *calumet,* and raised his eyes and arms to the *Sun,* and invoked the forgiveness of M. de Bienville." "Annals of Louisiana . . . By M. Penicaut," p. 131.

twenty men, of whom I was of the number to act as his interpreter. We arrived at the Natchez village with our weapons in good condition, as it is always necessary to be suspicious of savages, who are greatly addicted to betrayal of their word. We marched in with our drum beating, our flag unfurled, in proper order, so that all the savages were attracted from their other villages; when they learned of our arrival, they came. All of them seemed quite satisfied to see us arrive for the purpose of concluding the peace there, as the common run of the people liked the French very much and had had no part in the murder of the five Frenchmen that had been killed.

When M. Pailloux had read the articles of peace to the Grand Chief before all the other chiefs who were there present, the Grand Chief approved the terms his brother had accepted and said to M. Pailloux that he would have the work started on the fort whenever M. de Bienville would command and that we had only to choose the spot.

We remained a week in the village, where we were very well entertained by the savages during that time. Afterwards we went to M. de Bienville at the fort of the Tonicas, where we remained only two days, after which we returned to the Natchez with M. de Bienville and fifty men in order to talk with the Grand Chief and the other chiefs. The Grand Chief—accompanied by other chiefs and followed by nearly all the Natchez—came to the landing to meet M. de Bienville. He straightway ratified the articles of peace, upon the same terms that had been laid down to the young chief, his brother. M. de Bienville chose a spot on a height close to the village for the site of the fort, which they commenced the very next day after he had prescribed the form of it and had had the *enceinte* marked off.

A few days later he returned to the fort of the Tonicas, leaving M. Pailloux with twelve Frenchmen to carry on the work on the fort. It took a full six weeks to finish it; and as soon as it was finished, M. de Bienville was notified and he came there with MM. de Tissenet and de la Loire, the two brothers, and all the Frenchmen who were with him at the fort of the Tonicas. As soon as he got there he ordered still more officers' quarters and more soldiers' barracks inside the fort, and magazines to hold munitions and food supplies and the merchandise belonging to the Company, which the savages had brought back. This fort was named Roselie [15] by M. de Bienville. The Grand Chief came with all the other chiefs and almost all the Natchez savages to sing their calumet of peace in front of the fort, which lasted three days.

All this year M. de Bienville remained at the Natchez.

---

[15] Of Fort Rosalie, named for Mme de Pontchartrain, there is scarcely a vestige left to mark the place where the Natchez Indians massacred the entire garrison in 1729. There is a clumsy restoration of a palisade and one inner building set high above the crust of land where the Mississippi has eaten away Natchez-under-the-Hill. The path through the weeds and tangled brush is so little worn that one may feel certain that the spot is visited by few of the thousands of tourists who come to see ante-bellum Natchez. Down the hill, a few hundred yards toward town, sits the namesake of Fort Rosalie—one of the mansions of American days before the War, well-kept and beautiful Rosalie. In all the province of Old Louisiana, "the Natchez" was the place of richest prospects for Frenchmen during those first wild years of the Company of the Indies.

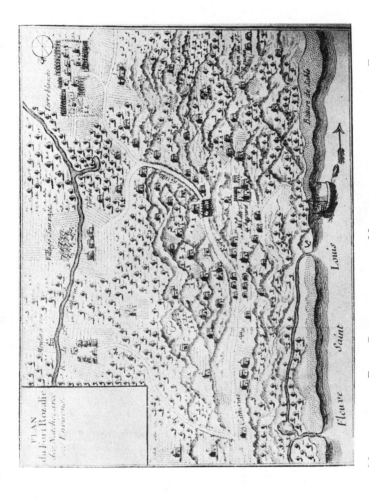

Map showing Fort Rosalie at the Natchez and neighboring French settlements and native villages. From Louis François Benjamin Dumont de Montigny, *Mémoires Historiques sur la Louisiane* (Paris, 1753).

Chapter 17

The Year 1715

M. de Bienville comes down to Mobile—M. de St. Denis returns from Mexico; his marriage to the daughter of Captain Dom Pedros de Vilesca—Fort established at the Nassitoches—The Spaniards come down to the Assinaïs

. DE BIENVILLE left M. Pailloux as commandant of Fort Roselie and M. de Tissenet as lieutenant and went down to Mobile to give an account of what he had done at the Natchez and, at the same time, to obtain munitions, food supplies, and merchandise to carry back to Fort Roselie. He remained only two weeks at Mobile and returned to the Natchez to take all these supplies and to have the living quarters finished which were yet to be built inside the fort.

M. de St. Denis arrived at Mobile during this year with Segnor Dom Juan de Vilesca,[1] uncle of his wife, and three other Spaniards. He had been away three years on his Mexican voyage, an account of which he gave to M. de la Mothe, as follows:

He said that he had been escorted by an officer and twenty-four Spanish cavalrymen from Caoüil Village two hundred and fifty leagues to Mexico City, the capital

---

[1] The biographer of St. Denis, Ross Phares, gives Diego Ramón, St. Denis' father-in-law, as the member of the family who came to Mobile, where he engaged in horse-trading. Alférez Domingo Ramón was the only uncle mentioned by Phares. (*Cavalier in the Wilderness*, p. 54 and p. 111.) Notice *Dom* as the French form of *Don*.

of Mexico, where he spoke to the Viceroy [2] and showed him his passport. He said then that the Viceroy, after examining his passport, told him that he had made an ill-conceived voyage, and he had him put in prison without being willing to hear more. M. de St. Denis, being quite astonished at such treatment, was no little puzzled. He remained in this prison for more than three months; but, luckily for him, several Frenchmen spoke in his behalf [3] to the Viceroy. They were in Mexico in the service of the Spaniards and were acquainted with M. d'Hyberville, who was related to M. de St. Denis through marriage with M. de St. Denis' niece. Sending for him a second time, the Viceroy tried to persuade him to serve the King of Spain by offering him a company of cavalry. But M. de St. Denis—far indeed from being attracted enough by the Viceroy's offers to be persuaded to quit the service of the King of France—told him that he had taken an oath of fidelity to his King, whose service he would quit only at death.

It had already been reported to the Viceroy that, during the time M. de St. Denis had stayed at Rivière du Nord, he had made love to the daughter of Captain Dom Pedros de Vilesca. The Viceroy said to him: "You are already more than a half-naturalized Spaniard, since you are to be married to Dona Maria, the elder daughter of Dom Pedros de Vilesca, when you return."

"I will not conceal from you, Monsieur," M. de St. Denis replied to him, "that I love Dona Maria, since it

[2] The Duke de Linares.

[3] Gayarré identified St. Denis' chief benefactor among French officers in Mexico City as the Marquis de Larnage, the favorite aide-de-camp of the Viceroy. *History of Louisiana*, I, 173.

has been told to Your Excellency, but I have never fancied myself as worthy to marry her."

The Viceroy told him he could be assured that, if he accepted the offer made him of a company of cavalry in the service of the King of Spain, Dom Pedros would be delighted to give him his daughter in marriage. "And I give you my word for that," added the Viceroy. "Therefore you can remain here two months. Think of what I am proposing to you. You will be free to walk out into town during that time. You will meet several French officers in town who are in the service of the King of Spain, with which they are quite satisfied."

[M. de St. Denis' account continued]: [4] "I expressed my great thanks to Monseigneur the Viceroy for all his kindness and especially for the freedom that he gave me. On leaving his suite I found a Spanish officer who, speaking rather bad French, told me that he had been ordered to take me to lodge at his house and to be my companion in town when I wished to go out for a walk. I told him, in Spanish, which I spoke better than he spoke our language, that I was very much obliged to him and that that would give me a great deal of pleasure. I knew from experience that, to get along well with Spaniards, one had to heap honors upon them and show them much deference. After escorting me to his home, which was a house in the

---

[4] Much of the story about St. Denis is told in the first person. There is a slight possibility that Pénicaut, through his friendship with St. Denis' valet Jalot, had unauthorized access to the memoirs of St. Denis. One sentence yet to come in this book is better evidence. In his will, dated March 26, 1744, St. Denis left 1,500 livres to M. de la Frénière, presumably to pay for the publication of his memoirs. Some one among St. Denis' many descendants may still locate the manuscript. But Ross Phares, the latest biographer, was unable to locate it. The memoirs have not been published so far. *Cavalier in the Wilderness*, p. 262.

Spanish style—that is, a chalet with linen curtains and with walls all bare, with chairs entirely of wood as the only appointments—he showed me another room at the side of his, which opened upon a garden; it was a little cleaner and bigger, and in it he told me I was to sleep.

"We were on the point of going out when the Viceroy's master of the horse, or, in French, *le grand écuyer*, entered the room. As a gift from His Excellency, he presented me with a bag containing three hundred piastres, which His Excellency was sending me for me to use during the time I would be in Mexico. I thanked him very much and requested him to tell His Excellency that I was overwhelmed by all his generosities; and then I accompanied him downstairs, where, after a great many compliments, he made his departure.

"I then told the Spanish officer with me to direct me to a house where one could buy something to eat, for I wished to have the honor of taking him to dinner. He did not require much pressing: he took me to a hostelry where most of the officers usually ate, both French and Spanish. Here we had very good food without being fleeced, as it was at a set price of one piastre per person. I dined there always afterwards during the two months that I remained in Mexico. I found several French officers there in the King of Spain's service, with whom I became acquainted or, rather, who knew me without my knowing them, as most of them had been friends of M. d'Hyberville. They were the ones who had spoken in my behalf to the Viceroy, for which I thanked them profusely. I also made the acquaintance of several of the most eminent Spaniards of the town, who endeavored to persuade me to enter the service of the King of Spain. I was also invited several times to go to dinner at the home of Monseigneur the Viceroy, and I went. He gave sumptuous dinners, having people in to dine every day, especially the main officers. Never have I seen anything so rich as his silver services; his furniture, his wardrobes, his tables, on down to the fire-dogs in his rooms—everything was of massive silver of an extraordinary thickness and weight, but crudely wrought. During all the time I was in Mexico I took great care to guard my words and to say nothing that would be prejudicial to myself, although I daily enjoyed the good cheer with the officers, French and Spanish, who did all they could to persuade me to enter the service of the King of Spain, being egged on, I think, by the Viceroy; but they were never able to persuade me. That is what determined Monseigneur the Viceroy to give me my dismissal audience.

"He invited me to dine at his home, where I had received such courtesy before; and after dinner, taking me aside into a large, splendid study, which I had not yet been able to enter, he told me that, since he had not succeeded in inducing me to remain in Mexico in the service of the King, his master, I was free to go back to Louisiana and that I was to leave the next day with the officer with whom I had been staying. At the same time he presented me with a purse containing one thousand piastres, which he was granting me, he said laughing, to pay the expenses of my wedding. He added that he hoped Dona Maria would persuade me, perhaps better than he, to take the offers that he was making me. I thanked him again and again for all his generosities. But I was not able to obtain free trade from him. I left him at the door of his study, to which he returned after wishing me a good journey.

"I returned with the Spanish officer to our living quarters to prepare to leave on the next day. Afterwards I went to say goodby to all the French officers I had met and to several titled Spaniards who had shown me great friendship during my stay in Mexico. I supped once more with them that evening, and after supper we embraced one another and I went away to take my rest in order to get ready to leave.

"Next morning I was beginning to dress when Monseigneur the Viceroy's master of the horse entered my room and told me that His Excellency was sending me a horse from his stable, which he was giving me to use on my journey. I thanked him courteously and told him, in the Spanish language, that I was ever under obligation to His Excellency for all the good things he had heaped upon me, that I would not fail to acquaint the Governor of Louisiana and all the French with the magnitude of his generosities and of his magnificence. Then I went downstairs to see him off and to receive my horse, which a page of the Viceroy was holding by the bridle. I exclaimed, and exclaimed, about the value and the beauty of this present. The master of the horse, having heard the word *magnificence,* which I had let slip in my first flattery, seized the occasion to unfold to me the riches of his master, whom he elevated to equality at least with the grandest kings in the world. He gave me a detailed account of the great number of his servants and his horses, saying that he had more than two thousand more, handsomer than the one he had given me, not to mention the prodigious quantity of furniture and services of silver. I did not dare interrupt him, although his speech had already lasted nearly half an hour and I was beginning to be quite bored, when, luckily for me, the officer with whom I was lodged, who had the order to escort me, called through the window to tell me that I must go to breakfast, as we had to leave within an hour. I then left that big talker of an equerry, thanking him for having acquainted me with the might of Monseigneur the Viceroy, which I would not fail to proclaim to all the French officers when I got back to Louisiana.

"As soon as he had left me, I had my horse stabled and then went to have breakfast with the Spanish officer with whom I was staying. And afterwards we left together with only ten cavalrymen to escort us to Caoüil. It took us nearly three months to get there, as we went by easy stages. The horse which Monseigneur the Viceroy had given me was a bay horse, one of the handsomest and best that I have ever ridden.

"When we arrived at Caoüil, we went to see the Governor, who gave me the privilege of staying there one week. In this place I found Jalot, my valet and surgeon, who had stayed there waiting for me. During all that time, he had lived there from his surgeon's trade and had gained a great reputation for himself among the Spaniards by treating a great many of them, whom he had cured completely of several diseases, such as quartan fevers and dysentery, to which they are greatly subject. I went to lodge with the officer, who had taken me to the best inn in town. Here our fare would not have been so unduly good if Jalot had not cooked our food himself. A week later, the Governor of Caoüil gave me an officer and six cavalrymen to escort me to Rivière du Nord. I had permission from the Governor of Caoüil to buy my valet a horse, which cost only ten piastres, although a very good one. In a week we reached Rivière du Nord Village, where I went to stay at the home of Segnor Dom Pedros de Vilesca. The officer who brought me delivered a packet of letters to him and returned to Caoüil three days later.

"After I had stayed a week at Dom Pedros', something happened that greatly advanced my marriage. Here is how the thing occurred:

"Four villages of savages who were disheartened by Spanish rule decided to abandon their homes and go off and settle outside of Spanish territory. They loaded all that they could get of their best belongings and their grains upon their beasts and began moving off in the direction of the Cadodaquioux,[5] who are almost two hundred leagues from there. Segnor Dom Pedros was notified at once and was greatly distressed. He was partly to blame for this, as he had given too much freedom to his troopers, who were forever among the savages, pillaging them and annoying them without the savages' daring to defend themselves. He did not know what to do to stop the savages or to get them back; besides, no one dared go there, as these four villages together made more than a thousand men armed with bows and arrows."

Seeing Dom Pedros' difficulty, M. de St. Denis told him that if he was willing to permit him to go there alone, he would promise him to see to it that they returned. Segnor Dom Pedros embraced him and told him that he

[5] They lived near the Red River, in northwest Louisiana.

would not dare expose him in that way because in those villages there were two nations, the most wicked savages to be found, that would not fail to stab him; but M. de St. Denis was not disturbed by that. He mounted his horse and, followed by his valet Jalot, went to them. He tied a handkerchief to the end of a stick, which he showed them from a distance as a sign of peace; and, approaching them, speaking to them in Spanish, which they understood well, he told them to come back and all they wanted would be granted to them, and promised them in the name of Captain Dom Pedros that they would not be disturbed in the future, and pointed out to them that beyond Spanish territory they would daily be in danger of war with the Assinaïs or the Cadodaquioux, who cruelly put to death all the people they capture. He added that all soldiers would be forbidden to set foot at any time inside their village for the purpose of disturbing them, upon penalty of death, and that they had only to follow him and they would themselves hear this interdiction made out loud to the soldiers. The four chiefs of these nations told him that they asked nothing better than to return to their villages if no one wished to trouble them. M. de St. Denis, after promising them a second time, told them to follow him and they would hear the interdiction made to all the troopers; and immediately all these poor savages followed M. de St. Denis in order to come and talk to Captain Dom Pedros. Everybody in the village was very much astonished to see M. de St. Denis coming there at the head of more than four thousand persons, as many men as women and children of the savages.

M. de St. Denis dismounted and spoke a moment to Dom Pedros, who was delighted to be beholden to M. de St. Denis, because the Governor of Caoüil, who would not have failed to learn that the desertion of the savages was due to Segnor Dom Pedros' negligence, would have written about it to the Viceroy, damaging the Captain's reputation. Wherefore, following M. de St. Denis' advice, he had all his troopers assembled and had a proclamation published aloud in the presence of the chiefs of the savages, by which the troopers were forbidden henceforth to go among the savages to pillage them or to annoy them in any manner whatsoever, upon pain of death; and then he exhorted the savages to return to their village, which they did not abandon at any time afterwards.

This little service which M. de St. Denis rendered to Captain Dom Pedros greatly advanced his marriage to Segnora Dona Maria, his daughter. It was performed two months afterwards in the village church, which is ministered to by seven Spanish Cordelier Fathers. When the marriage articles had been signed by both parties, Dom Pedros went to Caoüil at once to buy wedding clothes. Along with him, too, M. de St. Denis sent Jalot to make several purchases, which he brought back to M. de St. Denis a month later when he returned with Segnor Dom Pedros. A week after Dom Pedros' return from Caoüil, the marriage was celebrated splendidly: M. de St. Denis gave each Spanish trooper three piastres and a cockade of yellow ribbon to stick in his hat and presented his wife with a very fine diamond which he had brought from France; and the Spanish soldiers celebrated with a lavish discharge of their muskets during the three days the wedding festivities lasted.

After the wedding M. de St. Denis remained in the village in his father-in-law's house for eight months more, after which he left with his father-in-law's brother Dom Juan de Vilesca, and three other Spaniards kin to him. He left his wife pregnant. His going was not without much shedding of tears. He promised her to come back soon to get her and take her with him to Mobile.

When M. de St. Denis had concluded his account, M. de la Mothe well knew that there were no grounds for hope of open trade with the Spaniards; therefore, he decided to have a fort built on the Rivière Rouge, among the Nassitoches, to prevent incursions that the Spaniards might make by way of this river as far as the Missicipy. For this purpose he sent twenty-five soldiers off with one sergeant and three boats loaded with merchandise, munitions, and food supplies, with a letter to M. de Bienville, who was at the Natchez. In the letter he requested M. de Bienville to send M. de Tissenet—a retired Canadian officer,[6] who understood the savage languages very well—at the head of this detachment that was to go up the Rivière Rouge to build a fort at the Nassitoches. As soon as M. de Bienville received this order, he notified M. de Tissenet, who set out three days later.

As soon as M. de Tissenet reached the Nassitoches, he gave presents to the savages, such as axes and picks. The

---

[6] ". . . ancien officier canadien." An *ancien officier* is not necessarily one retired because of age. Sometimes it means no more than a person who once served as officer. I find it difficult to translate.

Nassitoches were delighted to have a French post in their village. They sang their calumet of peace to M. de Tissenet, which lasted three days; and on the fourth they cut down many trees and carried them to the place that M. de Tissenet had chosen as the site of the fort; [7] it was finished in a short while. Quarters for the officers and the soldiers were then constructed on the inside and a magazine to hold the merchandise, the munitions, and the food supplies that had been brought. When all this building was done, M. de Tissenet sent two soldiers to the Yatacez—forty leagues farther, on the right of the Nassitoches if one is coming downstream from the north— to notify the chiefs still remaining at their village to come and talk to him at the Nassitoches. Two weeks later the two soldiers returned with two. M. de Tissenet told them that they ought to come with the rest of their village and settle at the Nassitoches. They would be undisturbed there, whereas at their own village they were in danger of attacks from the Cadodaquioux. [They would be given fields in which to sow their grains],[8] and the French would pay for the food they brought the French.

They did not fail to come back two weeks later, all together, with their women, children, and beasts laden with grain, bringing their personal belongings. They were located at the village of the Nassitoches, next to the Nassitoches, with whom they have stayed ever since, and with whom they live in fine harmony.

The fort which M. de la Mothe had ordered built at

---

[7] Thus Charles Claude du Tisné and Louis Juchereau de St. Denis are the founders of Natchitoches, the oldest town in present-day Louisiana.

[8] Supplied from Spofford, p. 351.

the Nassitoches was built quite opportunely, as the Viceroy of Mexico had ordered the Governor of the town of Caoüil to send troops to the French frontier with the intention of advancing in that direction as far as they could. They had come as far as the Assinaïs, with sixty cavalrymen and a captain. That is what M. de Tissenet learned from two Cordeliers of the four whom that captain had brought along to say Mass to his troopers and who had come down to the Nassitoches to pick up what they could, not expecting to find Frenchmen there. They were seized and taken to M. de Tissenet, who received them quite well, however, and gave them some presents, begging them to come there Sundays and feast days to say Mass, with pay for their trouble. After this, they went back to the Assinaïs and told the Spanish captain that the French had a fort at the Nassitoches. This stopped the Spaniards from advancing farther in the direction of Louisiana.[9]

[9] The farthest point the Spaniards reached was Los Adaes, fifteen miles from the French post at Natchitoches, where for nearly a generation M. de St. Denis, like a doughty marquis of the old world, was keeper of the marches.

Chapter 18

The Year 1716

M. de la Mothe sends a detachment to the Nassitoches—M. de
St. Denis' second trip to the Nassitoches—His second trip to
Rivière du Nord and the continuation of his story

HEN M. DE LA MOTHE received a letter
from M. de Tissenet informing him that the
Spaniards had come down to the Assinaïs, he
decided to send a second detachment to the
Nassitoches to reinforce the garrison of the fort. To this
end he ordered a sergeant to take twenty-five soldiers and
go there with provisions, with which four boats were
loaded. M. de St. Denis, who was indeed glad to go and
accompany Segnor Dom Juan de Vilesca, his father-in-
law's brother, on the way home, took advantage of this
occasion to go with him as far as the Nassitoches on the
Rivière Rouge, because this was his route back to Rivière
du Nord Village. They said goodby to M. de la Mothe and
left together in one of the boats for the Nassitoches. They
did not get there till three months later, as the currents
they had to stem were quite rapid.

When they reached the fort at the Nassitoches they
saw M. de Tissenet there. He was quite delighted to have
them. Segnor Dom Juan rested there for two weeks and
then left to return home to Rivière du Nord village with
his relatives, three Spaniards whom he had brought with
him to Mobile. Segnor Dom Juan, having left M. de St.
Denis at the Nassitoches with much show of esteem, took

his way through the Assinaïs and then went overland to his home.

M. de St. Denis remained three months at the fort at the Nassitoches after the departure of Segnor Dom Juan; he was quite troubled at being unable to go with him to his father-in-law's and have the pleasure of seeing his wife, Dona Maria. He had well foreseen that the Spanish captain of cavalry who was at the Assinaïs would assuredly have arrested him. He had, however, plenty of time and liberty to go there because, being a volunteer officer, responsible to no authority, being without employment, he did nothing except of his own free will. Yet, for all his freedom and the great longing he had to see his wife again, he considered that a second attempt to go into Mexico, where he had already been arrested, would put him in great danger even if he should have a second passport from the Governor-General of Louisiana, since the pretense of trade would no longer be a good excuse, all the more since the Viceroy had told him personally that he would never permit it unless he had first received an order from the Spanish King.

One day M. de St. Denis was in a deep reverie in a little wood which is at the point of the Nassitoches' island on the bank of the Rivière Rouge, where he had the habit of going for a walk, often alone. Jalot, his valet, who was having a good time picking strawberries in this little wood, noticed his master in that reverie. After watching him a long time from behind a bush, where he was standing, Jalot became aware of M. de St. Denis' depressed spirits and, to cheer him up, took him some of the strawberries he had gathered in a little basket.

M. de St. Denis asked him where he had found them. "All the woods," Jalot told him, "are full of them now, and especially the woods of Mexico," Jalot added, ["where big ones are found, and better ones than these"].[1] "I should think so," M. de St. Denis told him. "Since the region is warmer, the fruit there should be better. And so I will tell you, Jalot, that I have a great yearning to go through these woods, not for that fruit, but to go and see my wife and her fruit, who is [my child that I have not yet seen.][2] Dona Maria was pregnant when I left her to go to Mobile with Dom Juan, her uncle, who accompanied me, as you know. Dom Juan left more than three months ago, but I have received no news of my wife or of Dom Pedros, my father-in-law, to whom I sent letters by Dom Juan. To tell the truth, I am so distressed that I have decided to go to see Dona Maria, even if I lose my life in the attempt, rather than languish here as I am doing."

"Why disturb yourself and worry for such a long time?" Jalot told him. "This journey is not so difficult or so dangerous as you imagine. I know all the roads through the woods to take you right into Dom Pedros' house without our ever being observed by anyone."

"You are crazy," M. de St. Denis told him. "Is there any likelihood of our being able to make a journey of nearly two hundred leagues [3] without being discovered?"

"I know it so well," Jalot told him, "because I have made this trip more than four times in my life without ever having any unhappy experience. And if you wish,"

---

[1] Supplied from Spofford, p. 357.   [2] Supplied from Parkman, p. 301.
[3] ". . . deux cents lieues." Margry gives "douze cents lieues," which is wrong. *Découvertes*, V, 540.

Jalot added, "we shall go by boat four leagues upstream under pretext of hunting. At that place we shall land on the right side of the river, in woods that extend as far as Rivière du Nord, where Dom Pedros' village stands." [4]

M. de St. Denis, after pondering a moment, told Jalot that he was willing to trust things to him and that he should make his arrangements well and try to succeed on this voyage, on which they ran the risk, both of them, of losing their lives if they happened to be discovered. As far as he was concerned, he had made up his mind to risk his life and to leave within three days. That was the time that he was giving Jalot to get ready for the voyage. M. de St. Denis said no more to him.

One morning three days later, he went to have breakfast with M. de Tissenet and told him, on getting up from the table, that he had made arrangements to go to the woods hunting with Jalot; and afterwards he left M. de Tissenet and came back to Jalot, whom he found busy filling a sack with cooked meat and bread on which to subsist during the first days of travel after they left the village. Next they took a gun each, with supplies of powder and shot, and went off in a boat, in which they ascended the river for four leagues. When they got to the place where Jalot had told him they would have to land, Jalot tied the boat to a tree at the edge of the river; and together they went off to the right into the woods and walked for two hours. Then they rested in the woods till night. After they had eaten a bit of their small supply, when night came they began to continue their way and kept on till day, when they rested.

[4] This sentence is taken from Spofford, p. 359.

The fourth day, the provisions began to fail them; so Jalot told M. de St. Denis that they would have to go deeper into the woods if they were to find game, for he knew a spot where there usually were some deer. He took M. de St. Denis to a place farther away. They found a creek along which they ran across several deer. M. de St. Denis killed one, which Jalot skinned; and after cutting it up into pieces he built a fire at that place and roasted a part of the best pieces, which lasted them for four days. This is the way they lived during the four months they were on the road: living off the ends of their guns, traveling at night, and resting during the day.

The last day, when they were taking their rest in a wood that was no more than a league and a half from Dom Pedros', M. de St. Denis asked Jalot how he was going to manage to get him into his father-in-law's house without being detected.

"We must wait," Jalot told him, "until it is past midnight, since the Spaniards walk around very late in summer. As for the rest," he told him, "you just leave things to me and follow me; I shall get you in through the garden behind Dom Pedros' house. It is surrounded by a hedge. At one end of the hedge is a place through which I have often got in at night when I returned from making a call on a little Spanish girl whom I used to know at the time of your marriage."

M. de St. Denis began to laugh and said to him: "Our trip has progressed well, and I have a good omen about it, since love leads the way."

Jalot replied to him: "This journey has different fates in store for us: you are assured of finding Dona Maria, a wife whom you love; and I—I am not certain of finding my mistress; she may be married."

They talked to each other until about midnight; then Jalot took from his sack a piece of roasted venison wrapped in a napkin, which he unfolded before his master. But M. de St. Denis couldn't eat it. As for Jalot, who always had a good appetite, he ate a great deal of it and immediately fell into a deep sleep.

M. de St. Denis was too restless to sleep: every minute he woke up Jalot, telling him that it was time to go. At last Jalot went beyond the woods and saw by the stars that it was nearly midnight. He went back into the woods and told M. de St. Denis to wait for him and he would be back soon. He went off very speedily to Dom Pedros' village to find out whether he could see anyone; then he came back, still running. During that time, M. de St. Denis was extremely impatient: he could not understand why Jalot did not return and he swore great oaths against him. When Jalot did get back two hours later, he said nothing other than to tell his master to follow him.

He guided M. de St. Denis for one league, walking very fast over a sunken road between two slightly elevated banks, on which there was a double row of trees leading up to a country house. They passed by this and went half a league farther into open country, where the back of the garden of Dom Pedros' house extended.[5] Jalot stepped down into a little dry ditch and came up on the other side at the corner of the garden hedge. Here there was a bundle

<hr/>

[5] *Rendoit,* or *tendoit* as in Margry, *Découvertes,* V, 543. *Rendre* means to stretch or extend; but this nonreflexive use of it seems odd. *Se rendre* is equivalent to *aboutir à.* Parkman, p. 306, has "encore une demie lieu[e] de là dans une campagne ou aboutissoit le jardin de dom pedros."

of thorn-bush, [which shut in the end of the hedge. This he pushed down with the end of his gun]; [6] then after climbing up on the bank at the edge of the garden, he gave his hand to M. de St. Denis and drew him into the garden with him.

While Jalot was putting the thorn-bundle back up, M. de St. Denis moved forward very slowly into the garden. In the little moonlight that was shining he saw his wife out walking there alone. He went to her to take her in his arms, but she was frightened and cried out and fell in a faint. Luckily M. de St. Denis had on his person a bottle of *eau de la Reine d'Hongrie;* [7] he put some to her nose and revived her. She threw her arms around his neck, and after they had kissed each other, he led her— supporting her under her arms—to a little room which opened upon this garden, below the bedroom where she slept in summer; and, after talking with M. de St. Denis there for a short while, she went to her father's bedroom and her uncle's. They came and embraced M. de St. Denis. Together they went up to Dona Maria's bedroom, to which they had supper brought for M. de St. Denis. He ate very little with his father-in-law and his uncle, who stayed there only a short time, seeing that he was tired. They went back to their rooms to let him rest, and there we too shall let them rest until the year 1718, when for the second time he returned to Louisiana from Rivière du Nord Village.

---

[6] Supplied from Parkman, p. 306. [7] Spirits of rosemary.

Chapter 19

The Year 1717

M. de l'Épinet, M. Hubert, and several other officers arrive
in Louisiana—M. de Bienville comes down to Isle Dauphine—
M. de Gosseville's trip to Vera Cruz—An English ship comes to
Isle Dauphine—Calumet of peace sung to M. de l'Épinet by more
than twenty-four savage nations—New Biloxi established—The
town of New Orleans is begun

T THE beginning of this year, on the ninth
of March, three ships arrived from France at
the Isle Dauphine roadstead, namely: *Le Dudlot*,[1] commanded by M. de Gosseville;[2] *Le
Pan*,[3] by M. Dussaut;[4] and the frigate *La Paix*, by M.
Jary.[5] They brought M. de l'Épinet[6] as Commander-in-

---

[1] Commonly written *Dudlow*, as in Margry (*Découvertes*, V, 545). The name
may have been *Ludlow*. That the name gave trouble is evident from the spelling
Le Luelou on "Carte de L'Jsle Dauphine" by Lieutenant Du Sault, who commanded
the sister ship *Le Paon* at the time of the spring storm in 1717. On the ms. chart
"Idée ou plan du chenal par lequel est sorty le navire la *Paix* et le vaisseau du Roy
le *Pan* [*sic*] du port de lile Dauphine le 15e may 1717" (Bibliothèque Nationale),
the name is written *Le Lud Louu*.

[2] Margry reports his name from some other ms. as "Godeville, capitaine de brûlot
[captain of a fire-ship]." *Découvertes*, V, 545 and note.

[3] Correctly written *Le Paon* (the Peacock); but since *Paon* and *Pan* have the same
pronunciation, many people, including naval officers, wrote the name as *Pan*. See
n. 1, above.

[4] Margry (*Découvertes*, V, 545 and note) reports the name as given in some other
ms. as Dussaut-Santille. But it is spelled Du Sault on "Carte de L'Jsle Dauphine . . .
Par le Sr. Du Sault Lieutᵗ. Commandᵗ. le Vaisseau du Roy *Le Paon*," published in
this book.

[5] Given as M. Japy by Margry (*Découvertes*, V, 545). Margry recalls seeing
Chapy also. Pénicaut gives Japy too, but in command of the *Marie* at a later date.
The names may be the same. Bienville's nephew, M. de Noyan, gave even a third
spelling of the name of the officer commanding the *Marie* in August, 1719—Sieur
Japil. Rowland and Sanders, *MPA*, III, 254.

[6] Governor of Louisiana from March 3, 1716, to September 20, 1717. Surrey,
Calendar of Manuscripts in Paris Archives, I, ix.

Chief of Louisiana, replacing M. de la Mothe de Cadillac, and as commissary-general M. Hubert,[7] who came to relieve M. Duclos. Also, there were M. Artus,[8] as captain, and many other officers and a great number of soldiers and a great deal of munitions, food supplies, and all kinds of merchandise, which were unloaded and stored in the warehouses at Mobile and on Isle Dauphine.

From a boat that stopped at the Natchez on its way up to the Illinois, M. de Bienville learned that M. de l'Épinet had come to Mobile as Commandant-General, replacing M. de la Mothe de Cadillac, and a little later M. de Bienville came down to Mobile to pay his respects to M. de l'Épinet. When he got there, M. de l'Épinet gave him the cross of Chevalier de St. Louis, which His Majesty had sent him in recognition of his good services. On setting out from the Natchez, he had left M. de Pailloux as commandant of Fort Roselie during his absence and M. de Villers [9] as lieutenant, with sixty men.

Several days later, M. de l'Épinet sent M. de Gosseville —the captain of the ship named *Le Dudlot*, from which

[7] Marc Antoine Hubert was *ordonnateur*, or commissary-general, of Louisiana from November 12, 1716, to September 15, 1720. (*Ibid.*, I, x.) On May 18, 1718, when a child of his was baptized, his wife was Dame Elizabet Cesteri. Mobile Baptismal Records.

[8] Often written Dartus or D'Artus. This captain of infantry and engineers, who had served under Crozat's monopoly, was commandant of Dauphin Island in 1717. Complaints were made about his petty acts of discipline. He was at one time ordered back to France. See Company of the West to the Navy Council, [1716?], in Rowland and Sanders, *MPA*, III, 190; and [Hubert] to the Council, [1717], *ibid.*, II, 227.

[9] There may be a connection between this De Villers and the De Villiers brothers with whom George Washington fought just before and at the time of the surrender of Fort Necessity, in 1754. A Nyon de Villiers was commandant in the Illinois Country in 1764. See Fortier, *History of Louisiana*, I, 134 and 151.

the goods had not been unloaded—to Vera Cruz to try to sell them. M. de Gosseville did not go directly to Vera Cruz, but twelve leagues to one side, between Vera Cruz and a little town called Villarica.[10] When he got there, he secretly sent out two of our soldiers, who spoke Spanish, with a price list of the goods on board the ship. These two soldiers talked to three Spanish merchants and came back with them at night. They got into the longboat, which was at the beach, and came in it out to the ship, where the Spanish merchants looked at the goods that were on board. When they had agreed with M. de Gosseville about the price, they had the goods carried ashore, after paying cash for them. M. de Gosseville, greatly pleased over the outcome, then returned to Isle Dauphine. He sailed a week later to go back to France with the other two ships. MM. de la Mothe and Duclos went to France with him.

A few days later, M. de l'Épinet had a fort built on Isle Dauphine and some barracks for the soldiers. This fort was located two musket shots from the seashore, to protect the warehouse and prevent any landings in that direction.

While people were busy constructing this fort, an English ship landed at Isle Dauphine to take on water and wood. We took advantage of this opportunity to turn over to them the English men and English women who had been at Mobile for two and a half years. They had been ransomed by M. de Bienville from the Alibamons and Canapouces savages when they returned from Caro-

---

[10] Usually Villa Rica.

lina, where they had made an irruption. All the English men and English women that wanted to go back to their homes were put on the English captain's ship.

During that time the savages friendly to the French, those nearest to Mobile, learned that M. de l'Épinet had arrived as Governor-General of Louisiana, replacing M. de la Mothe de Cadillac, who had returned to France; and all the chiefs of more than twenty-four nations [11] came down to Isle Dauphine and sang their calumet of peace to M. de l'Épinet. These savages are named the Chaqtos,[12] the Taoüachas, the Apalaches, the Tinssas, the Mobiliens, the Tomez, the Gens des Fourches,[13] the Chactas, the Pascagoulas, the Passacolas, the Capinans, the Colapissas, the Bayagoulas, the Oumas, the Tonicas, the Chaoüachas, the Natchez, the Chicachas, the Nassitoches, the Yatacez, the Alibamons, the Canapouces, and others.[14] These calumets of peace lasted more than two months because the savages, being too badly separated one from another, could not all be there at the same time. They were all well received by M. de l'Épinet, who sent them back home with presents.

[11] Parkman, p. 311, gives ". . . les chefs de ces sauvages avec leurs femmes."

[12] Erroneously given as Chactas by Margry (*Découvertes*, V, 547); therefore, when he found Chactas coming lower in the list—after Gens des Fourches—he omitted the name.

[13] The first seven tribes named are small tribes living near Fort Louis de la Mobile. The Naniabas, who lived at the Forks (Fourches) of the Tombigbee and Alabama rivers, are omitted from this list. Surely they came to sing the calumet to the new governor and share in French largess. The deduction is that the Gens des Fourches were the Naniabas.

[14] I have twenty-two tribes listed. But I had to supply Chactas, Pascagoulas, and Passacolas from Spofford, p. 372. Margry has nineteen in his list. (*Découvertes*, V, 547.) Several of these tribes had come from a great distance: the Chicachas from north Mississippi and Tennessee; the Nassitoches and Yatacez from the Red River; the Canapouces (Catawba) from Carolina. But French presents no doubt paid them well for the effort.

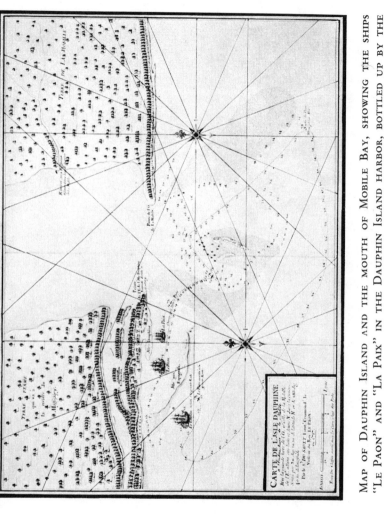

MAP OF DAUPHIN ISLAND AND THE MOUTH OF MOBILE BAY, SHOWING THE SHIPS "LE PAON" AND "LA PAIX" IN THE DAUPHIN ISLAND HARBOR, BOTTLED UP BY THE 1717 STORM. NOTE THE ESCAPE ROUTE CHARTED ACROSS THE BAR. THE PASS BETWEEN ISLE AUX ESPAGNOLS AND DAUPHIN ISLAND IS ERRONEOUSLY LEFT OPEN. FROM THE Bibliothèque Nationale, Paris.

Toward the end of August, the entrance to the Isle Dauphine harbor was blocked by a stupendous mass of sand, which a dreadful storm piled up there. This was the reason that no ship has ever since been able to get in.[15] The waves from the sea drowned a great deal of livestock on Isle Dauphine. MM. de l'Épinet and de Bienville, seeing that the ships which would henceforth come from France would be able to anchor only in the Isle-aux-Vaisseaux roadstead,[16] where there is a good anchorage, decided to have a fort built on the mainland opposite this roadstead, which is only five leagues distant and is protected on the east by Isle-aux-Vaisseaux, from which it is only a quarter of a league distant, and on the west by Isle-aux-Chats, half a league away. The place they chose on the mainland for the site of the fort is one league west of Old Biloxi, going toward the point of the bay, opposite Vaisseaux roadstead. About the end of this year they began to build the fort; it was named New Biloxi.

During this same time there arrived at the Isle Dauphine roadstead the flûte named *La Dauphine*, com-

[15] See Lieutenant Du Sault's "Carte de L'Jsle Dauphine," facing page 206. It shows the beautiful little harbor at Dauphin Island and charts the route taken by the *Paon* in escaping from the blocked harbor after the storm. The fifteen-foot pass, on Du Sault's chart still shown open between Isle aux Espagnols and Dauphin, was entirely blocked by sand. Without doubt this damage to Port Dauphin influenced the French in the decision to move the capital from Mobile, now without a port, to New Biloxi and then to New Orleans. Mobile, which could not be reached by ships through the shallow bay, was in danger of being abandoned. Pénicaut says the storm came in August, which suggests a hurricane. But Lieutenant Du Sault in the escaping *Paon* crossed the bar safely on May 15, 1717. The *Paix*, a smaller ship, apparently had less trouble; and the *Ludlow* or *Dudlow*, which had remained anchored in the roadstead south of Isle aux Espagnols, outside the harbor, was not involved in this difficult navigation.

[16] Ship Island roadstead. "Carte de la Coste du Nouveau Biloxy," published in this book, shows twenty feet of water close to the beach on the northwest cove of Ship Island. French ships drew twelve to fifteen feet.

manded by Captain Belanger. He had brought a great many workmen, among them some carpenters and also a great many salt smugglers. All those people were disembarked in longboats [17] and taken to the new fort at Biloxi to work and to build barracks and houses for the residents and soldiers from Isle Dauphine. Also some warehouses were built in which to store the merchandise that would henceforth come from France.

M. de Bienville had told M. de l'Épinet that on his last trip down from the Natchez he had noticed a place quite suitable for the site of a settlement on the bank of the Missicipy thirty leagues above the embouchure of the river, on the right side going upstream. As soon as the fort at New Biloxi was finished, M. de l'Épinet sent the eighty salt smugglers [18] over there at the beginning of winter and a great many carpenters with M. de Bienville to show them the place he had chosen on the bank of the Missicipy for this new post. At the same time he gave an order to M. Blondel, [19] a captain, to go to the Natchez and replace M. Pailloux and send him down to New Orleans to join M. de Bienville and draw the plan of it. But this year only some living quarters were built and two large

[17] Between the Ship Island roadstead and New Biloxi the water was too shallow for ships to approach the new capital. *Traversiers* ventured three fourths of the way in and then anchored; longboats, serving as lighters, transferred freight and passengers to the shore. The decision to move the capital to New Biloxi proved to be one of the poorest made by a none-too-wise government.

[18] Though their morals were faulty, these smugglers, who at least were not lacking in initiative, were potentially better colonists than the many vagabonds and criminals shipped to the colony by the Company of the Indies. The quality of pressed colonists fell so low that on September 24, 1719, the *Achille,* the *Mercure,* and the *Content* were ordered to treat one hundred smugglers (*cent fraudeurs*) "avec douceur et humanité." Henri Gravier, *La Colonization de La Louisiane à L'Époque de Law* (Paris, 1904), p. 36.

[19] This seems to be Philippe Blondel, who was later commandant at Natchitoches.

warehouses in which to store the munitions and food supplies which M. de l'Épinet sent over.

Toward the end of this year, a little boat named *Le Neptune* arrived at Vaisseaux roadstead, bringing a great deal of merchandise and munitions and several soldiers. This little boat remained afterwards in Louisiana and in the following years was used to transport the essential food supplies for the workmen engaged in the building of New Orleans.

M. de Bienville wrote several days afterwards to M. de Chateaugué, his brother, who was commanding officer at Mobile, to send a detachment to the fort we had at the Alibamons,[20] with munitions and food supplies. He wrote also to M. de la Tour, the commandant of the fort, telling him to keep himself on good terms with the Alibamons and Canapouces savages.

[20] Fort Toulouse.

Chapter 20

The Year 1718

M. de Bienville comes down to Isle Dauphine—Concessions
established—M. de Boisbrian leaves for the Illinois—Fort established near the Yasoux—Peace made with the Chetimachas—M.
de St. Denis arrives at Isle Dauphine, and his galante story is continued

T THE beginning of this year M. de Bienville returned to Isle Dauphine, leaving M.
Pailloux as commandant at New Orleans to
keep the construction work going. He reached
an agreement with M. de l'Épinet to have the passes
sounded at the entrance to the Missicipy, so that an attempt could be made to bring *Le Neptune* in fully loaded
with munitions and merchandise which it had brought
from France, with the troops that were aboard. The three
arms of the river's embouchure were sounded, and the
narrowest, which is at the right of its embouchure, was
found to be the deepest, with thirteen feet of water. This
was more than enough for that vessel to come in; it went
on upstream as high as New Orleans, where it came safely
to port. Afterwards much heavier craft came through,
and proceeded right up to the landing at New Orleans.

The Commissary, M. Hubert, likewise went to New
Orleans at the same time, by way of Lake Pontchartrain,
into which flows a little river that has been named Rivière
d'Orléans [1] since that time. People ascend it from the lake

---

[1] Now Bayou St. John.

to this place, about three quarters of a league. A few days after M. Hubert got there, he chose a place two musket shots from the *enceinte* around New Orleans, in the direction of the little river of the same name, and had a very pretty house built there. Several families who were living at Isle Dauphine came also and settled at New Orleans. MM. de l'Épinet and de Bienville sent many soldiers and workmen there to speed up the construction. They sent an order to M. Pailloux to have two main buildings constructed for barracks, big enough to quarter a thousand soldiers each, because this year a great many troops were to arrive from France, not to mention a number of families for concessions in the area, as indeed came.

At the beginning of March, two ships arrived at the Isle Dauphine roadstead, one named *La Duchesse de Noailles,* commanded by M. de la Salle,[2] and the other a flûte named *La Marie,* commanded by Captain Japy.[3] On these two ships there were at least five hundred persons who were going to stay in the region—officers, soldiers, and other persons who had come to obtain concessions,[4] which were established this very year.

The first concession established was that of MM. Paris,[5]

[2] I do not know whether this officer was a relative of the explorer La Salle. His nephew Nicholas de la Salle had already died.

[3] Written Jary by the penman of Parkman, p. 319. Here is further evidence that Jary and Japy are the same man.

[4] Pénicaut is a primary source of the history of the concession phase of Louisiana under John Law's companies. He is the chief source of Henri Gravier's information about concessions given in *La Colonization de La Louisiane à L'Époque de Law.* Pénicaut should be more dependable as an authority on the colonization under Law's companies than on, say, the discovery of the Mississippi by Iberville, since the writer's memory was less likely to be faulty over recent events.

[5] The Paris brothers—Antoine, Claude, Joseph, and Jean—were prominent financiers in France. (Paul Augé [comp.], *Larousse du XXme Siècle* [Paris, 1928–33], V, 381–382.) The most prominent brother, Paris *dit* Duverney, was a director of

managed by M. Dubuisson,[6] who had brought his brother and his two sisters with him, with twenty-five persons and many personal possessions. It was located twenty-eight leagues above New Orleans on the left bank of the Missicipy going upstream, in the old village of the Bayagoulas. In addition to the tilling of fields, they established a silkworm factory there; for that reason they planted a great many mulberry seedlings.

That of M. de Moeuve,[7] managed by M. de Laire [8] and his two nephews, with two other persons named MM. de Chastan and de la Roüe,[9] who had eighty men, both labor-

---

the Company of the West. After the fall of John Law, Paris-Duverney was in 1724 made *syndic-général* of the weakened Company of the Indies. He had played no small part in discrediting the stock of the Company. Gayarré (*History of Louisiana*, I, 241) locates the Paris-Duverney concession on the west bank of the Mississippi, opposite Bayou Manchac. Both Pénicaut and Du Pratz locate it at the old Bayogoula village. [Antoine Simon] Le Page Du Pratz, *History of Louisiana* (reprint of English ed., New Orleans, n.d.), p. 52.

[6] The Sieur de Pauger had serious arguments with a certain Dubuisson, "habitant de la Nouvelle-Orléans," in March, 1721, about the irregular development of houses and streets. (Gravier, *La Colonization de La Louisiane*, p. 44.) A Sieur Dubuisson was killed on June 6, 1728, or 1729, by one Bernaudat (Rowland and Sanders, *MPA*, II, 659, 664, and 670) in a drunken brawl in celebration of Dubuisson's saint's day, St. Claude's day. The younger Dubuisson brother is requesting, by June 4, 1729, that his sister return to Louisiana from France. Minutes of the Directors of the Company of the Indies, June 4, 1729, *ibid.*, II, 656–57.

[7] Gayarré (*History of Louisiana*, I, 241) gives a plantation owner named De Meuse, whose concession was at Pointe Coupée. But the mss. all support M. de Moeuve as Pénicaut's spelling of this name. On January 2, 1721, a M. Desmeuves was made a director of the Company of the Indies. Surrey, *Calendar of Manuscripts in Paris Archives*, I, vii.

[8] The Parkman ms., p. 320, is different: "Celle de Mr de Moeuve dirigée par Mrs de Laire ses deux neveux." This reading makes Messrs. Laire the two nephews of De Moeuve. De la Chaise mentions a Sieur de l'Aire as a concessionaire whose provisions had been commandeered by Bienville. De la Chaise to the Directors of the Company of the Indies, September 6 and 10, 1723, in Rowland and Sanders, *MPA*, II, 338.

[9] I cannot identify Chastan and De la Roüe. An Antoine Roux, living at Cannes Brûlées, was granted 100 livres by the Superior Council to tide him over till the next harvest. Minutes for May 9, 1724, *ibid.*, III, 397.

ers and servants. It was placed eleven leagues beyond New Orleans on the left of the Missicipy going upstream, in the old village of the Tinssas.

That of MM. Brossart, merchants from Lion, who came themselves. They had only ten persons with them. It was established at the village of the Nassitoches—above New Orleans for sixty-six leagues, going upstream on the left to the mouth of the Rivière Rouge, which one has to enter and ascend for seventy leagues more in order to get to the Nassitoches.

That of M. de la Harpe,[10] of St. Malo, who came himself with twenty-five persons. It was located two hundred and thirty-six leagues beyond New Orleans, to the left of the Missicipy, in the village of the Cadodaquioux, one hundred leagues above the Nassitoches. M. de la Harpe went up there in spite of all the bad roads and the unbelievable difficulties he met with upon the Rivière Rouge.

That of M. de la Houssaye,[11] a gentleman from Picardie, with fifteen persons, among whom were MM. Tisserands,[12] two brothers, who were partners of M. de la Houssaye. It is established close to the village of the Natchez, on the bank of their little river, eighty-eight

[10] Bénard de la Harpe, the prominent officer and explorer whose *Journal Historique de l'Établissement des Français à la Louisiane* (New Orleans and Paris, 1831) is often cited as one of the most authoritative books about early Louisiana.

[11] According to Gayarré (*History of Louisiana*, I, 242), Messrs. Scouvion de la Houssaye and their eighty-two followers were settled on land on the Yazoo. Apparently there were at least two Houssaye concessions or two or more families.

[12] Tixerant may be another spelling of this name. There was a Tixerant in the colony in 1741. (Bienville and Salmon to Maurepas, April 24, 1741, in Rowland and Sanders, *MPA*, III, 745.) One Sieur Tixerand was a warehouse keeper at New Biloxi and New Orleans; there were complaints about his poor accounts. See Messrs. Périer and De la Chaise to the Directors of the Company of the Indies, March 25, 1729, *ibid.*, II, 637, and marginal note, which shows there were two Tixerands.

leagues above New Orleans, and on the same side. It now belongs to Sieur Pénicaut, the author of this narrative, who bought it from them.

That of M. de Chantour,[13] who came with eight persons, is established a quarter of a league from New Orleans, on the same side—on the right of the Missicipy going upstream.

That of MM. Le Page [14] and Legras,[15] in partnership, who came with six persons: near New Orleans, next to M. Chantour's.

M. de Boisbrian had arrived aboard the ship named *La Duchesse de Noailles*. On leaving the ship at Isle Dauphine, he had delivered a packet of letters to M. de Bienville from His Majesty, who gave him the commission of Commandant-General of Louisiana. Also, there was another letter which commissioned M. Pailloux as adjutant-general of troops and commissioned M. Diron,[16] the brother of M. Dartaguet,[17] as captain of a company at the Illinois. Before leaving France, M. de Boisbrian had

[13] The last letter in this name is hard to read. Margry (*Découvertes*, V, 553) has "M. de Chantoux (?)." The six entries I have examined strongly support Chantour. Parkman, p. 322, has two clear entries as Chantour. B. F. French ("Annals of Louisiana . . . By M. Pénicaut," p. 141) has Chantous as the name of a concessionnaire at the old Choupitoulas village.

[14] Antoine Simon Le Page Du Pratz, a Dutchman, who arrived in the colony August 25, 1718. He stayed sixteen years, chiefly in the Natchez area. His *Histoire de la Louisiane* is excellent for Louisiana fauna and flora. See Stanley Clisby Arthur's Preface to the reprint of the 1774 English edition.

[15] This name is hard to read. It may be Legros.

[16] I believe this Diron is the one who became inspector-general of troops in Louisiana. Bernar Diron was a cadet in Chateaugué's company on March 16, 1709, when Dartaguette was *ordonnateur* at Mobile. Mobile Baptismal Records.

[17] The old *ordonnateur* who replaced the scrivener La Salle. He left Louisiana in 1711 and was tax collector of the district of Auch in 1723. Pénicaut dedicated his narrative to him, and I believe that the Clermont ms., from which this edition has been translated, was the personal copy of this member of the Diron-Dartaguette family.

been made a Chevalier de St. Louis and Governor of the Illinois; therefore, he left a few days later to go up to the Illinois with ten boats. He took one hundred soldiers with him and several officers, among whom were MM. Diron, the two brothers, one a captain, as I have already said, and the other a lieutenant,[18] and M. Bauchart,[19] also a lieutenant.

M. Barnaval [20] went up with them as far as the Natchez to take the place of M. Blondel,[21] who had been ordered to go up to the Nassitoches upon the Rivière Rouge to relieve M. de Tissenet so that he could come down and join M. de Boisbrian at the Natchez and the two could go up to the Illinois together.

M. de la Loire, who was at the Natchez, went to the Illinois with them, too, to be manager of the office and the warehouses belonging to the Company.

During this same time M. de Bienville sent M. de la Boulaye, a lieutenant, with thirty men and a great deal

[18] This is Pierre Dartaguette, the third member of the Diron-Dartaguette family. Notice that he went to the Illinois Country with Boisbriant. When Captain Diron was made inspector-general of troops in Louisiana he came back down river and held commands at Mobile and elsewhere. How long Pierre stayed at the Illinois, I do not know; but he was returning in charge of the 1733 convoy up river; he was commandant at the Illinois from 1733 till his death, probably on the fire-cadre, at a Chickasaw village just before the battle of Ackia, 1736. (See Belting, *Kaskaskia under the French Regime*, p. 76.) The other brother, Bernar Diron (if my identification is correct), stayed in the colony until 1742. He died at Cap François. See Rowland and Sanders' long note on the Dartaguettes, in *MPA*, I, 56–57. My account of the Dartaguettes does not agree with Rowland and Sanders'.

[19] Given as Bauchard in Margry, *Découvertes*, V, 554. The name may be Bouchart, as in Parkman, p. 323.

[20] Erroneously given as Bienville in Margry, *Découvertes*, V, 554. This officer, who once commanded Fort Rosalie at Natchez, appears in various documents as Bernaval. For Barnaval as commandant of Rosalie at the time of Bienville's attack on the so-called Terre Blanche village, see Dumont de Montigny, *Mémoires Historiques sur la Louisiane*, II, 100.

[21] Philippe Blondel.

of munitions and merchandise to establish a fort [22] close
to the village of the Yasoux. When he got there, he chose
the highest place he could find on the bank of their river,
on the right side four leagues inland from its mouth, two
musket shots from their village, and there he had his fort
built.

A few days after M. de Boisbrian had gone up to the
Illinois, the two ships, *La Duchesse de Noailles* and *La
Marie*, went back to France, taking M. de l'Épinet and
M. Artus. After they had gone, M. de Bienville sent M. de
Laubinière [23] with forty men and the necessary provisions
to the Nassitoches upon the Rivière Rouge to be in com-
mand there along with M. Blondel.

A little while later, M. de Bienville received a letter
from M. Dubuisson, who was in control of MM. Paris'
concession, established in the old village of the Bayagoulas
on the bank of the Missicipy. In this letter he pointed out
that he was not free of danger on his concession as long as
the French were at war with the savage nation named the
Chetimachas, who daily came in war parties to the neighborhood of his concession; and he stated that, if his men
went out ever so little, they were daily in danger of seizure
or death, as had already happened to two of his men,[24]

---

[22] Gayarré (*History of Louisiana*, I, 418) gives the name of the French fort
among the Yazoo as St. Claude in [1729–30], at the time the Yazoo, following
Natchez leadership, massacred the twenty men of the garrison, January 1 or 2,
1730. But Fort St. Pierre des Yazous shows on D'Anville's "Carte de la Louisiane
. . . Dressée en Mai 1732."

[23] This name appears as Sieur Lotbinière in Minutes of the Council of Commerce
Assembled at Dauphine Island on the Eighteenth of October, 1719. Rowland and
Sanders, *MPA*, III, 263.

[24] ". . . deux de ses gens," which Margry misread as "deux des sergents."
(*Découvertes*, V, 555). Margry's "two sergeants" have thence made their way into
secondary sources.

and that they were forced to hold themselves with weapons in hand night and day, which prevented them from working at their concession. Acting upon this information, M. de Bienville sent me alone among the Chetimachas to talk to their chief and persuade him to make peace with the French.

Although this mission seemed to me highly dangerous, I did not fail to undertake it because I spoke their language fairly well and was acquainted with several of the savages. I made my plan, not to go straight to the Chetimachas village, but to go on up to the Oumas village, where I expected to run across several of the Chetimachas savages, who come there quite often, as they are the Oumas' nearest neighbors.

I was not at all mistaken in my expectations: I found three of them and talked with them. I told them that I had M. de Bienville's orders to go to their chief for the purpose of making peace between them and the French. These three savages were quite delighted to learn this news because as long as they have been at war with the French they have had as enemies the savages friendly to the French, who were always on war parties against them, following M. de Bienville's orders, and have killed a great many of their people; therefore, these three savages did not hesitate to follow me when I told them to come with me as far as the concession of MM. Paris, which was only seven leagues away.

When we got there, M. Dubuisson gave them some little presents to take to their chiefs and some food for their trip. I requested them to come back in ten days at the latest, giving them ten little pieces of wood, which are tallies by which the savages reckon by nights, the same as we reckon by days. They did not fail to return ten days later, but they held back on the bank of their river,[25] which is five leagues from MM. Paris' concession. Only the three savages whom I had sent off came to the concession and informed me that the Grand Chief, with his wife and forty Chetimachas, was awaiting me at that place to talk with me. I hesitated somewhat to take the risk of going there alone; however, I made up my mind to do so, seeing no one that wished to accompany me. I went away with the three savages.

As soon as I got to the bank of their river and they saw me, they uttered a dreadful shout. I thought then that I was betrayed and that this was the last day of my life; but this strange shout was only a shout of joy, for the Grand Chief received me with perfect manners and told me that it would give him and all his nation great pleasure to make peace with the French. I told him that, to make peace, they would have to come to New Orleans to sing their calumet of peace to M. de Bienville, our commandant. They said they would follow me wherever I wanted to lead them. I led them first to MM. Paris' concession, where M. Dubuisson gave them some food; and after they had spent the night there, we set off with daybreak the next day to go downstream to New Orleans. They stayed there a week, as it was necessary to await the reply of M. de Bienville, who instructed M. de Pailloux to make them sing their calumet of peace and to grant peace on the following terms:

[25] Bayou Lafourche.

INDIANS OF THE FOX, ILLINOIS, AND ATTAKAPA TRIBES. THE NEGRO SLAVE GIRL, AS WELL AS THE COMMODITIES, IS A SIGN OF ACCULTURATION. NOTE THE PET CRANE BESIDE THE CHIEF. From Bushnell, "Drawings by A. DeBatz."

First, that the Chetimachas taken as slaves during the war would not be returned to them and they would return whatever French people they might have taken or that might be in their villages.

Second, that they would leave their homes on the river where they were and come and settle on the bank of the Missicipy River in a place that was marked off for them, one league below MM. Paris' concession.

They all accepted these terms and kept them faithfully; for a fortnight later, with their families and their livestock loaded with their possessions, they came downstream to settle. Before dismissing them, M. Pailloux gave them the presents which M. de Bienville had indicated should be given them. With these they were quite satisfied.

This peace made with the Chetimachas, which compelled them to come and settle on the bank of the Missicipy, caused other savage nations to make several changes of dwelling place. They came and settled on the bank of the Missicipy. The first were the Chaoüachas,[26] twenty leagues away from the river bank, who came and settled on the bank of the Missicipy three leagues below New Orleans, on the right going upstream. The Oüachas [27] also, who were twenty-five leagues from the river, came and settled eleven leagues above New Orleans, on the left side going upstream, three quarters above M. de Moeuve's concession. The Colapissas, who lived on the shore of Lake Pontchartrain, came and made their settlement likewise on the bank of the Missicipy, thirteen leagues above New

[26] The Chawasha.

[27] The Washa Indians, a small tribe living near the Chawasha, with whom they later united. Hodge, *Handbook,* II, 918–19.

Orleans, on the right. All these nations are highly industrious and all are quite helpful in furnishing food to the
French, to the troops as well as to the people on the concessions.

Toward the end of this year, M. de St. Denis, with his
valet Jalot, arrived at Isle Dauphine. He embraced M. de
Bienville, but did not give him much of an account of his
voyage because at that time he was quite reserved with
M. de Bienville, following a pique that they had had with
each other. That is what made him keep quiet about the
circumstances, which his valet Jalot related to me and
about which I began to talk within the year 1716. Here is
the continuation:

M. de St. Denis had reached the home of his father-in-
law, Dom Pedros de Vilesca, at Rivière du Nord Village,
and had surprised Dona Maria in the garden. When she re-
gained consciousness and recognized her husband, they
entered Dom Pedros' house, and she went to tell Dom
Pedros and her uncle, Dom Juan, that M. de St. Denis had
arrived. They joined him at once in the little garden room,
where Dona Maria had left him; and after they had embraced one another again and again, they went together
up to Dona Maria's room, which was above this one, and
supper was brought up to M. de St. Denis. He ate very
little, and after a great many felicitations on both sides,
they left him to rest, seeing plainly that he had need of
rest, being quite exhausted.

The next day he remained in bed till very late; so, Dom
Pedros and Dom Juan did not go to his room till about
midday, when they had dinner brought and all dined with
Dona Maria. After dinner Dom Pedros drew M. de St.

Denis aside and after showing his son-in-law much affection and indicating that he was delighted to welcome him to his home, he told him that he begged him earnestly to grant him one favor. M. de St. Denis, who could deny him nothing, replied that he was ready to give him all the services that he could, even at the expense of his life. "I would not have made this request of you," added Dom Pedros, "if your life, as well as mine, were not in danger —in case you should not follow the advice I must give you." At the same time Dom Pedros informed him that an order to arrest him if he should visit Dona Maria had been received from the Viceroy of Mexico.[28] A cavalry officer with twenty-five cavalrymen from the Governor of Caoüil had been waiting for him in the village for six months; it was absolutely necessary to forbid him and his valet, too, to go out of the house. "Because otherwise," his father-in-law told him, "if you are noticed, you will be taken to the Viceroy, from whose hands you will not get away so easily as you did the first time. I myself have an order to arrest you; this I shall never do, even if it should cost me my life; therefore," Dom Pedros repeated once more, "I beg you not to go outside my house, which no one has seen you enter, and where you will surely not be discovered, especially in Dona Maria's bedroom, where no one ever goes." M. de St. Denis thanked him for his advice and at the same time forbad his valet Jalot to go, day or night, out of the little room where he slept underneath M. de St. Denis' bedroom.

"The surprising thing," Jalot said to me, "is that M. de

---

[28] Baltasar de Zúñiga, Marquis de Valero, who was free of the influence of St. Denis' friends. Phares, *Cavalier in the Wilderness*, p. 119.

St. Denis spent nearly a year in this manner, without ever going out of his wife's bedroom except very late at night when he went to walk with her under the trees of a garden path at the house. During that time, his wife, Dona Maria, became pregnant with her second child. I believe that this is what kept M. de St. Denis from becoming bored, for they loved each other more tenderly than ever.

"As for me," Jalot told me, "I have never spent any time that seemed to me longer, especially in winter when one could no longer walk in the garden because of the cold. Sometimes in the evening, when the door of the house was shut, I warmed myself by the fire in the kitchen, with a tall, lean and ugly serving girl named Luce, who had more pride than the daughter of the most famous barber [29] in Mexico City."

Ten months later Dona Maria was delivered of a boy, who was named Dom Juan for the uncle of M. de St. Denis' wife, who was the child's godfather. Dona Isabella, his wife's sister, was godmother. The child was secretly baptized within the house, in Dom Pedros' room, by a Cordelier. During the baptism of his son, M. de St. Denis remained in his wife's room and did not appear before this monk, for fear of being discovered. Dona Maria chose to nurse her baby herself. It looked exactly like M. de St. Denis.

Six weeks later, spring being already well advanced, Dom Pedros came one morning to M. de St. Denis in his wife's room and told him, with a face that appeared quite disturbed, that he had been warned that there was suspicion that M. de St. Denis was hiding in his house. The

[29] Jalot was himself a surgeon-barber.

officer in the village had called on him, asking to see his daughter, Dona Maria, but he had replied that she was indisposed and was resting, and therefore could not see any one.

Toward evening of the same day, Dom Juan, Dom Pedros' brother, came in Dona Maria's room and told Dom Pedros, in the presence of M. de St. Denis, that he had just learned from one of his friends that the cavalry officer in the village had sent one of his troopers to Caoüil with a letter addressed to the Governor. Dom Juan was afraid the letter was sent to obtain a warrant to search Dom Pedros' house. Because of the confinement of Dona Maria, Dom Pedros was suspected of having M. de St. Denis in his house. Some one certainly must have disclosed it, and M. de St. Denis would have to leave without delay.

Upon the advice of Dom Pedros and Dom Juan, it was decided that he would leave at nightfall of the second day. This he was compelled to do after a great many tears had been shed by both of them, and after Dom Pedros and Dom Juan de Vilesca had given him expressions of affection, promising him before he left that in a short while they would take his wife to him at Mobile.

He and Jalot left through the rear of the house about midnight and went as far as the woods along the sunken road over which they had come—without meeting any one. They walked until day, and when day came they pushed deep into a wood, to eat and to rest there during the day. Thus they traveled for six weeks without having any unpleasant encounter or making any great headway each night, living, as is usual in that region, off the ends of their guns when the food Jalot had provided ran short after only six days.

They had already passed more than eight leagues beyond the Assinaïs, where the Spaniards have their last outpost, and were no more than fifty leagues from the Nassitoches, where the French have their first fort in that direction. That day while they were resting near a creek in a wood, Jalot caught sight of a deer on its way to the creek. He shot at it with a bullet, but the deer ran on, although struck clear through the body, and fell at some distance near the road. M. de St. Denis and Jalot followed it by the trail of blood stained on the grasses and leaves through which it had passed. After they had found it and were beginning to skin it so that they could cut some pieces for roasting, two Spanish cavalrymen came into the wood, pistol in hand, shouting, "To the death! To the death!" [30] One of the cavalrymen headed for Jalot, firing his pistol at him from a distance, but missing him. M. de St. Denis, who had his gun loaded, fired it at the other cavalryman and knocked him to the ground with the shot. Jalot got behind a tree and poured a handful of powder into his gun and slipped a bullet on top of the powder. But the cavalryman who had fired his pistol at

---

[30] "Amath, amath," Parkman, p. 339, and Spofford, p. 404. Clermont has "Amatti! Amatti!" This exclamation of the Spanish troopers proved a puzzler to the penmen and to Margry too. *Découvertes*, V, 562, has ". . . à mata! à mata!" Margry's form of the expression led me to believe that Pénicaut was trying to write some part of the Spanish verb *matar*, "to slay." My colleague Dr. Gustavo René Hernández suggested *ármate*, "arm!" said by one trooper to the other. If Pénicaut was writing Spanish, he wrote bad Spanish indeed, merely a representation of *ármate* or of *mátale*, "kill him!" But if he was writing French, which has the stronger claim, he meant *à math* or *à mat*, "to the death!" or "to a finish," or "we've got you!" Cf. Fr. *faire mat*, "to checkmate," which in a figurative sense is the equivalent of *abattre*, "to slaughter." The French verb *mater*, "(check)mate," goes ultimately back to Persian *châh mat*, "the king is dead." See *Larousse du XXme Siècle*, IV, 734.

him, having seen his comrade fall, did not wait for Jalot to prime his gun; he fled as fast as he could at full gallop. Having emptied his gun, M. de St. Denis was no little disconcerted, and Jalot too, because they feared there might be still more cavalrymen besides those two. Jalot went outside the woods to find out, but he did not see any cavalrymen in the road other than the one that had fired his pistol at him, and he was fleeing at full gallop in the direction of the Assinaïs and was already quite far off. When Jalot returned and told M. de St. Denis, they went to the cavalryman who had fallen from M. de St. Denis' shot; but he was already dead, the bullet having passed through his stomach. Jalot caught his horse, the reins having passed under the cavalryman's arm in the fall.

On the horse's croup was a little bag containing bread and cooked meat, which Jalot took charge of. They quickly decided that they would not remain longer in that place, and although it was broad daylight, M. de St. Denis mounted the horse and insisted that Jalot should ride behind him. They traveled on until night; they rested a full three hours in a wood at a place where they found a great deal of grass to feed to the horse. They traveled on for the remainder of the night, until daybreak, when they went more than a league and a half into the wood with the horse. They found a small lake on the shore of which were six huts of savages, in which there were three women and one man, with four small children entirely naked. The man fled as soon as he saw them coming. Jalot spoke to these savages' women in the Nassitoches language, which they understood well, and told them that he and M. de St. Denis were Frenchmen from the fort at the

Nassitoches and that they should go and fetch their husbands, for no one wanted to harm them. One of the women ran after the savage and brought him back. "He told us, trembling, that he had been afraid that we were Spaniards from the Assinaïs, who were their enemies and who had captured three of his comrades, whom the Assinaïs had eaten." [31] They were of the Yatacez nation, the majority of whom had settled with the Nassitoches. For that reason M. de St. Denis told them to come and join the other savages of their nation who were living at the Nassitoches, where they would not be in danger of being seized by the Assinaïs. Jalot asked them how many nights it was from there to the Nassitoches. They replied three nights and a half—that is, according to our way of computing, thirty-five leagues—and just as far to the Assinaïs. M. de St. Denis took the horse into one of their huts, and with the savage's help Jalot gathered some grass for the horse. M. de St. Denis and Jalot ate the sagamité which the savage women gave them. After this they took a rest for the remainder of the day.

Half an hour before nightfall they set out and three days later reached the Nassitoches. M. de St. Denis was

[31] This sentence, which I have put in quotation marks because it contains *we* and *us* as proof of a first-person narrator, seems to be a last vestige inadvertently left by the author after changing a first-person narrative to the objective point of view. How did this come about? It may represent no more than evidence that the author first wrote in the first person and then changed his plan. But there are two other possible explanations. One of them—that Pénicaut had access to St. Denis' memoirs—is given in Chapter XVII, n. 4. The other, advanced by Charles B. Reed, is that Pénicaut has copied a romantic narrative that Jalot wrote about his master in order to protect him from an accusation of treason, since St. Denis accepted, and did not reject, the Viceroy's offer of employment. Serving Spain on a salary, St. Denis acted as quartermaster and guide of the Domingo Ramón expedition to present-day Texas. See Reed, "Sieur de St. Denis and Jallot, his Valet de Chambre," *Northwestern University Bulletin; The Medical School*, XXXIV (March 19, 1934), 13-15.

surprised at not finding M. de Tissenet there, whom he had left there when he went away to visit his wife. He remained there for two weeks to rest with MM. Blondel and de Laubinière, and afterwards returned with Jalot in a boat to New Orleans, where he paid his respects to M. Pailloux. He remained there twelve days, examining the construction in progress and then went back to Isle Dauphine to M. de Bienville.

Those are the details Jalot gives me of his master's *amours*. M. de St. Denis did not stay long at Isle Dauphine. He went away and settled at old Fort Biloxi, making all his slaves come and live there and having all his belongings brought.

Chapter 21

The Year 1719

M. de Sérigny and three ships arrive at Isle Dauphine—War declared with the Spaniards and Fort Passacol captured—Treachery of the Spaniards: they lay siege to Passacol and retake it—The Spaniards come to make a raid on Isle Dauphine and are repulsed—Arrival of M. de Chamelin's squadron and the second capture of Fort Passacol by the French and the destruction of it —Isle Dauphine abandoned

N FEBRUARY there arrived at the Isle Dauphine roadstead three ships from France named *Le Comte de Toulouze, Le Maréchal de Villars*, and *Le St. Louis*, commanded by M. de Sérigny.[1] MM. de Villardeau,[2] de Gaque,[3] and du Chambeau [4] came on them as directors in place of M. Rogeon,[5]

[1] Joseph Le Moyne de Sérigny, brother of Iberville. Along with Bienville he governed Louisiana in 1718-20. He became governor of Rochefort; and of the many Le Moyne brothers, only he founded a family. Surrey, *Calendar of Manuscripts in French Archives*, I, ix, and Rowland and Sanders, *MPA*, II, 550 and n. 3.

[2] Minutes of the Council of Commerce of Louisiana for 1719 and 1720 carry his signature. Rowland and Sanders, *MPA*, III, 268 ff.

[3] Charles Legac, whose signature, C. Legac, is on Minutes of the Council of Commerce as a member and apparently as secretary in 1719 and 1720. (*Ibid.*, III, 268.) These meetings were held at Mobile and at Dauphin Island. Gayarré has his name as Legas. *History of Louisiana*, I, 253.

[4] It was not a Du Chambeau, but Larubault who, with the director C. Legac, signed the Minutes of the Council of Commerce in April, 1719. (Rowland and Sanders, *MPA*, III, 240-41). Larubault was at Pensacola, presumably a prisoner of the Spaniards, when Chateaugué as prisoner wrote his letter to Bienville on August 9, 1719. (Chateaugué to Bienville, *ibid.*, III, 251-52). Pénicaut tells on p. 232 that Du Chambeau was sent to Havana as prisoner along with Chateaugué. Fortier (*History of Louisiana*, I, 68) and Gayarré (*History of Louisiana*, I, 251-54) both have this agent-director of the Company as L'Archambault.

[5] Raujon.

whom they relieved. Also, there was M. de Montplaisir,[6] heading a party of thirty workmen from Clérac,[7] coming to work in a tobacco factory, and M. de Catillon,[8] an Irish gentleman who had brought sixty men under his orders to work on a concession which he came to establish. This concession was placed at La Fourche des Oüachitas, on the bank of the Rivière Rouge, on the right side of this river, eight leagues above the mouth, and seventy-four leagues from New Orleans.

The concession of M. de Bonne [9]—who had come with the rank of attorney-general, bringing his whole family and fifteen persons—was placed on the right side two leagues above Rivière d'Orléans.

MM. Pellerin [10] and Bellecourt's [11] concession, with fifteen persons and their family, was placed at the village of the Natchez.

On these three ships M. de Sérigny had brought a great

[6] De la Chaise reported that a Sieur La Bro had taken the place of De Montplaisir as manager of the Clairacs' tobacco plantation at Natchez by the time the plantation was being granted or sold to M. Le Blanc, September 6 and 10, 1723. Rowland and Sanders, *MPA*, II, 294 and 335.

[7] Glossed by Margry as "Ouvriers de la manufacture du tabac, établie sur le territoire de Clérac (Charente-Inférieure)." *Découvertes,* V, 573.

[8] Given as Catillou by Margry (*Découvertes,* V, 565). He suggests Cantillon. The Parkman ms. (p. 346 and p. 364) gives de Catillon. A Jaque Chatillon [*sic*] signed the Mobile Baptismal Records on January 23, 1711. And a Sieur Cantillon is mentioned in De la Chaise's letter of September 6, 1723. Rowland and Sanders, *MPA*, II, 294 and 354.

[9] Parkman, p. 346, has de Borme or de Boume. Gayarré gives this attorney-general as Cartier de Baune. *History of Louisiana,* I, 252–53.

[10] Minutes of the Council, March 23, 1725, mention a Sieur Guyot, of Natchez, as being the partner of Sieur Pellerin. Rowland and Sanders, *MPA*, II, 420.

[11] This partner of Pellerin may have moved to the Illinois Country, for in 1725 Sieur Guyot is Pellerin's partner. (*Ibid.*) I have been unable to find a Bellecourt among the well-indexed documents in *MPA*. But in the Illinois Country there was an L. Belcour as *huissier* in 1728; and a Bellecourt family lived at Kaskaskia. Joseph Bellecourt's will is dated October 11, 1740. Belting, *Kaskaskia under the French Regime,* pp. 111–12.

many soldiers, workmen, and two hundred and fifty Negroes, who were from the very first used in unloading the ships and moving the munitions and merchandise to the warehouses on Isle Dauphine.

A few days after M. de Sérigny had gone ashore at Isle Dauphine, he announced that war had been declared with Spain; therefore, with M. de Bienville and the other officers he held a council at which it was decided that they would go and lay siege to Fort Passacol,[12] which is the closest fort the Spaniards have to Mobile. With this in mind, he sent M. de Bienville to Mobile to have all the residents living there warned to be ready to go on this expedition. At the same time he sent word to our friends among the savages, those living closest to us, and set a day for them to go to Mobile. When all the French soldiers and the savages got there, MM. de Bienville and de Chateaugué, with the other officers and all the troops, left Mobile to go by land and lay siege to Passacol, while M. de Sérigny went by sea with four ships to enter the harbor. The Spaniards put up scarcely any resistance and surrendered the very first day, according to the following terms:

First, two ships would be provided to take them to Havana, with the necessary food;

Second, they would leave all their weapons and ammunition, cannons as well as guns, cannon balls, powder, and food supplies that were in the fort.

As the capture of this fort had cost so little and the fortifications were scarcely damaged at all, M. de Cha-

[12] Fort Pensacola.

teaugué was left there as governor, with three hundred Frenchmen and the necessary munitions and provisions. All the savages were sent home, and MM. de Sérigny and de Bienville brought the troops back to Mobile and Isle Dauphine.

A few days later, the fourteen hundred Spaniards who, according to the terms, had to be returned, were sent back to Havana; they were sent in the two ships, Le Comte de Toulouze and Le Maréchal de Villars; [13] but the Governor of Havana had had ten bilanders [14] armed and had made the prisoners revolt whom we had taken there in our two vessels. They seized control of them, making prisoners of our men, and immediately returned and laid siege to Passacol. MM. de Sérigny and de Bienville, who had not expected such treachery, did not have enough time to assemble the troops and the savages, whom they had disbanded, and to go to relieve Passacol. On the other hand, M. de Chateaugué had not made preparations to withstand a siege so soon: he suffered the further grief of seeing ninety of the three hundred men he had as his whole garrison desert the very first day he was under siege; and in spite of all his admonishments to the two hundred who remained—encouraging them as best he could, both by his words and his example to resist strongly—they nevertheless resisted so poorly during the four days he

[13] This ship, or possibly the Toulouse, was commanded by the Chevalier de Grieux, which is the same name as the one chosen by Prévost for the hero of Histoire du Chevalier Des Grieux et de Manon Lescaut. The real De Grieux was captured at Havana. (Rowland and Sanders, MPA, III, 246 and 269.) Harry Kurz, who edited Prévost's novel, gives a possible identification of the hero as Charles Des Grieux, "écuyer, chevalier de St. Louis et lieutenant de carabiniers, mort en 1723." Histoire du Chevalier Des Grieux et de Manon Lescaut (New York, 1929), p. 234.

[14] A bilander is a small two masted merchant vessel that operates chiefly in coastal waters, "by land."

held out that he was compelled to surrender as a prisoner of war with his garrison.

The Spaniards put our soldiers in the bottom of the hold, their hands and their feet tied. As for MM. de Chateaugué and du Chambeau, they were immediately taken to Havana in one of the Spaniards' bilanders.

After the Spaniards had retaken Passacol, they followed the advice of the French deserters and came down in the direction of Isle Dauphine, boasting of coming there and getting a foothold to pillage by means of the nine bilanders they manned and our two ships which they had armed and equipped with a great many troops. M. de Bienville, having foreseen this emergency, had sent an order to several different nations of the Mobile area to come down to Isle Dauphine. M. de St. Denis came, too, from Biloxi, leading a great many savages from the neighborhood where he lived. This proved to be of great help to Isle Dauphine. There came, too, a great many people from the concessions, who with great courage defended the island in the places where they were posted, so that the Spaniards were repulsed from all sides of the island at every landing they attempted during twelve consecutive days and nights.

One of the most powerful of their bilanders, on which were the eighty French deserters, landed at a place called Miragouin,[15] at the beginning of Baye de la Mobile, where they knew there was some merchandise belonging to several persons of the concessions. They pillaged a part of this and carried it in rowboats to their bilander; but when

[15] On Mon Louis Island. Nicolas Bodin, Sieur de Miragouanne, owned the land there.

they came back a second time, they were surprised by a party of Mobilien savages, who killed some thirty of them and captured seventeen. These they escorted to Mobile, where their heads were broken. After twelve days the Spaniards went back to Passacol in their bilanders, having failed in their attempt on Isle Dauphine.

At that same time, [fortunately], Commodore de Chamelin [16] arrived at the Isle Dauphine roadstead with five warships and immediately had M. de Sérigny notified to have his troops assembled to go by land to Passacol, while he would go with his squadron and enter the harbor to attack the fort. As soon as M. de Sérigny received this news, he wrote about it to M. de Bienville, who was at Mobile. M. de St. Denis came over also, leading several savage nations. M. de Sérigny, having learned that all the troops had assembled there, left Isle Dauphine to go to Mobile and lead all these troops by land to invest Passacol.

When M. de Chamelin had been informed that M. de Sérigny had invested Fort Passacol by land, he led the way into the harbor with his ship named *L'Hercule*, followed by four others, which went in without firing a single cannon shot. Only the last ship, named *Le Mars*, fired at the little fort, from both her sides, for two hours, knocking it down completely. Only this little fort [17] resisted. The Spanish governor, who was in command of it, saw that his fort was no longer in condition to hold out and sounded a parley two hours later.

[16] His signature was Desnos de Champmeslin. (Copy of the Minutes of the Navy Council Held on Board the Vessel "Hercule" in the Roadstead of Dauphine Island, September 5, 1719, in Rowland and Sanders, MPA, III, 262.) One word in this sentence, "fortunately," is supplied from Parkman, p. 351.

[17] Built on the western tip of Santa Rosa Island. Bienville to the Council, Dauphine Island, October 20, 1719, *ibid.*, III, 273.

M. de Chamelin had had his guns trained on the big fort, but it did not put up any resistance and straightway surrendered without firing one cannon shot. So, the recapture of Passacol lasted no longer than three hours. MM. de Sérigny and de Bienville had the savages go inside the big fort and the little one, which they were permitted to plunder as a reward for their efforts. The nine bilanders belonging to the Spaniards and our two ships, which they had treacherously seized and armed, were taken after a little fight, which lasted one hour at most. In the big and the little Fort Passacol there were fifteen hundred Spaniards, who were sent back to Havana in two bilanders. After the savages had plundered all there was in Passacol, the two forts were completely razed.

At this time M. de St. Denis arranged to entertain M. de Chamelin and the captains and officers of marine with a dance of the savages, who sang a calumet of peace to him. Next, in the name of M. de Chamelin, M. de St. Denis made them an oration in their own language, exhorting them to be friends of the French forever. After this speech, M. de Chamelin had presents given to them all, with which they were quite satisfied.

A few days after the demolition of Fort Passacol, M. de Chamelin took his squadron back to France. The Spanish bilanders and our two ships were brought to Isle Dauphine. MM. de Bienville and de St. Denis disbanded the savages and led the French troops to Mobile and Isle Dauphine. Since Passacol was an advanced post, a sergeant was left there with twelve soldiers to give warning of ships approaching land from that direction. When M. de Chamelin had come to Isle Dauphine, a flûte named

La Marie had come with his squadron. Aboard *La Marie* was M. Arnaud,[18] in charge of a party of fifty miners whom he had brought along with him, and a great many soldiers, some ammunition, and merchandise.

Upon arrival the captain in command of *La Marie*, named Sieur Japy, had given a letter to M. de Bienville by which the Company ordered him to have several flat boats built to transport the personal effects of a great many persons who would arrive in Louisiana the following year, to whom the Company had granted concessions. This forced M. de Bienville to send orders to the workmen at Mobile, Biloxi, New Orleans, and everywhere else to construct some flat boats as quickly as possible and take them over to Biloxi.

M. de Sérigny sailed about that time on the ships *Le Comte de Toulouze* and *Le Maréchal de Villars* to go back to France. One month after the departure of M. de Sérigny, a vessel named *Les Deux Frères* arrived, with a great number of German men and German women on board. It was further loaded with all kinds of merchandise and personal possessions which belonged to them. This vessel anchored in the Isle-aux-Vaisseaux roadstead, and their personal effects and merchandise were unloaded at New Biloxi, to which they were brought in flatboats along with all the people that were on the ship.

Toward the end of this year, several of the Isle Dauphine families left to go to New Biloxi and settle. At the same time a great deal of merchandise and munitions and

[18] I suspect this is a penman's error for Renault, which in script can be taken for Arnault. The man in question was Philippe François Renault, who had been a banker in Paris. He became the Company's director-general for mines and was quite active in the Illinois Country. See Alvord, *The Illinois Country*, p. 154.

provisions that were in the warehouses on the island and a great number of families that lived there were loaded aboard *Le Neptune,* a small ship, which was to take them to New Orleans.

Near the end of this year, M. Hubert, the commissary-general at New Orleans, had bought a great supply of corn from the savages and had had it stored in the warehouses. Finally this year all the warehouses on Isle Dauphine were emptied and moved to New Orleans and Biloxi, where M. de Bienville and the officers went to live, with all the troops that were on Isle Dauphine. Left on the island were only one sergeant with twelve soldiers and a coastal pilot to land ships from France at the Isle-aux-Vaisseaux roadstead, situated opposite New Biloxi.

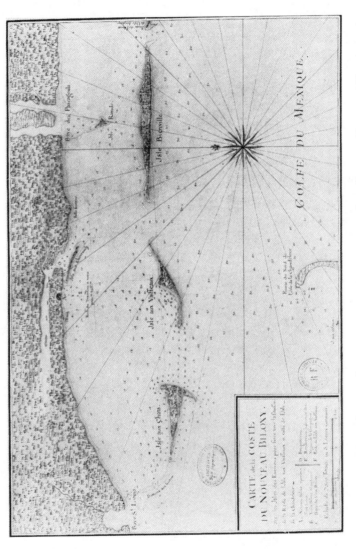

MAP OF MISSISSIPPI SOUND. SOUNDINGS MARKED BETWEEN SHIP ISLAND (ISLE AUX VAISSEAUX) AND NEW BILOXI TO THE NORTH TESTIFY TO THE POOR CHOICE OF NEW BILOXI AS CAPITAL OF LOUISIANA. From the Bibliothèque Nationale, Paris.

Chapter 22

The Year 1720

M. Hubert's trip to the Natchez and the establishment of a
tobacco factory by M. de Montplaisir—Seven ships arrive in
Louisiana—Several concessions established—Convoy sent to the
Alibamons—M. de St. Denis receives the commission of captain
and commandant of the fort at the Nassitoches

A T THE beginning of this year M. Hubert,
the commissary-general, left New Orleans,
where he lived, to go up to the Natchez. At
the same time he had eight boats taken there
loaded with merchandise and his belongings. He had his
whole family with him and sixty servants whom he had
brought from France. The head of the Cléracs, M. de
Montplaisir, who had been instructed by the Company
to establish a tobacco factory in Louisiana, went to the
Natchez, too, by means of the same accommodations,
with thirty tobacco workers. On the way up they ran
into M. de la Harpe, of St. Malo, on his way down from
the Cadodaquioux, to go to Biloxi and from there to
France, having established his concession. Upon reaching
the Natchez, M. Hubert took his whole family to stay
with M. de la Loire, the manager of the warehouses; and
the next day he had all the merchandise belonging to the
Company and his own personal effects moved there. He
held back two of the biggest boats, loaded with merchandise and munitions, and dispatched them the next day to
M. de Boisbrian at the Illinois.

Several days after the Commissary, M. Hubert, had rested at the Natchez in the house of the Chevalier de la Loire, he went out and inspected the land in the area. He found a spot near the small Rivière des Natchez, half a league from the main village, which he chose as the site of a quite large house to be built by the carpenters he had brought over from France in addition to more than twenty workmen of different trades. The land that he chose for his concession he established around his house. This land extended in one direction for one league, to where Fort Roselie stood, which M. de Bienville had had built, and where we kept a French garrison, and in the other direction as far as M. Hubert chose to extend into the prairies. That very year he had his fields plowed with plows he had taken the trouble to bring from France, and these he sowed to French wheat, which grew there as fine as the finest wheat of France. This concession is now one of the most delightful along the Missicipy, for M. Hubert improved it by adding a water mill to grind grain on the place, since he had taken the precautions of bringing several millstones from France and had a very smart miller among his workmen. This mill saw service that very year both with the troops and with the savages, who came to it in droves carrying their grains, which made this concession very rich. He also had a forge mill built on this river so that he could work in it a gunsmith and an edge-tool worker he had brought. They proved to be of great service in the area, on weapons and in the making of plowshares and other iron things. At the same time the Commissary, M. Hubert, gave a quite fine and comfortable dwelling place, one league away, to M. de Montplaisir, so that he could put his thirty tobacco workers to work there. This factory succeeded very well, for as early as the second year they made more than a hundred thousand pounds of tobacco.

The noble chiefs of the Natchez, seeing the Commissary, M. Hubert, established near the village, came in a body and sang their calumet of peace to him with great ceremony. After it had ended, they begged the Commissary, M. Hubert, to obtain a pardon from M. de Bienville for the Chief of La Terre Blanche,[1] who had been forbidden by M. de Bienville ever to make an appearance in their village, under pain of having his head broken if he was caught there, because he had had a hand in the murder of four Frenchmen killed by the Natchez in 1713. The Commissary, M. Hubert, wrote about this to M. de Bienville, and a while later M. de Bienville sent him the pardon he had requested for the Chief of La Terre Blanche. The Natchez were so delighted that the noble Grand Chief proclaimed a festival of dancing in the nine villages, which lasted one week.

At the same time the Yasoux, the Chacxoumas,[2] the Arcanssas, the Chactas, the Chicachas, all of them savages of the Upper [3] Missicipy, came down to the Natchez and sang their calumet of peace to the Commissary, M. Hubert. He gave substantial presents to all of them before dismissing them.

[1] Here La Terre Blanche seems to be given as the name of the village—White Earth.

[2] The Chakchiuma, a Muskhogean tribe, whose name comes from Choctaw *saktchi*, "crawfish," and *huma*, "red," was one of the largest of the Yazoo River nations. They later merged with the Chickasaw confederation. Hodge, *Handbook*, I, 231–32.

[3] Upper Mississippi usually means the Illinois Country and above. Here *upper* represents the point of view of a Frenchman at Mobile or New Biloxi.

At the beginning of this year seven ships from France, named *La Gironde, L'Éléphant, La Loire, La Seine, Le Dromadaire, Le Traversier,* and *La Vénus,* had arrived at the Isle-aux-Vaisseaux roadstead, opposite New Biloxi. These ships had brought over more than four thousand persons on their decks—Frenchmen, Germans, and Swiss.[4] There were also sixty girls from the Hôpital-Général [5] of Paris to be married in the country, and among all these persons there were a great number for concessions which were established this year. Here are the names and the places where they were established:

First, that of M. Colis,[6] managed by MM. Dumanoirs [7]

[4] Margry (*Découvertes,* V, 576) makes the important error of giving *Juifs,* "Jews." The error was caused by old-fashioned double *s*'s in *Suisses.* Moreover, other evidence indicates Swiss. That Jews were not wanted is patently evident in the first article in the so-called Black Code of 1724, which prohibited Jews. And Swiss, many of them, were indeed sent to Louisiana. By January 4, 1720, John Law, the head of the Company of the Indies, had sent a company of 210 "ouvriers suisses . . . pour la coupe des bois, reunie par la capitulation passée avec le sieur Wonwarderlich." Gravier, *La Colonization de La Louisiane à L'Époque de Law,* p. 65 and note.

[5] These were not the best women for founding a colony; for the Hôpital-Général, a house of detention and correction, held 3,000 prisoners in these years of the eighteenth century—vagrants, kept women, prostitutes and other criminals, and some women held under *lettres de cachet.* Some of the prisoners were considered capable of reform; yet, treatment of prisoners was a poor road to rehabilitation: they were flogged, and their heads were shaved. (Kurz [ed.], Prévost's *Histoire du Chevalier Des Grieux et de Manon Lescaut,* pp. 241–42.) Statistics of the Company of the Indies and police records show that of the 1,215 women put aboard ships for Louisiana between October, 1717, and May, 1721, more than half were prostitutes. Kurz quotes a song of the times aimed at these women shipped to Louisiana:

> Alors toute personne sage
> Fera des voeux pour leur passage,
> Priera les flots, Neptune aussi,
> De les porter bien loin d'ici.
> (*Ibid.,* pp. 245–46. Quoted with permission of the Oxford University Press.)

[6] Usually written Kolly or Koly. According to Delanglez, Kolly, and not Bienville, owned the house in which the Ursuline nuns were temporarily lodged when they came to New Orleans. (*French Jesuits,* p. 135.) Kolly was one of the most prominent concessionnaires; he later bought M. Hubert's plantation at the Natchez.

[7] Also commonly written Du Manoir (e.g., in Rowland and Sanders, *MPA,* II,

and Scear,[8] who remained at Biloxi during all this year with seventy men they had brought from France. That of M. Laur,[9] well enough known in France for the invention of paper money,[10] managed by M. Lias,[11] with one hundred men under him. It is established on the Rivière des Arcanssas, one hundred and ninety-two leagues above New Orleans, on the right going upstream.

343). One Du Manoir, or possibly two, acted as agent, or even partner, of Kolly. (*Ibid.*, III, 364.) See also p. 252.

[8] Apparently the same name appears as Sieur Ceard in the letter of Périer and De la Chaise to the Directors of the Company of the Indies, July 31, 1728, and in the same sentence with Kolly. (*Ibid.*, II, 584.) Pénicaut identifies Scear as Kolly's manager. In 1724 a M. Céard won a decision before the Superior Council that forced Nicolas Chauvin de Lafrénière to build a "coffer dike" to protect Céard's land from overflow. (King, *Creole Families of New Orleans*, pp. 171–72.) The Chauvins then lived in the Tchoupitoulas district.

[9] A rather good phonetic spelling of Law. This man is John Law, one of the most spectacular operators in the history of business and high finance. Frenchmen soon called him Las, and still opprobriously pronounce the name Las, the *s* sound coming from the *s* in "*Law's* Money." (*Larousse du XXᵐᵉ Siècle*, IV, 371.) When the *s* was not sounded there may have been a pun on the name, too, since *las* means "sick and tired"; thousands of Frenchmen were doubtless sick and tired of Law's Money, Law's whole system of finance, which destroyed the financial structure of France in 1720. Through the Company of the West and its sequel the Company of the Indies, which John Law controlled, he held a commercial monopoly of Louisiana from September 12, 1717, till his Company collapsed in 1720 and he fled France in fear of his life. Much of Law's system—including the use of paper money not supported by matching cash in the treasury of the issuer of the paper, and the principle that wealth is credit or is the equivalent of money in circulation—is commonly accepted practice nowadays in both government and private finance. The Scot John Law was a pioneer in big business.

[10] Parkman, p. 362, has: "Celle de Mʳ Lauu linventeur des billets de Banque en france, ou du joly commerce de La rue Quinquempoix." This reference to the mad speculation in Law's stock and to the run on his bank, in which many persons were trampled to death, appears to me to be a spurious invention of the Parkman penman. Pénicaut, writing a book he hoped would win a gratuity for him, partly through the help of Dartaguette, would have been more cautious than to direct satire at the Company of the Indies, of which Dartaguette-Diron had been a director.

[11] Given as Elias by Margry (*Découvertes*, V, 576). By December 12, 1721, a Sieur Dufresne had been appointed to fill the place of overseer at Law's Arkansas concession. Minutes of the Council of Commerce, December 12, 1721, in Rowland and Sanders, *MPA*, II, 265.

They had such a great amount of goods and other belongings that they loaded thirty boats with them to go up to their concession.

That of M. Le Blanc, state minister [12] in France, managed by M. de la Tour,[13] an engineer who had come with sixty persons, was located on the Rivière des Yasoux,[14] two hundred and twenty leagues beyond New Orleans, four leagues inland upon the Rivière des Yasoux, on the right, at the same place where M. de la Boulaye's fort stands. M. de la Boulaye was ordered to go and build a fort on the Rivière des Arcanssas and settle there.

That of Count d'Artagnan,[15] managed by M. d'Artiguière,[16] with eighty men and a great many belongings, was placed six leagues above New Orleans, on the same side, at a place called Cannes Brûlées.

That of the Duke de Chârost [17] and the Marquis d'An-

[12] Of war. De la Chaise to the Directors of the Company of the Indies, New Orleans, October 18, 1723, in Rowland and Sanders, *MPA*, II, 373.

[13] Le Blond de la Tour, chief engineer at the building of New Orleans. By the time De la Chaise wrote his long letter cited in note 12, De la Tour had died "d'une maladie de chagrin et de langueur." The implication is that Bienville's meanness had caused his death. But, since De la Chaise is prejudiced, the only fact is that the lieutenant-general, the partner of Le Blanc, had died.

[14] Written Hyasoux by the Parkman penman, p. 362 and elsewhere.

[15] The D'Artagnan or D'Artaignan family was of the Gascon house of Montesquiou-Fezenzac. The most celebrated member of the family was the brilliant Charles de Baatz, Seigneur d'Artagnan, slain at Maastricht. Dumas, père, used him as a character in *Les Trois Mousquetaires*. Pierre de Montesquiou (1645–1725) was Count d'Artagnan and *maréchal* of France. As he gave up the name D'Artagnan after about 1709, preferring Montesquiou, I do not know whether he or his son or some other member of the family was the concessionnaire in Louisiana. *Larousse du XXme Siècle*, I, 366; IV, 965.

[16] Minutes of the Superior Council, May 9, 1724 (Rowland and Sanders, *MPA*, III, 397), show that D'Artagnan had two managers, M. de Benac and M. d'Artillières, the latter being without doubt the same as Pénicaut's D'Artiguière.

[17] The correct spelling comes from Parkman, p. 363. Clermont has Charo. The Duchy of Chârost was established in 1672 for Louis de Béthune, a nephew of Sully. The Béthune family held it into the eighteenth century. *Larousse du XXme Siècle*, II, 157.

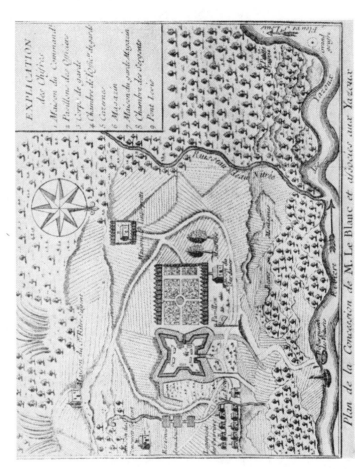

MAP OF A FRENCH CONCESSION NEAR THE MOUTH OF THE YAZOO RIVER. From
Dumont de Montigny, *Mémoires Historiques sur la Louisiane.*

ceny, his son, was managed by M. de l'Épinet,[18] who had one hundred persons with him and a great many belongings. It was placed sixteen leagues from New Orleans, on the right side going upstream, three leagues above the village of the Colapissas savages, on the same side. That of M. Dartaguet, who sent to his brother, M. Diron, the inspector-general of troops in Louisiana,[19] forty-five persons to cultivate it. It was placed next to Count d'Artagnan five leagues above New Orleans, on the right going upstream, at the place named Cannes Brûlées.

That of M. de Mézières,[20] managed by M. Marié [with thirty men, was placed] [21] in La Fourche des Oüachitas, near M. de Catillon's, seventy-four leagues up from New Orleans, to the left going up river, and eight leagues on up the Rivière Rouge above its mouth.

That of M. de Villemont,[22] who came himself with

[18] I can not find the connection, if there is one, between M. de l'Épinet, Chârost's manager, and the governor of Louisiana, L'Épinay. The Company of the West asked the Navy Council to order Governor L'Épinay to leave the colony in 1716. Company of the West to the Navy Council, Paris, [1716], in Rowland and Sanders, *MPA,* III, 190.

[19] Here is evidence that the old *ordonnateur,* located at Mobile from 1708 to 1711, is not the same person as the inspector-general. The brother, here identified as the inspector-general, is commonly called Diron-Dartaguette. For evidence that his given name may have been Bernar, see Chapter X, n. 1. The third brother, identified with certainty by many historians, was Pierre Dartaguette, slain by the Chickasaws. For the confusion in the relationship of the Dartaguette brothers, see Hamilton, *Colonial Mobile,* p. 108, and Rowland and Sanders' notes in *MPA,* I, 56–57.

[20] One Mézières, a concession holder, is mentioned as the Marquis de Mézières in Minutes of the Superior Council, June 15, 1724 (Rowland and Sanders, *MPA,* III, 416–17). The same document names his director as the Sieur de Laye. There may be a relationship between the concession holder and Athanaze de Mézières, the French officer who married St. Denis' daughter at Natchitoches, but I don't know it.

[21] Supplied from Parkman, p. 364. Parkman gives Marie instead of Marié.

[22] A Villemont was once commandant of Fort Toulouse (Gayarré, *History of Louisiana,* I, 281) after Marchand was murdered *c.* 1722.

all his family and fifteen persons, was placed at the same spot, next to M. Marié's.

That of Madame de Chaumont [23] F. A., managed by M. de Reüeillon,[24] who had come with thirty men, was placed upon the Rivière des Pascagoulas, forty leagues from New Orleans, twelve leagues on up this river above its mouth. This concession was able to harvest grain that very year.[25]

That of MM. Chauvin, three brothers,[26] who have more than one hundred Negroes to work on their concession, is established three leagues from New Orleans, on the right going upstream, on the bank of the Missicipy at a place called Choupitoula. This is the finest and best cultivated of the concessions in the country, with mill and forges.

That of M. de Breüil,[27] with his family and ten persons,

[23] For four years Mme de Chaumont neglected her plantation and her workmen. Her manager, Sieur de la Garde, being dunned by creditors, was selling her cattle and Negroes. (Périer and De la Chaise to the Directors of the Company of the Indies, November 2, 1727, in Rowland and Sanders, *MPA*, II, 557.) She finally sent her power of attorney to M. de Kolly so that he could take care of her concessions. Périer and De la Chaise to the Directors of the Company of the Indies, November 3, 1728, *ibid.*, II, 600.

[24] This name is uncertain: Parkman, p. 364, has Reueillon or Reveillon; Margry has Révillon. *Découvertes*, V, 577.

[25] Parkman, p. 364, adds a detail: ". . . non seulement de recueillir des grains pour subsister mais meme d'en vendre aux troupes du pais."

[26] There were four Chauvin brothers in Louisiana: Jacques, Joseph, Nicholas, and Louis. Pénicaut says three because three had plantations in the Tchoupitoulas tract. The brothers had lived at Mobile, and their names as well as the names of several wives appear in Mobile Baptismal Records prior to the concession period. Nicholas Chauvin *dit* de Lafrénière was the sire of the heroic attorney-general of the same name who was executed by the Spaniards on October 25, 1769. For a full account of the Chauvin brothers, see King, *Creole Families of New Orleans*, p. 169 ff.

[27] Fortier (*History of Louisiana*, I, 63) called Dubreuil the richest planter in Louisiana. This is Claude Joseph du Breuil, who at one time owned as many as five hundred Negroes. He came to the colony in 1719 on the *Comte de Toulouse*. He died in November, 1757. See Georges Oudard, *Four Cents an Acre* (New York, 1931), pp. 209–10; and Delanglez, *French Jesuits*, pp. 389–91.

was placed on the bank next to MM. de Chauvin's, on this side of it coming down the Missicipy River. That of MM. Guenots [28] and Préfontaine, [29] two brothers in partnership, with M. Macy [30] and sixty persons, above MM. de Chauvin.

These three concessions, which are side by side, are cultivated from Lake Pontchartrain to the bank of the Missicipy and are plowed with the plow, which has been used in the Lower Missicipy only for the past two years, just as forges have been.

In short, M. de Bienville had concessions distributed that year to more than three thousand persons, a detailed account of which would be too long and too tedious to give here. I thought it sufficient to report only some of those that belong to the best qualified persons, who will perhaps be glad to learn, in this new narrative, the places where their concessions are established and the distances they are from the town of New Orleans, just as I have marked on the new map [31] I have made of Louisiana.

[28] Guenot is the common spelling of this name. After Kolly had bought Sainte Reine, the Tchoupitoulas plantation, he owed 23,600 livres to Massy and Guenot in August, 1729. (Périer and De la Chaise to the Directors of the Company of the Indies, August 26, 1729, in Rowland and Sanders, *MPA*, II, 667.) One Guenot was slain by a Natchez Indian before March 23, 1725. Minutes of the Council, March 23, 1725, *ibid.*, II, 421.

[29] This brother may be named Tréfontaine, for there are two signatures of a Guenot de Tréfontaine to Minutes of the Council of Commerce held at Mobile on May 6 or 9, 1720 (*ibid.*, III, 288 and 293). He was substituting for the attorney-general.

[30] Massy is the spelling used in all documents I have seen in transcription in *MPA*. This concessionaire was quite prominent.

[31] I have not been able to locate this map. But there is no doubt that it did exist, for at the end of the Pénicaut ms. in the Rouen Library there are key letters referring to this map; with the letters are given the names of concessionnaires whose plantations have been marked on the map. See the Appendix for a transcription of the appendage to the Rouen ms. Also with the Rouen ms. there is a map made by f[rançois] B[oüet] from Pénicaut's narrative. Boüet prepared the Rouen ms. Only

A few days after M. de Bienville had distributed the concessions, he sent to Mobile, by way of the river, one of the ships that had come from France—loaded with munitions and food supplies, and with the goods that were on it—so that they could be unloaded at Mobile and stored in the warehouses.

At the same time M. de Bienville wrote the commandant at Mobile to dispatch a convoy of food and munitions to M. de la Tour, the Governor of the fort at the Alibamons,[32] which was a post quite advanced in the direction of Carolina and very important in preventing the English from entering Louisiana, because, although Isle Dauphine has been abandoned, Mobile—on account of its connection with this post—will be retained for the purpose of checking the savages in that direction.

M. de Bienville also sent the ship named *Le Dromadaire* fully loaded to New Orleans so that the munitions and goods it had brought from France could be unloaded there and stored in the warehouses.

M. Arnaud,[33] a captain, went up to the Illinois about that time with his fifty miners and with six boats loaded with all kinds of belongings. Also, several families for concessions near the Illinois went up with him; to these M. de Bienville gave some Negroes to cultivate their fields.

When M. Arnaud had reached the Illinois, he delivered a letter to M. Diron [34] from M. de Bienville, ordering him

---

his initials are on the map. (I have seen only microfilm of the Gravier transcription of the Rouen ms. and a photostat of the map, both supplied to me through the courtesy of the Ayer Collection of the Newberry Library, Chicago.)

[32] Fort Toulouse.   [33] Philippe François Renault.

[34] Bernar Diron-Dartaguette.

to come down to New Orleans, for His Majesty had made him inspector-general of troops in Louisiana. This obliged him to come downstream, paying visits of inspection to all the posts along the Missicipy where troops were garrisoned.

At the same time M. de St. Denis received a letter from the Court with the commission of captain of a company and governor at the Nassitoches. This forced him to go to the Nassitoches sometime afterwards with a reinforcement of thirty men in six boats loaded with the munitions and the food supplies he was taking. For this he was beholden to M. de Chamelin, who, on returning to France, had reported to the Court that M. de St. Denis, who was one of the worthiest officers in Louisiana, was nevertheless without employment; that he had been partly responsible for saving Isle Dauphine, which he had aided of his own free will, leading a great number of savages there, by whom he was greatly loved, and at the head of whom he landed on the island just in time to repulse the Spaniards, who were beginning to make a landing. He added that M. de St. Denis had taken a hand in every difficulty whenever need for his help had arisen in the province, although he had neither pay nor rank. This determined the Court to send him the commission of captain and governor of the fort at the Nassitoches.[35]

Toward the end of the year, after M. de St. Denis' departure, three *traversiers* arrived at the Isle-aux-Vaisseaux roadstead. On them were still more people for the concessions and for service in the country, besides a

---

[35] For the remaining years of St. Denis' life see the biography by Ross Phares, *Cavalier in the Wilderness.*

great deal of munitions and goods. M. de Bienville sent two of the *traversiers* to New Orleans fully loaded and had the personal effects unloaded from the third one and stored in the warehouses at New Biloxi. Six of the seven ships that had come to Louisiana returned to France, only *Le Dromadaire* remaining in Louisiana.

For the rest of this year, work continued at New Orleans and much progress was being made.

Chapter 23

The Year 1721

M. de Chateaugué arrives in Louisiana—M. de Bienville tries to have a fort established upon the Rivière de la Madelaine—Several ships arrive in Louisiana—The author falls ill of an inflammation of the eyes, from which he loses his eyesight, and he leaves for France—End of the narrative

N THE eighth of January of the year 1721, a flûte named *La Baleine* came to the Isle-aux-Vaisseaux roadstead and anchored. M. de Chateaugué came on it, to whom His Majesty had given, in France, the cross of Chevalier de St. Louis and who was bringing another for M. de St. Denis. On this ship was M. de la Harpe, of St. Malo, who had a concession established at the Cadodaquioux.

Sister Gertrude, one of the officers of the Hôpital-Général de la Salpêtrière [1] of Paris, had also come on this ship, with eighty-eight girls from this hospital, all brought up in this house from infancy. Under Sister Gertrude's chaperonage, they had come to be married in the country; and each one had her dot,[2] which consisted of two

[1] La Salpêtrière, now a home for mentally ill and aged women, was in the eighteenth century a house of detention whose very name could terrify women addicted to social foibles. This is the prison that seemed so horrible to the Chevalier des Grieux, Manon Lescaut's lover, that he could not name it. "Ma malheureuse maîtresse [Manon] fut donc enlevée, à mes yeux, et menée dans une retraite que j'ai horreur de nommer." Kurz (ed.), Prévost's *Histoire du Chevalier Des Grieux et de Manon Lescaut*, p. 84.

[2] These are not the so-called *cassette* girls, who came to Louisiana in 1728, although these girls are similarly provided. There is great contrast in the provenience of the two shipments. These girls, Pénicaut says, had been brought up in La Salpêtrière from infancy. They must have been the abandoned children—orphans or

suits of clothing, two skirts and petticoats, six laced bod-
ices, six chemises, six headdresses, and all other necessary
accessories, with which they were well provided so that
they could be married as quickly as possible in legitimate
wedlock. This merchandise was soon distributed, so great
was the dearth of it in the country; and if Sister Gertrude
had brought ten times as much of it, she would have found
a market for it in a short time.

A few days later M. de Bienville had a brigantine armed,
under the command of Captain Belanger, to take M. de
la Harpe to the Rivière de la Madelaine.[3] Great supplies
of food and munitions were shipped off in this brigantine,
with workmen and soldiers to make an establishment on
the bank of this river. They went about twenty leagues
upstream, where they came upon a strong party of savages
entrenched on one side of this river, who stopped them
and never did consent for the French to build a fort there.
M. de la Harpe had an interpreter tell them that the
French had come to be their friends, that they wanted
to do nothing except what was to their good and to bring
them some of the conveniences of life; but they were
unwilling to hear any of the proposals that were made to
them, which they rejected, telling us that they were satisfied with their condition and that they wished to live free
and off to themselves, without taking any other nation
among them. M. de la Harpe had them told further that
if any of their chiefs wished to go with the French to

---

illegitimates—of prostitutes or "kept" women who had been inmates in that house
of correction. (See Delanglez, *French Jesuits*, p. 53 and note.) With Sister Gertrude
came two other Grey sisters, Louise and Bergère. Delanglez gives the number of girls
in the shipment as ninety-six instead of eighty-eight.

[3] The Sabine River.

Biloxi, they would be given an opportunity to talk to
M. de Bienville, who would not fail to give them some
presents as evidence that we wanted a fort on the bank of
their river solely as a service to them. Nine presented
themselves and, getting in the brigantine, were conducted
to Biloxi.

During that time a ship named *Le Maréchal d'Estrées*
arrived at the Isle-aux-Vaisseaux roadstead under the
command of Captain Prudhomme, who came from
Sénégal.[4] He had brought on his ship one hundred and
seventy-five Negroes, who got off the ship at New Biloxi
and were allotted to all the residents of New Orleans, to
whom they were sent, as well as to several persons of the
concessions. The flûte named *La Baleine* returned to
France at that time. Sister Gertrude sailed on this ship to
return to France, too.

One month after the sailing of *La Baleine* there arrived
at the Isle-aux-Vaisseaux roadstead a ship named *Le St.
André*, loaded with five hundred barrels of flour. Also on
this ship were one hundred German families that had
come to settle in the region; they were scattered over
several concessions that had been granted them in different places along the Missicipy River. Some Negroes were
given them to aid them in establishing their concessions.
Some of the flour was put in the warehouses at New Biloxi
and the rest was carried to New Orleans.

A few days later, still another flûte arrived named *La
Durance*, on which there were thirteen hundred barrels
of flour. This ship was sent on up to New Orleans fully
loaded. Also, concessions were distributed to one hundred

---

[4] Supplied from Parkman, p. 373. Clermont and Spofford both have Sénéchal.

other German families that had come on this last ship. These concessions were placed beyond the Illinois on the Upper Missicipy.

The Commissary, M. Hubert, had wanted to return to France and had asked to be relieved. This year he sold his concession at the Natchez to MM. Dumanoirs, who bought it for M. Colis,[5] for whom they acted as managers. All the workmen M. Hubert had there they retained at the same wages they had agreed to with M. Hubert. He let MM. Dumanoirs have, also, several pieces of his furniture, among them those pieces that he did not wish to save and take back to France.

During this time Sieur Pénicaut, the author of this narrative, fell ill of an inflammation of the eyes, from which he lost his eyesight. Having tried in vain to have himself cured in the country, he was advised by M. de Bienville, the Governor-General [6] of the Province, and by what chief officers there were, to go to France to try to have himself cured. He sailed away on the ship named

[5] This purchase of Natchez property seems to account for Kolly's being at Natchez on November 28, 1729. M. Kolly and his son and their clerk, all from New Orleans, are listed by the Capuchin Philibert as being among the slain in the great massacre. Father Mathurin Le Petit, S.J., lists the father and son among the eight "best known" victims. See Le Petit, *The Natchez Massacre* (New Orleans, 1950), p. 18 and p. 42 with Father Philibert's list of victims.

[6] Although Bienville had the title of governor in the sense of commandant of a post and the title of commandant-general, I cannot find evidence to show that he received the title of governor-general before he was recalled to Louisiana in 1732. In Bienville to Maurepas, September 30, 1732 (Rowland and Sanders, *MPA*, III, 576–80), Bienville pleads for the right to wear the red ribbon of the order of St. Louis and to be promoted to the rank of captain, since he wishes to impress the Indians with his advanced status upon resuming control of the colony. At the end of that letter there is an extract of another written by the Company of the Indies to Bienville in March, 1720, conferring upon him, from the Company of the Indies, the title of governor-general of Louisiana. But, judging by Bienville's letter of September 30, 1732, that title had not been validated.

Le Maréchal d'Estrées on the third of October of that year, 1721,[7] leaving his wife [8] and his slaves in the country.

For nearly two years he has been in Paris, without being able to recover his sight following a great many different surgical operations that have been performed upon him at great cost to him without curing him, which has forced him to petition the Count de Toulouze [9] to try to get him a pension as reward for twenty-two years of service he has rendered His Majesty in the capacity of master ship's carpenter for the King in this country, testimonials to which he holds from all the chief officers of Louisiana, namely: the Count de Surgère; M. de la Mothe de Cadillac; M. Diron, the inspector-general; M. de Bienville, the Governor-General of the Province; M. de St. Denis, *ancien officier,* captain and governor of the fort at the Nassitoches.

He was a member of all the expeditions he mentions in his narrative, as he was really needed on them, not only to repair the longboats and the rowboats of the expeditions that went off as war parties or as convoys, but even to act as interpreter in explaining the questions and answers of the savages, whose languages he speaks quite

[7] Parkman, p. 376, has "le huit octobre de lannée 1701 [*sic*]."

[8] The wife of André Pénigault was Marguerite Catherine Prévôt, or Prévost, when his child René André was baptized on Oct. 27, 1708, and was Marie Prévôt when the child Jacque was baptized on March 28 (20 or 29?), 1710. I do not know what became of these children. André Pénicaut, the writer, does not mention children that he has left in the colony. The dates as given are the best guides to entries in Mobile Baptismal Records.

[9] Louis Alexandre de Bourbon, natural son of Louis XIV and Mme de Montespan. He had been legitimated and had served as a member of the Conseil de Marine, which acted as the Ministry from September 10, 1715, to September 24, 1718. See Rowland and Sanders, MPA, II, 209, n. 1.

well. Several times he has ascended the Missicipy from its embouchure, where it empties into the sea, as high as the Saut de St. Anthoine, which is nine hundred leagues from the embouchure. Likewise, he has been far up the tributaries that flow into the Missicipy, to right and to left of its banks, having visited nearly all the nations on both sides of this river for more than sixty leagues from its banks in the direction of Mexico, Canada, and Carolina.

Although the author has not recovered his eyesight with all the treatments which several surgeons and oculists have used without results, he still intends to go back to Louisiana,[10] where his wife is, after he has petitioned His Royal Highness, the Duke d'Orléans,[11] to have the kindness to have him granted a gratuity by the Company of the Indies, to which the Count de Toulouze sent him, since he was transferred in 1712 from His Majesty's service to service with the Company, His Majesty having ceded the commerce of Louisiana that year to the Company,[12] which he served continually until he lost his eyesight in 1721.

All that he reports in his narrative is quite true, whether about wars with the savages, of which he was an eyewitness, or about the vast extent of the country and the course of the Missicipy and the fertility of its banks. He avows that, if the excessive growth of trees with which

[10] I cannot prove that Pénicaut ever returned to Louisiana. For Fortier's opinion, see Editor's Introduction, p. xiii.

[11] Philippe, Duke of Orleans, the nephew of Louis XIV, was Regent of France from 1715 to 1723.

[12] Crozat's company is meant. Pénicaut uses Company rather loosely in referring to Crozat's monopoly (1713) and John Law's two companies, the Company of the West (1717) and the Company of the Indies (1719).

it is filled were cleared away, the country of Louisiana would be a terrestrial paradise with the agriculture that would be developed there, where wheat grows a great deal bigger than in France. In this country there is an astonishing abundance of game of every kind of species and fish in the rivers just as plentiful. There are fruits in great quantity and of a better taste than the fruits in France, the climate in Louisiana being a little bit warmer.

Those who read this narrative carefully will notice that it seems that God wills that Frenchmen live in this country in order to spread the Catholic religion to His glory and at the same time to found a second French empire to the glory of His Most Christian Majesty. It seems obvious that God is, so to speak, weary of the unheard-of cruelty the savages practise among themselves and that He wishes to give them rulers who will put a stop to it; for it is astonishing that a handful of people, whom M. d'Hyberville and the Count de Surgère brought into such a distant country, have established themselves among countless nations of the wildest savages and that men whom the savages had never seen—whose customs, religion, and language are altogether different—have nevertheless found the means of maintaining themselves in peace with the savages, of controlling them and of inducing them even to go to war with the other savages, their kinsmen and allies, who have dared to declare war on the French—throughout the twenty-five consecutive years of founding and maintaining this colony in this country.

Who will not recognize therein the hand of the Creator? And so, I shall end my narrative with these words of the Prophet:

Blessed be the Lord our God, who alone has done the greatest wonders. May His name be praised forever, and may all the earth be filled with knowledge of His divine majesty. So be it!

Benedictus Dominus Deus noster qui facit mirabilia solus, et benedictum nomen Majestatis ejus in aeternum, et replebitur Majestate ejus omnis terra. Fiat, fiat. Ps. 71.[13]

Fin

[13] Given as "psaume 70" at the end of the Parkman manuscript, but I find the quotation in Psalm LXXII: 18–20.

Bibliography

Manuscripts of Pénicaut's Relation

Clermont. This is the most authoritative manuscript. Collation shows no evidence that Margry used any other, although he knew two others. (*Découvertes,* V, 690.) B. F. French used this one, too, or a transcription of it. Evidence is strong that this is the dedicatory copy presented by Pénicaut to Dartaguiette Diron, to whom the book was dedicated. Only this manuscript has the dedication to Dartaguiette Diron. Dartaguiette lent or gave his copy to the Jesuit historian Charlevoix. (*La Nouvelle France,* II, lx–lxj). When the library of the Collège des Jésuites de Clermont, Paris, was auctioned, a Pénicaut manuscript was listed in the *Catalogus Manuscriptorum Codicum Collegii Claromontani.* (Elizabeth McCann, "Pénicaut and His Chronicle," *Mid-Amercia,* XXIII, n.s., p. 289.) The manuscript is stamped Bibliothèque Royale and is paraphed in accordance with the decree of July 5, 1763. (See W. Kane, "The End of a Jesuit Library," *Mid-America,* XXIII, n.s., pp. 190–213.) For the full title of Pénicaut's Relation see Appendix B. The Clermont manuscript is now in the Bibliothèque Nationale. Mss. Fr. 14613. 374 pp.

Parkman. John Meredith Read, Jr., American Consul-General in Paris, bought this manuscript on March 25, 1870, with the idea of making an edition. In deference to the great talent of Francis Parkman, Read gave

Parkman the manuscript on April 16, 1870. (Read's autograph on the ms.; also, Read to Parkman, April 15, 1870.) The title of the Parkman manuscript has these important additional words: "Dressé par francois Boüet sur les Memoires d'André Penicaut." It is now among the Parkman papers of the Massachusetts Historical Society. 380 pp.

Spofford. In 1869 Ainsworth Rand Spofford, the Librarian of Congress, bought this copy from Maisonneuve et Cie, Paris. The original title page is missing. Another hand has supplied a new one. The author's name is given as Sr Penicaud Rochelois (from Rochelle). This manuscript is now in the Library of Congress. 452 pp.

Rouen. I have not been able to examine the manuscript in the library of Rouen, France. I have used microfilm of a transcription of it made for M. Gravier. At the end of this manuscript there is a unique appendage that gives the names of prominent concessionnaires in Louisiana and letters of the alphabet corresponding to concessions marked on the map of Louisiana that Pénicaut made. This map is lost, but with the Rouen manuscript there is a map prepared by François Boüet. As in the Parkman manuscript, the title page contains the words "Dressé par françois Boüet sur les mémoires d'André Penicaut." The Gravier transcription of the Rouen manuscript is in the Ayer Collection of the Newberry Library, Chicago. Pages not numbered.

Editions

Margry, Pierre (ed. and comp.), "Relation de Pénicaut," in *Découvertes et Établissements des Français dans l'Ouest et dans le Sud de l'Amérique Septentrionale (1614–1754)*, V (Paris: Imprimerie de D. Jouaust, 1883), pp. 375–586. This French edition is complete except for a few passages, which were dropped by the Clermont penman. There is some evidence of hasty reading of Clermont. Also, there are some errors in place names and in Indian tribal names with which Margry was not familiar.

French, B. F. (ed. and tr.), "Annals of Louisiana, . . . from the establishment of the first colony under M. d'Iberville, to the departure of the author to France, in 1722 . . . by M. Penicaut. Translated from a copy of the original manuscript deposited in the Bibliothèque du Roi, Paris," in *Historical Collections of Louisiana and Florida*, n.s. (New York: J. Sabin and Sons, 1869), pp. 33–162.

Owen, Marie Bankhead, and Emmett Kilpatrick (eds.), "The Annals of Louisiana from 1698 to 1722. By M. Penicaut," in *Alabama Historical Quarterly* (Montgomery, 1930—), V (Fall, 1943), 261–355. This is a reprint of B. F. French's edition.

Primary and Secondary Sources

Adams, James Truslow (ed.), *Dictionary of American History*, 5 vols. (New York, 1942).

Alvord, Clarence Walworth, *The Illinois Country, 1673–1818* in Clarence W. Alvord (ed.), *The Centennial History of Illinois* (Springfield: Illinois Centennial Commission, 1920).

Bassett, John Spencer, and Sidney Bradshaw Fay (eds.), "Letters of Francis Parkman to Pierre Margry," with an Introductory Note by John Spencer Bassett, in *Smith College Studies in History,* VIII (April–July, 1923), 123–208.

Belting, Natalia Maree, *Kaskaskia under the French Regime,* in *Illinois Studies in the Social Sciences,* XXIX, No. 3 (Urbana: University of Illinois Press, 1948).

Bolton, Herbert E., *Rim of Christendom* (New York: Macmillan Company, 1936).

———, *The Spanish Border Lands* (New Haven: Yale University Press, 1921).

Butler, Ruth Lapham (ed. and tr.), *Journal of Paul du Ru* (Chicago: Caxton Club, 1934).

Chambers, Henry E. *A History of Louisiana,* I (Chicago and New York: American Historical Society, 1925).

Charlevoix, [Pierre François Xavier] Le P. de, *Histoire et Description Générale de la Nouvelle France, Avec Le Journal Historique d'un Voyage fait par ordre du Roi dans l'Amérique Septentrionale,* 3 Tomes (Paris: Chez Rolin Fils, Libraire, 1744).

Chateaubriand, [François René] M. le Vicomte de, *Les Natchez* (Paris: Librairie de Firmin-Didot et Cⁱᵉ, 1882).

Clark, Charles Upson, *Voyageurs, Robes Noires, et Coureurs de Bois* (New York: Institute of French Studies, Columbia University, 1934).

Crane, Vernon W., *The Southern Frontier, 1670–1732* (Durham: Duke University Press, 1928).

Delanglez, Jean, *The French Jesuits in Lower Louisiana (1700–1763)* in *Catholic University of America Studies in American Church History,* XXI (Washington: Catholic University of America, 1935).

Dumont [de Montigny, Louis François Benjamin], *Mémoires Historiques sur la Louisiane*, edited by M. L. L. M., 2 vols. (Paris: Chez Cl. J. B. Bauche, 1753).

Du Pratz, [Antoine Simon] Le Page, *Histoire de la Louisiane*, 3 vols. (Paris: De Bure, 1758).

———, *History of Louisiana*, with a Foreword by Stanley Clisby Arthur (Reprint of the London ed. of 1774, New Orleans: J. S. W. Harmanson, n.d.).

Fortier, Alcée, *A History of Louisiana*, 4 vols. (New York: Manzi, Joyant and Company, 1904).

——— (ed.), *Louisiana*, 3 vols. ([Madison, Wisconsin]: Century Historical Association, 1914).

Frégault, Guy, *Iberville le conquérant* (Montréal: Société des Éditions Pascal, 1944).

Gayarré, Charles, *History of Louisiana*, 4 vols. (3d ed., New Orleans: Armand Hawkins, Publisher, 1885).

Gravier, Henri, *La Colonization de La Louisiane à L'Époque de Law; Octobre 1717–Janvier 1721* (Paris: Masson et Cie, Éditeurs, 1904).

Hamilton, Peter J., *Colonial Mobile* (Boston and New York: Houghton, Mifflin and Company, 1897).

Hodge, Frederick Webb (ed.), *Handbook of American Indians North of Mexico* (Smithsonian Institution, Bureau of American Ethnology Bulletin 30, Washington: Government Printing Office, 1907, 1910), Parts 1 and 2 [cited as vols.].

Kane, W., "The End of a Jesuit Library" in *Mid-America*, XXIII, n.s. (July, 1941), 190–213.

King, Grace, *Creole Families of New Orleans* (New York: Macmillan Company, 1921).

King, Grace, *New Orleans, the Place and the People* (New York: Macmillan Company, 1928).

Laut, Agnes C., *Cadillac* (Indianapolis: Bobbs-Merrill Company, 1931).

Lauvrière, Émile, *Histoire de la Louisiane Française, 1673–1939,* in Louisiana State University, Romance Language Series, No. 3 (Baton Rouge: Louisiana State University Press, 1940).

Le Petit, Maturin, *The Natchez Massacre,* translated by Richard H. Hart (New Orleans: Poor Rich Press, 1950).

Margry, Pierre (ed. and comp.), *Découvertes et Établissements des Français dans l'Ouest et dans le Sud de l'Amérique Septentrionale (1614–1754)* (Paris: Imprimerie de D. Jouaust, 1880, 1883), Vols. IV and V.

McCann, Elizabeth, "Pénicaut and His Chronicle of Early Louisiana" in *Mid-America,* XXIII, n.s. (October, 1941), 288–304.

McDermott, John Francis, *Glossary of Mississippi Valley French, 1673–1850,* in Washington University Studies, Language and Literature, n.s., No. 12 (St. Louis: Washington University, 1941).

—— (ed.), *Old Cahokia* (St. Louis: St. Louis Historical Documents Foundation, 1949).

McWilliams, Richebourg, "Pénicaut as Alabama's First Literary Figure," in *Alabama Review,* V (January, 1952), 40–60.

Mobile Baptismal Records, 1704—— In the Residence of the Bishop of Mobile.

Murphy, Edmund Robert, *Henry de Tonty: Fur*

Trader of the Mississippi (Baltimore: Johns Hopkins Press, 1941).

Neill, E. D. and A. J. Hill, "Relation of M. Penicaut," in *Collections of the Minnesota Historical Society,* III (1870–80), 1–12.

Oudard, Georges, *The Amazing Life of John Law: The Man behind the Mississippi Bubble,* translated by G. E. C. Massé (New York: Payson and Clarke, Ltd., 1928).

————, *Four Cents an Acre: The Story of Louisiana under the French,* translated by Margery Bianco from "Notre Louisiane" (New York: Brewer and Warren, 1931).

Phares, Ross, *Cavalier in the Wilderness* (Baton Rouge: Louisiana State University Press, 1952).

Pickett, Albert James, *History of Alabama,* 2 vols. (2d ed., Charleston: Walker and James, 1851).

Pittman, Captain Philip, *The Present State of the European Settlements on the Mississippi,* edited by Frank Heywood Hodder (Cleveland: Arthur H. Clark Company, 1906).

Portré-Bobinski, Germaine, "French Civilization and Culture in Natchitoches" in *Natchitoches,* V (1941), 1–120.

Prévost, [Antoine François] L'Abbé, *Histoire du Chevalier Des Grieux et de Manon Lescaut,* edited by Harry Kurz (New York: Oxford University Press, 1929).

Read, John Meredith, Jr., Letter to Francis Parkman, April 15, 1870, in Parkman Papers, Massachusetts Historical Society, Boston.

Read, William A., *Louisiana-French* in Louisiana State University Studies No. 5 (Baton Rouge: Louisiana State University Press, 1931).

————, *Louisiana Place-Names of Indian Origin* in Louisiana State University and Agricultural and Mechanical College *Bulletin*, XIX, n.s., No. 2 (February, 1927). 72 pp.

Reed, Charles B., "Sieur de St. Denis and Jallot, his Valet de Chambre" in Northwestern University *Bulletin; The Medical School*, XXXIV (March 19, 1934), 1–20.

Reynolds, Jack A., "Louisiana Place Names of Romance Origin" (Unpublished Ph.D. thesis, Louisiana State University, 1942).

Richebourg, Captain de, "Mémoire de M. de Richebourg, sur la Première Guerre des Natchez," in *Historical Collections of Louisiana*, edited by B. F. French, III, n.s. (New York: D. Appleton and Company, 1851), pp. 241–52.

Rowland, Dunbar, and Albert Godfrey Sanders (ed. and tr.), *Mississippi Provincial Archives*, 3 vols. (Jackson, Mississippi: Press of the Mississippi Department of Archives and History, 1927–32).

Schlarman, J. H., *From Quebec to New Orleans* (Belleville, Illinois: Buechler Publishing Company, 1929).

School of Naval Administration, Stanford University, *Handbook on the Trust Territory of the Pacific Islands* (Washington: Naval Department, Office of the Chief of Naval Operations, 1948).

Schultz, Christian, *Travels on an Inland Voyage . . . 1807 and 1808*, 2 vols. published as one (New York: Isaac Riley, 1810).

Shea, John Gilmary, *Catholic Church in Colonial Days* (New York: John G. Shea, 1886).

Surrey, N. M. Miller, *Calendar of Manuscripts in Paris Archives and Libraries Relating to the History of the Mississippi Valley to 1803*, 2 vols. (Washington: Carnegie Institution of Washington, 1926–28).

Swanton, John R., *Indian Tribes of the Lower Mississippi Valley and Adjacent Coast of the Gulf of Mexico* in Smithsonian Institution, Bureau of American Ethnology *Bulletin*, No. 43 (Washington: Government Printing Office, 1911).

United States Coast Pilot: Gulf Coast, Key West to Rio Grande (3d ed., Washington: Government Printing Office, 1949).

War Department Corps of Engineers, U.S. Army, *The Middle and Upper Mississippi River*, Compiled under direction of the Division Engineer, Upper Mississippi Valley Division, St. Louis, Missouri (Washington: Government Printing Office, 1935).

Maps

American Atlas (Philadelphia: H. C. Carey and I. Lea, 1823).

[Boüet, François], "Carte de la Louisiane et du cours du Missisipy sur la Relation d'andré Penicaut, par f. B." (Photostat of a copy of this map in the Ayer Collection of the Newberry Library, Chicago. The original is with the Rouen manuscript of Pénicaut's Relation.)

D'Anville, [Jean Baptiste Bourgignon] Le Sr., "Carte de la Louisiane" (Dressée en Mai 1732, publiée en 1752).

Delisle, Guillaume, "Carte de La Louisiane et du Cours

du Mississipi Dressée sur un grand nombre de Mémoires entrau^tres sur ceux de M^r le Maire" (A Paris, Juin 1718).

Du Sault, Lieutenant, "Carte de L'Jsle Dauphine, avec la grande terre de l'O. & celle de la Mobille. . . . Par le S^r Du Sault Lieut^t Command^t le Vaisseau du Roy *Le Paon* en 1717." Photograph of Bibliothèque Nationale Ge. DD. 2987. No. 8809.

Moll, H., "A New Map of the North Parts of America Claimed by France," 1720.

Régis, M^r, "Carte du Cours de la Riviere aux Perles," in *Mississippi Provincial Archives*, I, 360.

Senex, John, "A Map of Louisiana and of the River Mississippi . . . Most humbly Inscribed to William Law of Lawreston, Esq." [London: Academy of Science, *c.* 1720].

U.S. Coast and Geodetic Survey, "Lake Borne and Approaches," No. 1268 (Washington: Government Printing Office, 1949).

Appendix A

The appendage to the Rouen manuscript, taken from the Gravier transcription in the Ayer Collection of the Newberry Library, Chicago

Lieux ou sont placées les concessions apartenantes a plusieurs personnes de qualité, marquez par lettre alphabetique sur la carte cy jointe.

Celle de M^r le Duc de Charost et de M le Marquis Danceny son fils a trois lieuës des Colapica, marquée   A

Celle de M. le comte D'Artagnan six lieues plus haut que la nouvelle Orleans   B

Celle de Mr Dartaguet a costé   C

Celle de M le Blanc ministre d'Estat dans la riviere des yasoux, ou estoit le fort   D

Celle de M. Laur anglois dans la riviere des Arcanças   E

Celle de Mrs Paris au vieux village des Bayagoulas   F

Celle de M. de Mezieres dans la fourche des ouachitas sur le bord de la riviere rouge   G

Celle de Mme de Chaumont dans la riviere des Pascagoulas douze lieues en montant   H [K?]

Celle de M. de Moeuve onze lieues par dela de la nouvelle orleans a lancien village des Tincats [Taensa]   I

Celle de M. Brossart au village des Nassitoches L
Celle de M de la Harpe Maloin aux Cadoda-
quioux M
Celle de M. de la Houssaye pres le village des
Natchez N
Celle de M de Catillon gentilhomme Irlandois
dans la fourche des ouachitas sur le bord de la
riviere rouge O
Celle de M de Bone a deux lieues dans la
riviere de la nouvelle orleans P
Celle de Mrs Pellerin et Bellecourt au village
des Natchez Q
Celle de Mr Colis sur la riviere des Natchez R
Celle de Mrs Chauvin trois lieues en deça de
nouvelle Orleans S
Celle de M. Dubreuil a costé T
Celle de Mrs Guenots a costé U [V?]
Celle de M. de Chantour a un quart de lieuë
de la nouvelle orleans du mesme costé X
Celle de M^{rs} le Page et le Gras a costé Y
Celle de Mr de Villemont dans la fourche des
ouachitas aupres de celle [de] M. de Mezieres sur
le bord de la riviere rouge Z

Appendix B

The full title of the Clermont manuscript of Pénicaut's Relation is translated: Narrative, OR TRUE AN-
NALS of what occurred in the country of Louisiana

during twenty-two consecutive years, from the beginning of French colonization in the region under Monsieur d'Hyberville and the Count de Surgère in 1699, up to 1721, WHEREIN ARE MENTIONED the wars of Frenchmen against the savages and of savages among themselves; the trade Frenchmen had with the savages; the course and the extent of the Missicipy; rivers that flow into this river: mines; the religion and customs of the savages; their foods, their hunting, their weddings, their festivals, and their funerals: concessions which Frenchmen hold there; together with THE GALANTE STORY of a French captain and the daughter of a Spanish captain of cavalry from Mexico.

Index

INDEX